Lost Cosmonaut

D1622811

LOST COSMONAUT

Travels to the republics that tourism forgot

Daniel Kalder

faber and faber

First published in 2006
by Faber and Faber Limited
3 Queen Square London WC1N 3AU
This paperback edition first published in 2007

Typeset by Faber and Faber Limited
Printed in England by Clays Ltd, St Ives plc

All rights reserved
© Daniel Kalder, 2006

The right of Daniel Kalder to be identified as author of this
work has been asserted in accordance with Section 77 of the
Copyright, Designs and Patents Act 1988

*This book is sold subject to the condition that it shall not, by
way of trade or otherwise, be lent, resold, hired out or otherwise
circulated without the publisher's prior consent in any form of
binding or cover other than that in which it is published and
without a similar condition including this condition being
imposed on the subsequent purchaser*

A CIP record for this book
is available from the British Library

ISBN 978-0-571-22781-5

10 9 8 7 6 5 4 3 2 1

To my parents

A note on this book:

This book is divided into four sections, four separate but interrelated journeys carried out over a period of several years. To fully capture this sense of time, one ought not to read continuously but rather, upon completion of each section, put the book down, go for a cup of tea, have a nap, take a stroll, that sort of thing. To achieve full results, one ought to put the book down for one year after reading Tatarstan, then for another year after reading about Kalmykia and for a full eighteen months before reading about Mari El. The last gap is much shorter: you need only wait four and a half months before reading about Udmurtia. In total then, it ought to take you almost four years to finish this book, which is not so ridiculous, when you consider that four years is approximately how much of our lives we spend shitting.

On the other hand, you can choose to ignore this advice and read the book in one sitting, forwards, backwards, sideways, or indeed upside down. It's entirely up to you. I was just trying to be helpful.

From The Shymkent Declarations

(Excerpts from the resolutions passed at the first international congress of Anti-Tourists at the Shymkent hotel, Shymkent, Kazakhstan October 1999)

. . . As the world has become smaller so its wonders have diminished. There is nothing amazing about the Taj Mahal, the Great Wall of China or the Pyramids of Egypt. They are as banal as the face of a Cornflakes packet.

Consequently the true unknown frontiers lie elsewhere.

The duty of the traveller, of the voyager is to open up new zones of experience. In our over explored world these must of necessity be wastelands, black holes, and grim urban blackspots: all the places which, ordinarily, people choose to avoid.

The only true voyagers, therefore, are anti-tourists. Following this logic we declare that:

The anti-tourist does not visit places that are in any way desirable.

The anti-tourist eschews comfort.

The anti-tourist embraces hunger and hallucinations and shit hotels.

The anti-tourist seeks locked doors and demolished buildings.

The anti-tourist scorns the bluster and bravado of the daredevil, who attempts to penetrate danger zones such as Afghanistan. The only thing that lies behind this is vanity and a desire to brag.

The anti-tourist travels at the wrong time of year.

The anti-tourist prefers dead things to living ones.

The anti-tourist is humble and seeks invisibility.

The anti-tourist is interested only in hidden histories, in delightful obscurities, in bad art.

The anti-tourist believes beauty is in the street.

The anti-tourist holds that whatever travel does, it rarely broadens the mind.

The anti-tourist values disorientation over enlightenment.

The anti-tourist loves truth, but he is also partial to lies. Especially his own.

TATARSTAN

1

It was my friend Joe who suggested going to Kazan, the capital of Tatarstan. He had a thing for the Golden Horde, for Grand Tartary and all that stuff. I didn't. I had once read a book about the Mongols by some old Oxbridge duffer and it put me off their history for ever. Joe, however, was planning a summer assault on Mongolia and Central Asia, perhaps a retracing of the Silk Road, and he wanted to get some practice in. The thing was, his Russian wasn't much cop and he was nervous about buying train tickets and visas and all that. He thought a trip to Kazan would be a good opportunity for him to rehearse. I agreed to go with him, as I am always ready for adventure, especially if someone else is willing to organize all the difficult bits.

2

Joe proposed the trip in Moscow in February. A few months passed while we waited for the weather to improve. Then, when the sun finally did come out, we went to get the tickets. One hot May day we queued in Kazan Station in Moscow for about half an hour, pushed and nudged on all sides by sweaty shuttle traders and dodgy characters. I was nervous because my Russian wasn't that great and I knew the women who worked in Russian train stations rarely had patience with foreigners who couldn't speak their language. I didn't think Joe was going to be able to do all the talking on his own and I was preparing to help him in spite of his promise I wouldn't have to do anything.

Suddenly we were at the front and Joe had disappeared. I looked around. He was standing behind me. 'Go on,' he said.

'Talk to her.' The jowly old hag behind the glass was already barking at me to hurry up or let the next person through. Her hair was the colour of Kia-Ora and it looked as though she had smeared pig's blood on her lips.

'What do you want?' she demanded.

I stammered out a request for two tickets to Kazan.

'When?'

'Tomorrow?'

'Not possible,' she said.

'Why?'

'I don't have information about those trains.'

'What do you mean?'

'I don't have any information about trains to Kazan leaving tomorrow.'

'But this is where you buy tickets for Kazan.'

'Yes.'

'Well, when will you have the information?'

'Tomorrow. Come back tomorrow.'

'But I want to go tomorrow.'

'I know. So come back tomorrow. NEXT!'

She refused to talk to me any more and an Armenian guy had already taken my place at the window. I turned to Joe. 'I thought you were going to do all the talking.'

'Thought I'd leave it to you,' he said. 'Never mind, why don't you come back to mine? I'll make you a cup of tea and show you a video of a dwarf getting a blow-job.'

A few weeks later, Yoshi, Joe's Japanese friend, arrived in town from Georgia. According to Joe, Yoshi was a professional photographer who had left Japan three years earlier to roam the globe and take pictures. He had lived all over the earth, in some of the worst hell-holes under the sun – places like Cambodia, Burma, Iran and Turkmenistan. He was a true world citizen. He was also probably insane, but very quiet with it.

Joe persuaded Yoshi to come to Kazan. When we went to get tickets the next time I also disappeared behind Yoshi and let him do all the talking. Although he barely spoke Russian we had tickets within a matter of minutes.

3

Tatarstan was Joe's idea, but I rapidly began to take an interest in it. Not so much because of its connections to the Mongol Horde, but more because it was a strange other zone in Europe. It had its own president, its own parliament, but nobody knew anything about it. Was it a country? Was it a nation? Was it a state? Was it, in actual fact, any different from the rest of Russia?

Few people realize the extent to which Russia is multi-ethnic, like no other country in Europe. It has seventy distinct nationalities, twenty-one of which have their own semi-autonomous 'republics' within the Russian Federation. At first glance this may look similar to the structure of Britain – one political union comprised of four nations – England, Scotland, Northern Ireland and Wales. Unlike Britain, however, Russia's republics were hastily created in 1918–20, by the Bolsheviks – prior to that they were mere provinces of the Tsarist empire.

Lenin created the republics as a sweetener to the regional ethnic elites, to keep them from seceding outright from the collapsing Tsarist empire. This does not mean he sympathized with their dreams of self-determination. He simply needed to make allies fast while at the same time holding Russia's vast territories together. To that end 'homelands' were given to the more important non-Russian nationalities, which had more autonomy to decide local questions than the other regions of Russia.

In most of these republics, however, Russians outnumber the people who give their names to the republic. In the Republic of Adygey, in southern Russia for example, less than 30 per cent of the populace is ethnic Adygey. Tatarstan is rare in that 48 per cent of the populace is Tatar, while only 43 per cent is Russian. Even then, only 23 per cent of Tatars actually live in their official homeland. The rest are dispersed around the former Soviet Union.

4

In the 1990s, however, the Tatars in Tatarstan were quick to grab as much autonomy as they could get their hands on. For example, Article 61 of the Constitution of Tatarstan states: 'The Republic of Tatarstan is a sovereign state, a subject of international law associated with the Russian Federation – Russia – on the basis of a Treaty on the mutual delegation of powers and areas of jurisdiction.'

The Russian Federation has never accepted that declaration of sovereignty. None the less, the Tatars insist on it. The Constitution also gives Tatarstan the right independently to conclude trade and economic agreements with foreign states and to form 'free economic zones' on the territory of the republic.

Wales and Scotland do not define themselves as 'sovereign states'. Nor are they free to establish tax-free zones. Is Tatarstan, then, although invisible internationally, more autonomous than some of the famous, ancient nations of the UK? And if so, why do we know nothing about it?

It was hard to fit Tatarstan into any categories, and this more than anything made it attractive. It was unknown, a black blot on the map, at the easternmost point of Europe. I knew it would be probably be impoverished and rather depressing, but this made it all the more attractive as, like many bourgeois Westerners, I like to look at poor foreigners. Unlike other bourgeois Westerners, however, I don't require picturesque settings to offset the poverty. In fact, the bleaker and more dismal the landscape, the more I enjoy it. I'm funny that way.

5

We were sharing the train carriage with Gulnara, a petite, fearful, forty-something Tatar lawyer. When she saw us come in, she turned pale and quickly left to find the conductor and asked for a new coupe. She indicated us: surely they didn't expect her to sleep with three strange men, foreigners no less. The conductor shrugged. There was nothing she could do. There were no vacancies. Gulnara sighed, rolled her eyes. Then she rejoined us, sat herself at the end of the bed and buried herself in a book. After about an hour, however, she grew curious, and engaged us in conversation. Or perhaps interrogation.

'Why are you going to Tatarstan?' she asked.

'For tourism,' I replied.

'Come on,' she said. 'Why are you really going?'

I looked at Joe and Yoshi, who were sitting opposite, for confirmation.

'No, really,' said Joe. 'For tourism.'

Gulnara looked at him warily. 'For tourism?'

'Yes,' said Joe. 'We're tourists.'

Gulnara couldn't believe anyone would go to Kazan, capital of Tatarstan, simply for a holiday. Nobody went there because they wanted to. The conductor was the same. She had never seen foreign passports before, and laughed when we said we were tourists. You didn't go to Kazan as a tourist.

7

There was nothing there. You were pushed to go. You had to go. For business, or to see your family. Take Gulnara, for example – she was going to see her mother, who lived there. Otherwise she would have stayed in Moscow for the weekend, in her luxury apartment on Tverskaya, in the centre of the city.

'So, you're tourists,' said Gulnara.

'Yes,' I said. 'We're tourists.'

She snorted, opened her book. I was obviously an idiot or a liar. Whichever, I was talking shit, and she didn't want anything more to do with me. She, a native of Tatarstan, could see no reason why anybody would ever choose to go there.

There was nothing extraordinary in Gulnara's reaction. When I told my Russian friends I was planning to visit Kazan, rather than be impressed by my desire to broaden my knowledge of their mysterious country, they were confused. 'Why don't you go to St Petersburg instead?' they suggested. 'It's a lot more interesting.' 'I've already been,' I replied. 'Many times.' Some tried vigorously to dissuade me. 'There is nothing to see in Tatarstan. You will waste your time.' 'That's why I'm going,' I said. 'To see nothing.' 'It is dangerous,' they said. 'Full of Mafia.' 'That's why I'm going,' I said. 'To find crime.' It was my friend Yura who got to the heart of the matter: 'For you Kazan is interesting. It's exotic. For Russians, however, it is different. No Russian would go there for a holiday, because it reminds them of what a poor, backward country this is.'

Only one guy, Gleb, spoke well of the city. He had done his military service there and remembered two years of shooting Kalashnikovs in the sunshine with pleasure. 'It is a pretty town,' he said. 'But totally boring. Why on earth do you want to go there?'

In 1236 Batu Khan, grandson of Genghis, crossed the Ural mountains and invaded Europe. In Batu's 'Golden Horde', Mongols and Turks from Central Asia fought side by side. First they subjugated the Bulgars of the Volga region, and then moved on to the Russian lands. They were an unstoppable force, toppling prince after prince, burning, raping, looting and pillaging in a spree of conquering that took them to the fringes of Western Europe. For the next two hundred and fifty years, the Russians lived under the Mongol–Tatar 'yoke'.

The Mongols formed the aristocracy of the Horde and ruled from the cities of Karakorum, in Inner Mongolia, and later Sarai, near the site of modern Volgograd. Russian princes would travel thousands of miles to Karakorum to pay their taxes, or gain approval from the Great Khan on questions of royal succession. There, deep in the desert, they met with the chiefs of the Mongol, Tatar, Tibetan, and Bokharian hordes, as well as the ambassadors of the Caliph of Baghdad, the Pope and even the King of France. They learned to speak Turkic, and to negotiate the court culture of the Horde. Eventually the princes of Muscovy ingratiated themselves with the Khan so well that they were made his agents, entrusted with the responsibility of collecting the taxes from the other Russian principalities.

The Horde, however, was unstable, and beset with internal struggles. In the fourteenth century it converted to Islam and under the Khan Oz Beg became Turkified. After him, however, other khans came and went, some strong, some weak. The Russians first stopped paying tribute in the late fourteenth century, and won a famous battle against the Horde at Kulikovo field, under the Muscovite Prince Dmitri Donskoy. But Tatar supremacy was soon re-established in the usual violent manner. It wasn't until almost a hundred years later that the Horde was finally beaten, in a stunning anti-climax to two hundred and fifty years of sustained brutality and extortion. It happened like this.

The Slav princes once again stopped paying their taxes. Khan Akhmad assembled a force to invade the Russian lands. He destroyed a few cities, and then sent a delegation to hammer out a peace deal. The negotiations broke down. So the Khan formed an alliance with the King of Poland and the Grand Duke of Lithuania, to deal with the Russians once and for all.

The leader of the Russian princes, Ivan III of Moscow, got together an army and went to meet Akhmad at the Ugra river, a stream on the border between Lithuania and Russia. The two armies lined up, facing each other across the river. And then –

And then nothing. They stood there, glaring at each other. This continued for several months. One day Akhmad retreated, without a fight.

What was the reason for this strange behaviour? First, the Poles and the Lithuanians failed to send the troops they had promised. Then, a rival chief attacked one of Akhmad's camps, containing his wives and family. Shortly thereafter, Akhmad was assassinated.

And that was the end of the Tatar yoke. The Golden Horde broke up into three separate khanates – one based in the Crimea, another in Siberia, and one centred around the city of Kazan. This last khanate was the ancestor of modern Tatarstan.

Tatar: A mini-phrasebook

Hello	sSAnmesez
Goodbye	SAU bulygiz
How are you?	khal LYAR ni CHEK
Please give me . . .	BIRegezche . . .
(Very) beautiful	(bik) maTUR
Boy	maLAI
I want	min telim
(Very) beautiful	(bik) maTUR
Boy	maLAI
Are you selling?	sez saTASyzmy?
(Very beautiful)	(bik) maTUR
Boy	maLAI
How much does it cost?	KUPme toRA?
Very good	kaiMAHK
Boy	maLAI
(Very) tasty	(bik) tamLE
Boy	maLAI
Honey	bahl
Cream	kaiMAHK
Chemist	darukhaNA
How do I get to . . .?	niCHEK baryrGAH . . .?
Hospital	shifakhaNA
(Very) good	(bik) yakhSHI
Many thanks	zur rakhMAT
Goodbye	SAU bulgyz

8

The train pulled into Kazan early in the morning. The sun was shining and the sky was blue, so I could see all the drunks staggering about on the cracked platform without difficulty. I looked around, and saw a banner spread across some rails. There was a statement in Cyrillic on it, but strangely, although I can read Russian reasonably well, I couldn't understand it at all. Suddenly I realized it was in Tatar. Yoshi had a Tatar–Japanese dictionary, so I asked him what it said. Slowly he spelt out his translation. It was a chilling message: 'Leave . . . now . . . white . . . devils.'*

Meanwhile, a flag I had never seen before was flying from the top of a nearby building. The flag was dark green and orange, divided horizontally by a thin white stripe. There was no Russian tricolour.

It was interesting: although much was familiar – the shabby concrete architecture, the weather-beaten faces, the little kiosks peddling cheap cigarettes and alcohol, for example – there had nonetheless been a shift. It wasn't as though I was in a different country – nothing so bold as that. It was something different. Something more unsettling: as though I was in another dimension, in a place that had developed along parallel lines to the rest of Russia up to a point, but had then suddenly diverged, although I didn't yet know what the differences were. I had felt this once before, in Almaty, the former capital of Kazakhstan. Almaty is a strange city, fringed by huge mountains, located in a small oasis in the midst of dry steppe. Its planners decided to make it green, too, and it looks like a city built inside a forest. When I lived there I would spend whole days wandering through its streets, periodically stumbling upon statues of Asiatic geniuses I had never heard of,

* See the last of the *Shymkent Declarations*. You have been warned.

with names like 'Abai' and 'Dzhambyl', authors of poems and songs I knew nothing of. It was almost magical enough to make up for the fact that the city was a dead concrete dust-bowl. Almost, but not quite . . .

Yoshi found the tram station and we rode, teetering on ancient tracks for a few minutes until we reached the city centre. The first hotel we tried, the enormous and gloomy Hotel Tatarstan offered us rooms for $50 a night, but without hot water – and the receptionist didn't even blink when she quoted us the price. This howling rip-off confirmed that we were definitely still in the Russian Federation. We passed on that and found rooms in the Hotel Duslyk – 'Friendship' – which also lacked hot water but cost five times less.

Lenin gazes upon the State Opera and Ballet Theatre, Kazan.

9

In the Middle Ages the merchants and ambassadors who made the journey to Kazan described it as a 'City of Wonders'

13

and 'Capital of the East'. After weeks trudging through Old Russia and its benighted villages of mud, dilapidated huts and sombre black-domed churches, where mumbling priests and cruel princes lorded it over lice-infested peasants, they suddenly found themselves in a city of pointed towers and minarets. Here there were beautiful palaces, ancient burial vaults, and vast libraries filled with philosophical manuscripts and poetry. Here they were guests in warm homes where the walls were covered in exotic carpets, and where the women, dark-eyed and mysterious, moved silent and subtle as the wind.

The city was a like mirage – fantastic, mystical, something from an Eastern folktale. In its bazaar you could buy fruit, silk, carpets, spices, porcelain and weapons, furs and wax from Russia, pure-bred horses and cattle from the steppes in the south, the homelands of the legendary Scythian tribes.* The Tatars, meanwhile, produced furs, leather goods, and jewellery. Strolling through the bazaar it seemed as though you could meet traders from every corner of the earth, and buy goods as beautiful as any from the sharp and witty devils, who spent their whole lives amid the pungent smells and the rich, rich colours, absorbing them, mixing with them, embodying them . . .

And Kazan was a city of scholars, of poets. The great Khan Mukhamad Amin filled his court with musicians and artists. There the legendary Tatar poet and philosopher Mukhammadyar recited *The Husband's Gift* and *Light of the Heart* for the first time to a rapturous response from the assembled courtiers, nobles and concubines. Such magic! Such beauty! They were carried aloft on the magical wings of

* An interesting titbit on the Scythians: they used to drink horse's milk, which is rich in oestrogen. As time went on the men would grow breasts, of which they were very proud. They were also very fond of hashish.

14

his rhetoric. And gathered there were other poets and artists, who dazzled the nobles of the city with their creations – it was as if their wits had been touched by angels.

And at the centre of it all was the walled fortress behind which stood the Khan Mosque itself, with its brilliant blue dome, and its many towers rising up, up to pierce the starry night sky. And, in the morning, the call to prayer would sound from those same towers, bringing the proud citizens of this brilliant city to their knees in veneration before God above . . .

10

This old Kazan was destroyed by Ivan the Terrible in 1552. He razed the city to the ground, destroying the towers and libraries spoken of by the medieval travellers. He put to the sword the men, the women, the children, the animals. Bodies lay rotting in the streets, a torrent of blood surged through the city. Death came to everything.

Fire came too. Ivan set the great Khan Mosque ablaze: how fiercely it burned! And how long the minarets stood, before finally collapsing, with a terrible crash, silencing for ever the call to prayer. It had taken Ivan three attempts to subdue the city: the Tatars were stubborn; they were fierce. He had to make certain there would be no rebellion. He had to crush them completely. He was ruthless that way: he had killed his own son, after all, struck him dead in a murderous rage. The Tatars, an alien people who had reigned over his ancestors with cruelty and rapacity, stood no chance of mercy at his hands.

And they received none. After Ivan's invasion, all the surviving Tatars were expelled from the city, and all the mosques were destroyed. Those who set foot within the walls of Kazan were executed. Tatar culture was suppressed and Orthodox missionaries were sent to convert the Tatars and other ethnic groups in the area – the Chuvash, the Mordvin, the Mari, the Udmurt – to the Russian Church.

Kazan started a new life, as an important Russian city. In 1708 it was made the centre of the vast Kazan province, the Tsarist precursor of the later Soviet republic.

Over time, Tsarist oppression lightened. Tatars joined the official administration, and some even gained entry to the Russian aristocracy. Then in 1767 Catherine the Great, in a fit of enlightenment and religious tolerance, granted permission for new stone mosques to be built. But the fires, the bloodshed, that Kazan knew so well, were only waiting round the corner.

In the east a peasant named Emelyan Pugachev declared himself tsar. He led a rebellion that began in the Ural mountains and raged through Eastern Russia, inspiring downtrodden serfs to throw down their ploughshares and pick up swords and smite their cruel masters. The Masters of the Empire in St Petersburg could feel the heat, could smell the charred wood of the burning cities. Pugachev reached Kazan in 1774, and set the city ablaze. His forces got as far as the Kremlin walls before the Imperial army defeated him. Then the rebel died horribly, in a most unenlightened way: he was hanged, drawn and quartered. Thus the regime dealt with its enemies.

Slowly, the city was built anew. But the turbulent life of Kazan was far from over. There were more fires in 1815, which led to yet more rebuilding, and, suddenly, a cultural flowering. Kazan University and the first Tatar grammar schools were established. The University became the centre of Asian studies in Russia, and counted among its famous students Lenin (who was expelled), Tolstoy and Lobachevsky, the founder of non-Euclidean geometry.

By the start of the twentieth century, nothing remained of the Tatar city, except perhaps for one tower in the Kremlin, of disputed origin. Nevertheless, a real renaissance in Tatar culture was under way. The Tatars were allowed their own press and began to publish in their own language. Artists produced paintings, writers wrote books, directors and actors made theatre, and composers created music. By 1908 there were thirty *madrasa*s, and Kazan had become the centre of Islam in Russia.

But history in this part of the world is not restful. Further revolution and destruction were waiting round the corner.

11

A walking tour of Kazan

From our hotel we walked down the river to (1) The State Theatre of Tatarstan. It was a large, white concrete building. Here, you could see Ibsen translated into Tatar, as well as works by local writers. It was covered in pigeon shit, and the pigeons were happily shitting away as we passed.

After the State Theatre we came to (2) Bauman Street which was notable for the presence of a McDonald's. I was surprised and pleased to find the Golden Arches so far from Moscow. I was even more surprised and impressed by the Tatar flag emblazoned on the door. It was the first time I had been witness to the marriage of nationalism and the world's largest fast-food franchise. It had no effect on the quality of my Royal Cheeseburger breakfast, either, except that the Coke tasted somewhat chemical.

About halfway down Bauman Street someone had built a wall to stop you from seeing the run-down part. So we crossed on to Kremlovskaya Street, which led us to (3) The

Kremlin. The walls of the Kazan Kremlin were painted a dazzling white. Inside we found some old bricks and a cathedral. I could also see the residential area of Kazan in the distance: long rows of identical concrete apartment buildings, identical to those in every other Russian city. It was a sunny day, however, and they looked clean and cheerful.

Behind the cathedral was the palatial residence of the president, and just down from it was the red Suyumbeki Tower, named after the Tatar princess who was married to all three of the last Kazan khans. There is a legend about Suyumbeki: that she was so beautiful, Ivan the Terrible wanted to marry her. She agreed to his proposal on the condition that within a week he build a tower higher than all the minarets in Kazan. Ivan obliged, but on the seventh day she reneged on the deal. She climbed to the top of the tower, said goodbye to her people and leapt to her death. Ivan, it is said, was so pissed off he invaded Kazan and razed it to the ground.

The most impressive thing about the Kremlin, however, was the enormous Kul Sherif Mosque they were building. It had a large blue dome, and four super-thin minarets shooting up into the sky. It was a reconstruction of the Khan Mosque Ivan had destroyed four centuries earlier.

I spent a while wandering around the Kul Sherif. They hadn't put the tiles on yet, so much of it was blank concrete. There were no security guards around, and I thought about sneaking inside as I was curious to see what an empty mosque looked like. But I was almost certain a guard would emerge if I tried, and wouldn't be amused. He might give me a beating, or take me to the police.

Setting a mosque next door to a church struck me as just asking for trouble. My guidebook stressed the party line: that Russians and Tatars had lived together in harmony for centuries, and that the branches of the faiths they followed were mutually liberal. But, in my naiveté, I thought maybe they had been at peace because the Russians had always ruthlessly asserted their dominance, quashed rebellions, and had spent four centuries Russifying the Tatars. But if the Tatars began to assert themselves, pushing further their declaration of sovereignty and Islam spread . . . well, perhaps under the current president Mintimir 'Iron Man' Shaimiyev – a strong leader and secularist – nothing would happen.

But if Tatarstan pressed for more autonomy, and the Russian population began to feel pressurized, ghettoized, it would only take a few extremists for bombs to start flying, and for emergency workers to start picking limbs up off pavements. Standing there, I thought I could smell on the wind whiffs of future confrontation, of riots and oppression. I inhaled deep, bracing draughts.

After the Kremlin we went into (4) The State Museum. They charged us more because we were foreigners. It was completely shite. They had a single Egyptian mummy and a few pens belonging to Musa Jalil, a local poet martyred by the Nazis. The paucity of exhibits was such that, imagining that couldn't possibly be it, I started taking the stairs to the next floor when I was yelled at by a fat, hairy woman: 'The first floor's closed!' she screamed. So that was that.

After the museum I looked over a wall and saw (5) The Circus. It looked like a silver flying saucer.

And that, pretty much, was Kazan: a fairly sleepy provincial Russian city distinguished by a big mosque.

The Kul Sherif Mosque, destroyed 450 years ago by Ivan the Terrible.
It's back.

Ten great Tatars (you've never heard of)

SHIGABUTDIN MARDZHANI (1818–1889)
A scholar and religious leader, he laid the foundations for contemporary research into the Kazan Tatars and the history of the region. His major work, *Reports on the History of Kazan and the Bulgar*, remains a valuable source for contemporary historians.

KAYUM NASYRI (1825–1902)
After the long period of severe cultural repression, Nasyri was one of the first Tatars to enrol at Kazan University. He wrote academic textbooks on the Tatar language, arithmetic, geometry, botany and history, and created the first scientific grammar of the Tatar language. He also compiled the first Tatar dictionary.

GALIMDZHAN BARUDI (1857–1921)
Barudi was a religious educator and reformer, who organized 'Mukhammadiya', an important Kazan *madrasa*. In the early days of the Soviet Union he was spiritual head of Russia's Muslims, elected mufti by the General Congress of Muslims in Moscow. He didn't live long enough to witness the destruction of the mosques, or the mass executions and exiles of the muftis.

GABDULLA TUKAI (1886–1913)
The most popular of Tatar poets, he wrote lyrical and tragic poetry, satire, children's poems and fairy tales. His fairy tales remain popular today and have inspired many pieces of music and paintings. He died in a hospital in Kazan at the age of twenty-seven.

MIRSAID SULTAN-GALIEV (1892–1940)

Sultan-Saliev was one of the leaders in building the nation states of the Soviet Union. He was a member of the board of Narkomnats, the state committee on questions of nationality, and also Head of the Eastern Section of the Red Army Political Organization. He helped prepare the joint Tatar–Bashkir Republic which was later replaced by two separate states. Deemed ideologically untrustworthy, he was first arrested in 1923. He survived another eighteen years before Stalin had him shot.

BAKI URMANCHE (1897–1990)

Urmanche is considered the greatest Tatar artist of the twentieth century. He was not only a sculptor, painter, draughtsman, but also an expert on languages and philosophy, on Tatar folklore and history. At one time a political prisoner in the Gulag, he survived to become a revered public figure.

SALIK SAIDASHEV (1900–1954)

Saidashev – 'The Founder of Professional Tatar Music' – composed songs, marches, musicals and tunes that are still played in Tatarstan during official celebrations.

MUSA JALIL (1906–1944)

Jalil was one of the dominant figures of Tatar culture in the 1930s, a dangerous time for intellectuals and artists. He was a poet, a publicist, a brilliant organizer; he wrote librettos; he was also a humorist and entertainer. Taken prisoner by the Germans in the Second World War, he became a leader of the underground resistance and was later guillotined. His most famous works are the *Moabit Notebooks,* which he wrote while imprisoned.

NAZIB ZHIGANOV (1911–1988)

Zhiganov was the greatest Tatar composer of the Soviet era.

Unlike Saidashev, who wrote ditties, he produced classical operas, symphonies and chamber music, and headed the Tatarstan Composers' Union from its inception in 1939 for many years. He was also the Rector of the Kazan Conservatory, which opened in 1945.

SOFIA GUBAIDULINA (1930–)
The only woman on this list and the only non-corpse. One of the most significant contemporary composers in the world, she was born in Chistopol (a Tatar town), but studied piano in the Kazan Conservatory, where she composed her first pieces. Her challenging, highly avant-garde music is now performed around the world. She lives in Germany.

13

The existence of these invisible geniuses disturbs me. We take no notice of their music, their books, their causes, or their history, although they are and it is European. But it is unknown, a whole other Europe, a shadow Europe that might as well not exist for all we Westerners care. In fact, it does not exist for us. They do not exist.

You will never read a poem by Musa Jalil. You will never hear a symphony by Nazib Zhiganov. If you weren't reading this book you would never have thought about the first academic textbook in the Tatar language.

I know people are regularly tortured and murdered for causes I've never heard of. So the existence of ghost canons and traditions shouldn't really disturb me at all. But it does. I shiver when I think about them. They are a mystery, an existential riddle I cannot solve.

It is 1917; the flames of revolution have left the Tsarist empire in disarray. In St Petersburg new rulers struggle to assert control over a rapidly disintegrating Russia. The Tatar elite seizes the moment to create the Idil–Ural Republic. This fully independent state will include the traditional lands not only of the Tatars, but also of the Mari, the Chuvash, and the Bashkirs – in short of everyone who lived on this part of the Volga before the Russians, with their swords and priests, established their hegemony. Thus set free, these long-oppressed peoples will live together in harmony and their cultures will flourish.

Fat chance. In 1918 the Bolsheviks move in and establish the Socialist Tatar–Bashkir Republic instead. And then two years later Lenin changes his mind. The Tatars and the Bashkirs are split and each nationality is given its own state. The lines on the map are drawn somewhat arbitrarily, however: 75 per cent of Tatars find themselves living outside what is nominally their homeland. Throughout the rest of the 1920s, the Bolsheviks execute the Tatar leadership, annihilate the intelligentsia, and shoot just about anybody who has an idea in his head.

The vice tightens yet further in the 1930s. Stalin embarks on a programme of wholesale Russification in Tatarstan and across the Soviet Union. His methods are brutal. Russians are settled en masse in the area, and all schooling is conducted in Russian. Religious buildings are destroyed. The Tatar alphabet, transcribed from Arabic into Latin in 1929, is retranscribed into Cyrillic, the alphabet of the colonial masters. The word 'Eastern', too suggestive of a separate identity, is dropped from all Tatar institutions and replaced with 'State'. And, of course, prodigious numbers of people are shot.

Meanwhile lots of industrial concerns open in Tatarstan:

engineering works, plastics, petrochemicals, heavy machinery, aeroplanes and oil are all produced in the Republic. Tatar areas are favoured over Russian ones as sites for the vast industrial complexes spewing smoke and toxins into the environment.

After World War II even the Volga changes. A reservoir is built, causing the river to flood its banks, bringing it right up to the Kremlin. The narrow, twisting Kazanka, which ran through the centre of town, becomes a broad, straight channel, hemmed in by concrete. New suburbs mushroom: long broad streets lined with identical multi-storey prefabricated housing. That's where the descendants of the Golden Horde live, looking out upon a city that shares a name and locale with the one their ancestors founded, but little else. The new Kazan, it must be admitted, does have a lot of towers. But they are higher, and made of concrete.

15

Architectural interlude

One of the most striking features of Kazan is the sheer volume of collapsed buildings in the city centre. In the central street and radiating outwards, everywhere you go you pass houses that have caved in on themselves. Sometimes you look in through a glassless window, and furniture and clothes are mixed in with the rubble. The house next door can be in perfect condition, but this one, for some reason, just collapsed one day. I wondered, as I was passing, how many of them had taken families – fathers, mothers, daughters, sons – with them.

Alex and Mike

Joe had a friend from Kazan. His name was Alex: he was Tatar, although fair-haired and pale-skinned. Alex meanwhile, had a friend called Mike: he was Russian, although dark-haired and swarthy. They were therefore a pretty representative pair, although all mixed up. Alex worked in Moscow, while Mike was a surgeon in Germany. But both of them had grown up in Kazan. I hoped that through them we'd somehow find a path 'into' the city. It's OK to wander around with a map and guidebook, but this rarely gives you much of a feel for life as it is lived. It's much better to talk to people. A few words exchanged in a café can tell you more about a place in seconds than any number of books and heritage centres.

The problem is that I don't much like talking to people. I'm scared that they'll turn out to be freaks and then won't leave me alone. There's nothing worse than having some weirdo suddenly become your new best friend and dog your steps for hours, or days. That was one of the reasons I liked travelling with Joe: not only was he clever and funny, but he was also good at picking up interesting characters. Freaks and alkies gravitated towards him. I, meanwhile, could study them in safety at a distance, using Joe for cover.

Alex and Mike took us on a desultory tour of Kazan, showing pretty much what we had already seen, plus the Tatar Parliament, which was a heavy grey concrete building on top of a hill, with a statue of Lenin standing in front of it. On the way I periodically paused to take pictures of piles of crap, crumbling buildings, graffiti and peeling paint.

'Why are you taking a picture of that?' asked Mike, as I aimed my camera at a ladder leaning against a yellow wall.

The Secret History of the World #15,053

'For my photographic project,' I answered.

'What project is that?' he asked, a smile at the corner of his lips.

'The secret history of the world.'

'What do you mean?'

'I take pictures of the things everybody sees but dismisses as unimportant.'

'Like a ladder leaning against a wall?'

'Or graffiti . . . or peeling paint . . . or a dead dog. There is beauty in all this stuff, if you stop and look at it – if you learn how to look at it. I am creating a vast archive of lost moments and neglected epiphanies.'

'And who do you show these pictures to?'

'No one. That's why it's called the secret history of the world.'

Mike laughed. He began walking alongside me, asking questions. I didn't really like it. Like I said, when I first meet someone I prefer to observe them from the safety of a bunker for a while, until I have ascertained they are not a freak or bore. Mike, however, didn't give me that opportunity. He wasn't interested in Joe or Yoshi, but he was interested in me. He kept looking into my eyes and laughing. Mike had mentioned an English ex-girlfriend, but that was not the vibe I was picking up. He looked like a trouser pilot to me. I suspected he wanted to stick his cock in my ass.

He made me nervous.

17

It was apparent that Alex and Mike didn't give a shit about Tatarstan. They had left and they were glad they had left. It was OK to come back for a weekend now and then – like Gulnara on the train – but that was enough. After our tour, we sat down on a patio next to a kiosk drinking beers. Alex, it transpired, was allergic to alcohol and quickly came out in red blotches. He insisted on drinking anyway. Mike, meanwhile, was sitting across from me, smiling and gazing into my eyes. I was half worried he might interpret any questions as a come on and start rubbing his leg against mine under the table, so I directed most of my cultural inquiries to Alex.

'What about the *Sabantui* festival?' I asked. I had read that this was a great event in the Tatar calendar.

'Oh that. You've missed it. It happens in May, I think. What do you think, Mike?'

'Yeah, maybe.'

'What's it about?'

'Oh, you know. Sack races, egg-and-spoon races and – what do you call them? – tug-o'-war contests. It's not very interesting.'

And that was that. He took another sip on his beer and another blotch appeared. I decided to try a different tack.

'What about traditional Tatar wrestling?'

'They wrestle.'

Thus Alex effortlessly batted away all questions about Tatarstan.

'What about your national cuisine? Do you have any special dishes?' asked Joe.

'Do we have any special dishes?' Alex asked Mike.

'I don't know. You're the Tatar, not me.'

'I'm only half Tatar,' said Alex. 'My mother was Russian.'

'But it says you're Tatar on your passport,' said Mike.

'Yes.' Alex explained that in Russia your ethnicity was written on your passport. 'It's stupid,' he sighed.

'Tatars eat *echpochmak*,' said Mike.

'Oh yeah,' said Alex.

'What's that?' I asked.

'How do you explain it?' asked Alex.

'It's a triangle of pastry,' said Mike, 'with meat, potato and onion.'

'Is it any good?'

'It's all right.'

Perhaps these questions about local traditions were a non-starter anyway. I would never, for example, ask a Frenchman about stripy jumpers and onions. Not unless I was trying to annoy him, that is. So I thought I'd try to probe a little more in depth and risk a potentially controversial but more urgent question.

'What about relations between Tatars and Russians?' I asked, not wanting to be any more specific, in case I were to tread on his toes.

'They're not bad,' said Alex, shrugging. 'There's a lot of intermarriage. It's the government that's terrible.'

'Why?'

'The Russians are very patient. Very patient. Shaimiyev is terrible. I don't know how the Russians can stand it.'

I was intrigued: why was Shaimiyev so terrible? Was there prejudice against Russians? Did they find it hard to get top government jobs, like in Kazakhstan? Did Shaimiyev push Tatar culture on them?

In fact, I already knew the answers to all these questions. Shaimiyev was an aggressive nepotist who had filled the government with relatives. He had also repeatedly stressed the importance of the goal of 'full Tatar sovereignty'. Nevertheless I felt a strange urge to hear Alex confirm what I had already read, as if that would make it more authentic somehow. But Alex was finished as far as politics and inter-ethnic relations were concerned. I asked him to elaborate, but he waved the question away.

Alex took another sip on his beer and then something interesting happened: the red blotches suddenly blinked white, and the rest of his face turned red. He also began sweating.

'So do you like Kazan?' asked Joe.

Alex shrugged. 'Not especially. It's OK, I suppose.'

Alex's lack of enthusiasm for the revival of Tatar traditions didn't surprise me. These things often originate at the top, and enthusiasm for them remains at the top, among the bureaucrats and politicians who make a living off them. In Scotland, for example, we have a parliament for the first time in three hundred years, but the only people who think it's a good idea are the ones getting paid to sit in it, the smug little nobodies, elevated local councillors living high on the hog on taxpayers' cash.

Suddenly Alex remembered something.

'Kazan was famous for its gangs in the 1970s.'

'What kind of gangs?'

'Street gangs.'

'Soviet street gangs?'

'Yes.'

'Who was in them?'

'Teenagers.'

'Were they dangerous?'

'No.'

'Do you still have them now?'

'No.'

'Were you in one?'

'No.'

Suddenly Mike interjected. 'Alex, can you speak Tatar?' he asked.

'No,' said Alex.

'So you can't even speak your own language?'

Alex shrugged. The blotches on his face were moving around now and he was sweating profusely.

'You shouldn't drink,' said Mike.

Alex shrugged. 'You're the doctor,' he said. And drank some more.

The conversation lagged. Every time I looked Mike was checking me out. I told myself I was just being paranoid. Then some gypsy kids started bothering us. They came up, hands outstretched, mouths open. One particularly insistent little girl homed in on Joe, who tried to ignore her.

'She's beginning to get on my tits,' he said, after a minute or so. 'She won't go away.' He turned to Mike. 'How do you tell a kid to get lost in Russian?'

Mike smiled. His eyes flashed. I suspected he rather liked to be cruel, in a Wildean way.

'Say *ot vali menya*.'

Joe practised the words, but found it difficult to get his tongue round them.

'Or you can try *pashol von*.'

'*Pashol von*?' Joe picked it up immediately.

Alex shook his head. He muttered something to Mike, whose eyes were glittering.

'Which is worse?' asked Joe.

'*Pashol von*,' said Alex.

'But it's not obscene?'

'No, no,' said Mike. 'Just rather direct.'

Joe turned to the gypsy girl.

'*Pashol von*,' he said.

The kid fucked off immediately.

Alex shook his head, remonstrating quietly in Russian with Mike. 'It's not right', he said, 'to talk to a child that way.' Mike, however continued to smile, staring me in the eyes.

Somehow the conversation got round to Stalin. Until this point Mike had been a detached observer at the table, wryly amused by the foreigners and occasionally offering an interjection. But when Joe started on about Stalin's victims Mike suddenly piped up.

'Yes, but Stalin was absolutely right.'

I was a little startled to hear this coming from a guy in his late twenties. The sentiment itself is banal enough: there are still millions of Russians who think Stalin was the country's greatest leader, a universal genius who won a war and transformed the Soviet Union into a superpower. But most of them are old and stupid. Not only would they deny, for example, that he engineered a famine in the Ukraine that killed 6 million people, they probably wouldn't even have heard of it.

Mike was different, however. He was well educated. He had lived abroad. He knew all of Stalin's crimes. He probably knew more about them than me.

'Stalin did what he had to do,' he said, his eyes flashing. 'The country was backwards. If he hadn't killed all those people, it would never have industrialized. He was building a country.'

'But don't you think it's a bit much to kill 20 million people to build a country?' I asked. 'To build *their* country? Isn't there a contradiction?'

'No,' he said, smiling.

I didn't pursue the conversation any further. It wasn't that I was outraged; I was simply unwilling. If this fool couldn't figure out for himself that Stalin was a bad man then I doubted I could persuade him. And if he thought he was being clever or shocking then I wasn't going to gratify him by rising to his bait. Nevertheless, I was a little surprised that a doctor, committed to preserving the sanctity of life by the Hippocratic oath, was able without any hesitation to write off so much of it as mere chaff.

Alex meanwhile was still drinking, and in greater pain than ever before.

'We're going to a club called *Banzai* later, if you'd like to join us.'

Mike looked over at me and smiled.

We went to a restaurant, the most prestigious in Kazan, Mike told us. It was an American-style steakhouse that had English menus, for foreign oil workers, I assumed. By this point, however, the conversation was really limping along, like a polio victim. Soon it would wheeze its last dismal breath and die. Alex, meanwhile, was too poor to afford anything except a bowl of soup. Mike helped him out, but it was still embarrassing to watch him sipping away, trying to drag out the bowl while the rest of us tucked into plates of meat.

We decided to skip the club, although I was curious about nightlife in Tatarstan. Alex and Mike displayed no signs of grief. We parted on the street.

'Thanks,' said Joe.

Alex shrugged. 'Don't mention it.'

As soon as they were out of earshot, Joe turned to me. 'That Mike was a right cockmuncher. And he *really* liked you,' he said.

'You noticed?' I said. 'I was wondering if I was just imagining it.'

'He couldn't take his eyes off you, man.'

It was nice to know I wasn't paranoid. But I was thinking of other things. After talking to Alex and Mike for three or four hours, I was no nearer to an idea of Tatarstan. It remained elusive.

18

A cabinet of curiosities

I

I came upon some exhibition rooms just down some steps from the Kremlin. They were built into a wall, and definitely

Peter the Great's bottled babies. Some people collect stamps . . .

pre-Revolutionary. There were no windows, and the ceilings were low: I suspected they had been store rooms for the nobles of the Kremlin in an earlier period. There was very little to draw your attention to them, just a placard on the pavement outside. But what I found there was one of the great wonders of Russia – bottled mutant babies from Peter the Great's collection of freaks.

Excuse me if I digress from Tatarstan for a moment, but these freaks are one of my favourite things in the world, and it was a great joy for me to find them in Kazan. The story is interesting, I promise you.

In his youth, Peter the Great travelled around Europe, studying ships and engineering and contemporary Western customs. He worked incognito in the shipyards of Holland, learning for himself the skills he planned to import to backwards Russia. Simultaneously, he indulged a fascination for the natural world. He haunted auction rooms and markets, buying fossils, seashells, and stuffed animals. Then, in 1697, in Amsterdam, he paid a visit to the workshop of Frederik Ruysch, who was renowned as the greatest embalmer in Europe. Peter's casual shopping for dead things was about to enter a new, darker, much more obsessive level.

For Ruysch was an artist of death. He liked to *do things* with the bodies and limbs he preserved. He looked at the corpses of children and saw that they were terribly pretty. So he dressed them in lace and placed them in little coffins, adorned with beads, flowers and small candles and made them beautiful. When Ruysch looked at the skeletons of foetuses, he thought they would look wonderful mounted in dioramas illustrating allegorical themes. So he took the little bones and stuck them together in morally instructive combinations. Most gruesome of all, however, was his collection of nature's own 'sports', or whimsies – stillborn mutant babies, floating in jars of his preserving fluid.

Ruysch opened his workshop to the public twice a week, and Peter's was only one of many famous signatures in the guest book. But the Tsar's fascination with what he saw there was both profound and intimate. He was so affected by the beauty of one dead infant 'embalmed so masterfully that it seemed the child was merely sleeping' that this giant of a man, who would later torture his own son to death, could not help but kiss her.

Twenty years after his first visit, Peter returned to Amsterdam and paid Ruysch 20,000 gulden for the entire collection, and had it transported to St Petersburg. It would become the foundation of his 'Kunstkamera' – the first public museum in all Russia.

Ruysch, although seventy-nine years old at the time, immediately set about assembling a new collection. Peter, meanwhile, began augmenting the original one. In 1718 he issued his famous 'monsters decree', obligating his subjects to bring 'monsters' and 'ugly ones' from all over the empire to his museum. For ten years, monsters, both living and dead, were delivered to the Kunstkamera, and Peter's collection came to include live specimens of dwarfs and mutated animals as well as dead ones. Those who attempted to conceal their monsters were subject to a hefty fine if discovered.

Among the exhibits were an eight-legged lamb, a three-legged infant, and a sheep with two mouths and two tongues. But the most celebrated freak of all was Foma Ignatiev, a dwarf who actually lived in the museum. Not only was Foma a mere 126 cm tall, but he suffered from *ectodactyly*, which meant that his hands and feet terminated in two clawlike digits. In the carnivals of the nineteenth and twentieth centuries a man with his condition would have been billed as a lobster boy.

Peter claimed his goal was 'to instruct and teach about Nature – living and dead – and about the artistry that flows from the hands of men'. Legend has it that visitors to the museum were even offered a free glass of vodka and a slice of salo (salted pig's fat) to entice them within, so keen was the Tsar for his people to come and learn.

II

I had been to the Kunstkamera in St Petersburg a couple of times. Unfortunately there were no longer any live exhibits, and what survived of Peter's collection was divided between two rooms. One was particularly atmospheric. It was circular, with multiple exits and entrances, and the walls were lined with old wooden cabinets. They contained, among other things, a stuffed, two-headed lamb, the skeleton of a two-headed baby, a severed hand made curiously elegant by the addition of a lacy frill, and a child's head with the cap of the skull sawn off. The child had glass eyes. They peered out through the aged, yellow glass, blank and somehow weary, as curious schoolchildren gazed into the twisting coils of its brain.

The best stuff, however, was the cabinet of bottled babies. These infants are now three hundred years old, and sleep an eerie and unsettling sleep. Drained of all colour, they float there, pale and soft and squishy, as if in suspended animation, awaiting the day they will be awoken.

I saw a wide variety of abnormalities, from microcephalics with tiny heads to macrocephalics with great, swollen, balloon skulls. There was a child born with his brain outside his skull, and infants whose faces appeared to have collapsed in on themselves. There was a fleshy mermaid, labelled a 'siren', and a cyclops. And then there were the grimacing Siamese twins, who appeared locked in a deadly struggle to wrench themselves free of one another.

The exhibit in Kazan was a lot smaller, but even more gruesome. In addition to a cyclops, a pumpkin head, and a baby with its vestigial twin embedded in its body, there were Siamese twins of every imaginable variety: babies joined at the face, at the waist, end to end, scalp to scalp.

For some reason, although I always enjoy the company of the dead babies in St Petersburg, it was difficult to spend much time with those in Kazan. I kept thinking of the grief and terror of the mother when she saw the monster that had come from her womb. How was she was treated by her community? Were the parents pitied, or shunned as sinners, bearers of the Devil's curse? These sleepers were blissfully oblivious to the pain and the horror they had brought.

I also found the corpses more nauseating, more shocking than the first time I saw them. Perhaps it was the element of surprise. I wasn't prepared.

I returned to the street where the sun was shining, relieved to escape that dark cavern of nature's horrors. Nonetheless, I was glad I had spent the time with the babies. It was a surprise, a bonus, something slightly magical, even. I wondered idly where else Peter's collection was stored. Perhaps, I thought, in some remote corner of cold Siberia there is a small town where you can pay to enter an old storage room and see the pickled remains of Foma, his dwarf.

19

Confessions of a Japanese photographer (part 1)

I had been in Yoshi's company for days and I was beginning to feel bad that I hadn't actually had a conversation with him yet. I hadn't even tried. In the Kremlin, in the hotel, in the restaurants, I'd been silent. He was Joe's friend, not mine, and he didn't say much anyway, but nonetheless I felt some obligation, some pressure to say something. Besides, he was the first Japanese I had spent any significant time with and he had an interesting job. I felt I might be missing out on some good stories if I didn't try to speak to him at least once.

Joe had told me that Yosh was a professional photographer, and that he travelled the world taking pictures of horrible places, and held exhibitions of his work in Tokyo. I was impressed; it sounded glamorous. What most impressed me, however, was Yoshi's complete autonomy: he had taken full control of his life – earned enough money to say goodbye to the motherland and then drift across the earth for years, supporting himself with his art. It sounded beautiful to me. However, when I spoke to him the truth was less marvellous.

'Joe tells me you're a photographer,' I said.

'Yes, it true.'

'What type of photography do you do?'

'Commercial. I take photo for advertisement, for magazine, for catalogue. I make video too.'

'Do you only do commercial photography? Joe told me you do art photography, travel photography.'

'No – only commercial. I make video too.'

So all that stuff about the self-supporting artist was one of Joe's tall tales. Joe was a Scheherazade – embellishing his dreams, weaving stories that made his own life more glamorous. He had friends who were Buddhist monks, musicians, photographers . . . in all of this there was a kernel of truth; I didn't think he ever lied outright . . . but nevertheless, when I dug around inside his stories a reality more prosaic, sometimes even slightly sad would always emerge.

That said, I had never met a Japanese commercial photographer before. I figured Yosh had to have one or two good stories. I asked what the strangest thing he had ever photographed was.

'Once I made advertisement for soap. I film girl washing hand for whole day. I film for five minute, then stop. Then I film again, and again, and again for eight hours. It very boring.'

'Did she have nice hands?' I asked.

'Ya. Very nice. But she have ugly face. We film other girl for face.'

'Commercial photography very well paid in Japan, but very hard. I work all day, seven days a week. It no life, life not possible. So I save money for three years. I save fifty thousand dollars. Then I leave. I don't go back for three years. I don't work for three years. I travel.'

I looked at Yosh. His face was scarred, the result of a bad motorcycle accident when he was a teenager. His life, I thought, had to be boring. And lonely. Drifting from country to country, without friends, never going home. He was like the Wandering Jew. But he was cheerful and laughed a lot. He, at least, had chosen this life.

Gangs of Kazan

I was fascinated by Alex's mention of youth gangs in Kazan in the 1970s and 1980s. The next day, while eating breakfast in McDonald's, an idea for a film entitled *Gangs of Kazan* unfolded in my head. Just like Harry Potter did in J. K. Rowling's.*

THE SCENE
The lost world of the Soviet Union in the 1970s, the shabbiest point of the post-war era, in both the East and the West. Kazan is a drab, crumbling shit heap, with a run-down city centre surrounded by poor-quality housing and massive factories belching out smoke. The only colour in this landscape comes from giant billboards featuring Lenin and happy workers, but these are faded and covered in dirt. Against this backdrop two gangs, the Stalins and the Trotskys, fight it out for supremacy.

THE PLOT
The Trotskys get stranded in enemy territory late at night. The film follows their attempt to make it back to their own turf without being killed by another gang along the way. Those gangs, meanwhile, grow increasingly surreal, and start wearing fancy dress. One gang dresses like Soviet pioneers in shorts and red neckerchiefs; they carry lead pipes. Another all dress like the Beatles-era Paul McCartney and wear Paul McCartney masks. They go for flick knives. The violence mounts as the film progresses, reaching a climax towards the

* Note to producers – there are four movie ideas placed in each section of this book. There's been a lot of interest in the film in section 3 in particular. I'm still open to offers on all of them, however. But please: no time-wasters.

end. A highlight is when six Paul McCartney lookalikes get their heads stoved in with baseball bats.

THE CHARACTERS

There's Pasha, the leader; Iskander, the lieutenant; Vova, the young and inexperienced guy; Marat, who's strong but slow and Sergei who's angry and unpredictable. The last two both die. Marat gets truncheoned to death by police and Sergei, after getting separated from the others, gets mauled by a bear that's roaming through the city at night. There's also a frightened girl with them. She's called Anna. She isn't a Trotsky – she's Vova's sister, who wants to persuade her younger brother to abandon the gang. She slows them down and causes problems. Pasha and Sergei both fancy her, creating sexual tension, but that's solved when the bear takes Sergei's head off. She almost gets raped by an evil Paul McCartney in a scene that gives male viewers a chance to ogle a pair of nice young breasts.

Samuel L. Jackson does a cameo, as a gang specialist from Chicago flown in by the troubled Soviet authorities to look at the problem. His eyes flame and he gets all righteous as he rails against the Soviet bureacrats for not giving the kids freedom.

THE STYLES

Brown, brown, brown. It's 1978 after all, and Comrade Hairy Eyebrows is in charge (sort of) drooling away in his wheelchair. Everything is brown. Brown flares, brown shoes, Bay City Roller haircuts, and cheap polyester shirts.

THE SOUNDTRACK

Bad disco and easy listening. In the 1970s Russian youth listened to Boney M, Smokie, Demis Roussos, Jean Michel Jarre and French pop like Mireille Mathieu and Joe Dassin. There's a quality scene where a Paul McCartney has his head kicked in to the strains of 'Brown Girl in the Ring'. In slow motion.

THE CLIMAX

It starts when one of the Stalins attacks Pasha from behind with an ice pick, but Pasha ducks, avoids the blow and then crushes the guy's balls with one brutal kick. Then he and Slava, the lead Stalin, have a bottle fight as everyone else looks on. Slava the Stalin gets glassed. His cohorts retreat. The Trotskys arrive home, safe and sound (minus Marat and Sergei of course).

THE PITCH

The film is a poem of freedom. The independent human spirit always triumphs over the deadening choices offered by society. Instead of joining the Young Communists and working on building sites on their weekends, these boys band together and live bravely, according to their own rules. My film would

The Secret History of the World #15,611

capture the reckless, carefree, exuberant violence of youth, in that last vital moment before adulthood darkens it.

It would, however, have no connection to reality.

21

In the early 1970s in Kazan, a Russian called Sergei Antipov organized a boxing club. It was well equipped, and soon he had thirty or forty boys attending regularly. Antipov was in his late teens, the boys younger. Their parents didn't mind. It kept them off the streets, made them tougher, it was good discipline. Besides, it never did a boy any harm to know how to defend himself. That the boys idolized Antipov was perhaps a little strange, but not startling in adolescents. They need role models. They grow out of it.

Antipov's boxing club was not typical for the Soviet Union, however. In fact it was a recruiting ground and training camp for the criminal gang he was forming. The gang was called Tyap Lyap, an abbreviation of 'Teplokontrol', the name of the main factory in the local area. It was a workers' part of town: the boys who lived there were not going to study in the prestigious halls of Kazan State University. Their parents' lives were brutal and hard, spent toiling with machines in the enormous industrial plants of the city. They expected their lives would be the same, coming home bored and exhausted to tiny flats. They would rarely eat meat. There was little to work for, little to live for in the Soviet Union. Life was hard, grimy and poor.

Antipov offered something else, however. Economic reforms in the mid-1960s had led to a large increase in the production of black-market goods, and a network of shops selling them. Antipov saw openings for a strong man. With his gang, Tyap Lyap, he initiated a crime spree like nothing the Soviet Union had ever seen: beatings, robberies, armed robberies, extortion, racketeering, fights, murders. Previously the state had had the monopoly on crime. Now youth was taking over.

The fire started by Tyap Lyap spread, and soon other gangs appeared. They took their names from local areas, and thus great writers. Hadi Taktash, Adel Qutuy, and Pervaki were all respected Tatar and Soviet literary names. Others, such as Jilplochadka, were not. The gangs transformed them all into symbols of terror.

The gangs were ethnically mixed and authoritarian in structure. The youngest members, around fifteen to sixteen years old, were *sheluha/scorlupa* – 'shell'/'peel'. They worked as scouts and pickpockets. Next came the *molodiye* – 'bride-grooms' – who, being seventeen or eighteen years old, were expected to participate in fights and robberies. After them came only *stariki* – 'old men'. They too fought, but they were the masterminds, the planners, the ideological leaders of the groups. Regardless of age or position, however, all had to contribute to the *obshak*, the common kitty, Karl Marx style – 'each according to his ability'– whether that be through stealing, intimidation or violence.

The gangs expanded aggressively. Boys would be forced to join or take a beating. Wars were common, too, as gangs challenged each other over territory. These wars were fought without rules. You could hit a man when he was down; in fact, it was foolish not to. What if he got up again? Two against one was fine. Weapons, if you could get them, were A-OK. Tyap Lyap built their own, out of spare parts they culled from the Teplokontrol factory. Other gangs used knives, pistols, clubs, even acid in their attacks. By the mid-1980s there were over a hundred juvenile gangs in Kazan, in a state of permanent warfare. In the first half of 1988 alone, five teenagers were murdered and many more were hospitalized with serious injuries. As the Soviet Union teetered on collapse, the streets of Kazan were awash with youthful violence.

22

In the 1990s, however, the gang wars ended. The reason was simple: capitalism.

Territorial conflicts were set aside as everybody concentrated on making money. The first to get in on the act were the Hadi Taktash mob, who dated back to 1970s. Originally inspired by Tyap Lyap, they soon outstripped their mentors at business. They took control of *Orgsintez*, the biggest polyethylene factory in the region. They quickly diversified, however, moving into the far more profitable areas of drugs, prostitution and graveyard control. This last area was a guaranteed money-earner, as graveyards are never affected by a crisis. On the contrary, they boom. As life expectancy in the Russian Federation plummeted, so, under Hadi Taktash, the price of a plot of land to bury your loved one skyrocketed. They claimed: 'All the city is ours.'

Although Hadi Taktash was pre-eminent, large or small, all the gangs got in on the act. The easiest way for a gang to make money is to extract *krisha* payments from the shops and businesses in their neighbourhoods. *Krisha* means 'roof': it is the insurance money you pay so your shop or office won't meet with a sudden accident. A street trader bringing home $200 a month can pay up to half of that in *krisha*. But there are services you can extract for your *krisha* payments. A rival business may burn down. Or a rival businessman might be found in his doorway with a bullet in his head.

Other gangs diversified into markets, breweries, casinos and nightclubs: in short, every sphere of Tatarstan's economic activity. The *Banzai* club Alex and Mike invited us to visit was controlled by the Pervaki mob, and it was rumoured that the boss of Krasni Vostok, the largest brewery in the region, was a mobster. In fact, according to Tatarstan's public prosecutor, twenty major gangs in Kazan control nine out of ten private businesses and numerous state ones besides.

23

And with this shift towards business, the culture of the gangs has changed. The nicknames have gone. Strangers are never recruited, and nobody is forced to join. Now members come through family or old-school connections only, just like in an English gentleman's club. And whereas strength and prison time used to bring respect, now a boss needs the qualities of an organizer or businessman. After all, a major gang will have between fifty and two hundred members, and they all want opportunities to earn money.

The *obshak,* however, is one thing that has not changed. It remains and everyone still has to contribute. But the largest *obshaks* now contain enormous amounts of money and the gangs have representatives in Moscow and St Petersburg, where it is laundered and invested.

What about the police, you ask? I've read it argued that the Russian police aren't very well equipped to fight crime. In the Soviet Union, it was not actually their job to catch criminals, but rather to frame and dispose of ideological dissenters. In actual fact, in 1978, members of Tyap Lyap were brought to trial for over sixty crimes, although another thirty-six were suppressed. As most of the beatings and murders affected only other criminals the police were content to let them take it out on each other.

In modern Russia, meanwhile, police corruption is endemic.

Partly, it's economics. The state pays police about $200 a month. The criminals pay $400, so the police work for the criminals. But they work for themselves too. It's well known that if you don't get your *krisha* from a gangster you buy it from the cops, and that works even better.

At the start of the 1990s Kazan was notorious even by the Russian Federation's standards. Contract murders went unsolved; the TV channels showed corpses morning, noon and night, and parents were afraid to let their children walk to school alone for fear they might be kidnapped.

Since then, things have become less blatant and on the surface at least, there is calm. Not all the police are corrupt, either. In fact, the leaders of both Tyap Lyap and Hadi Taktash, much to their own astonishment, were successfully prosecuted in the late 1990s and are now sitting in prison. The gangs have not vanished, however. A new generation has stepped in to take over, and Tatarstan's major businesses remain in the grip of organized crime.

24

I didn't see any crime when I was in Kazan. But it was all around me. While I was staring at mutant babies near the Kremlin, Rafael Valeyev was walking in Azov, a new area of wide streets and high buildings in the north of the city. Three boys in cheap leather jackets beat him with baseball bats and stole his money. A few hours later, as I was sitting in my hotel room reading about Ivan the Terrible's invasion, Andrei Silkin, a nasty little punk and drug addict from Salik Saidashev street, was slapping Sveta Lyukmanova in the face, just to teach the little slut a lesson. A few hours later, while I was watching Alsou, the Tatar pop sensation on Russian MTV, Sveta, with the bruises rising on her face was giving a blow-job to Rustam Shakhmuratov, a small-time dealer in counterfeit merchandise from Bashkiria. And then the next day, as Joe, Yoshi and I relaxed in the sun on the bank of the Volga, Alexei Tarasov was working in the casino he managed. He didn't suspect that a killer was waiting near the doorway of his apartment building, ready to dispatch him with a single control shot.

25

Confessions of a Japanese photographer (part 2)

I was staring at the back of Yoshi's green backpack. It was covered in the names of the countries he had visited. There were some truly appalling hell-holes there: Cambodia, Uzbekistan, Turkmenistan, Burma . . . I wondered why he never went to nice places. The answer was very simple. He wanted the $50,000 he had saved to last as long as possible. In the West it would vanish very quickly. But in war-ravaged Third World countries he could really make his savings go a long way.

He also thought that these places were somehow more spiritual than, say, America or Sweden. Perhaps he was attracted by the absence of material things people in his own country had in such abundance and slaved so hard to earn. Whatever, I was impressed by his ability to drift fearlessly from scabrous hole to scabrous hole. I asked him if he'd ever felt in danger of death.

'In Burma,' he said, 'I go for walk one morning. I see boy walk towards me, with gun in his hands. I, shitting pants, think: "This is the end, for real. I dead this time." Then he smile, show me bananas. He want sell.'

'Did you buy any?' I asked.

'I eat. They were most tasty bananas of my life.'
I asked what the friendliest country he had been to was.
'Iran,' he answered, without any hesitation.
And the least friendly?
'Probably Russia,' he said.

26

Parts of Tatarstan I never saw

I never saw Tsipya, a village of baptized Tatars and Udmurts. The native inhabitants of this area, the Udmurts, were converted to Christianity in the mid-eighteenth century. Various incentives were offered to those who would accept the new faith. In 1724–25, for example, new converts were given 50 kopeks to buy clothing and footwear. By 1729, the sum had doubled to a rouble. But perhaps this wasn't enticing enough, because a mere two years later it was ten roubles *plus* a silver cross. Someone in this town is also alleged to have invented a wooden motor car and it's in the local museum, but I never saw it, as I never visited Tsipya.

I also never visited Elabuga, in spite of the fact that I read a beggar was sacrificed to pagan gods there in the early nineteenth century, and I like that kind of thing. Fans of Russian poetry may be interested to know that Elabuga is where Marina Tsvetaeva killed herself in 1941. There's a museum devoted to her but, of course, I don't know anything about it.

I never saw Leninogorsk either. There's something for everyone in the 'youth centre' there: kids can play in the amusement park while their parents dine at candle-lit tables, or play billiards, if they wish. Friday nights they have a *Nostalgie* 1980s theme, for the over-thirties. Saturdays, however, are reserved for teenage discos. They even have live dancing in the can-can style, or so they say. Unfortunately I cannot confirm the veracity of the management's claims.

Lastly, I also never went to the museum preserve of Velikie Bulgary. This site contains many ruins of the Volga Bulgars, the power in the area before the Golden Horde. In addition to some old mausoleums and mosques you can see the remains of a bath-house. That might have been interesting. On the other hand, it might also have been excruciatingly dull. Generally speaking, if you want to get a feeling for ancient peoples, you're better off reading a book.

There are many other things I didn't see in Tatarstan, but unfortunately there is no room to list them here.

27

The women of Kazan

My guidebook stated that: 'The women of Kazan have long had a reputation both at home and abroad for being among the most attractive in the world . . . In Kazan, local girls have been drifting off to places like Cuba, the former GDR and more recently to other foreign countries. It is not unusual for these girls to be students who combine their studies with a modelling career.'

In actual fact, as I wandered around Kazan I saw more women with monobrows and ear hair than I ever had in my entire life.

Only joking. The only woman of Kazan I knew was a girl called Alla, who worked for the same company as me in Moscow. Alla should have been beautiful. She had long, thick dark hair, and black eyes with long lashes. She was slim, and loved music. She had studied the violin at the Moscow Conservatory. But she also had a moustache, uneven teeth and was crippled by shyness. I had known her for about five years and had maybe said about five words to her in that time. But she was always extremely pleasant, smiling with embarrassment each time we met.

One day I was waiting for a friend at the metro when I spotted her with a man. He was a new guy, Rob, who had come to Russia from Liverpool. He was an old-school, 1980s-style *Socialist Worker*-type militant. He didn't see me amid the throng, but she did. She was on his arm, leaning into him. Her eyes flashed and she nodded at me as she went past. She looked delighted.

I told Joe what I'd seen, as he lived with Rob. He knew all about it. They'd awoken him the night before, ringing the doorbell at 3 a.m. Rob had lost his keys. Alla flushed scarlet in front of Joe as she stood there in the doorway. Then Rob ushered her into his room, where, to quote Joe, he 'chewed on her moustache' in a night of passion.

Two weeks later and it was finished. Rob had thrown her over for a prettier girl. I saw Alla in the office. It was excruciating. Everybody knew what had happened. She was smiling, but mixed in with her shyness were new qualities of shame and humiliation.

Rob, meanwhile, was totally blasé. He knew she was still hung up on him, and even generously accompanied her to concerts from time to time. She always invited him. She could get free tickets through her connections, and Rob wasn't averse to a free show, even if it meant sitting next to an ugly girl with a moustache for a few hours.

Carved inscription on a mosque in the Tatar quarter. Tatars can't read it, either.

28

The spires of Kazan

I like to read about the Kazan of old: this oriental city on the edge of Europe, this gateway to the East, to a world of philosophers, traders, minarets and dark-eyed beauties. It sounded spectacular: a jewelled city, of mysteries, incense-filled rooms, hidden corners, of cruelty and beauty, of darkness and enlightenment.

But Ivan the Terrible washed all that away in a torrent of fire and blood, and what had taken its place was a provincial Russian city: pleasant, but rather dull, distinguished from other Russian towns only by the occasional minaret protruding from a mosque, which in turn was designed to resemble a Russian building as much as possible.

These cloaked mosques shrink from attention, and are rather small, and pathetic. They look like old sheds with spires.

I went walking in the Muslim quarter: a grid of abandoned streets, with dilapidated wooden huts. I walked and walked and saw no one, not even any animals. There was a moment when a call to prayer drifted towards me over the rooftops, but I couldn't discern what direction it was coming from, or who it was calling to.

I went on and passed into an industrial zone, a broad road lined with large Soviet factories: dirty boxes, with enormous funnels. I came to some train tracks and crossed them, saw buildings with balconies with bars on them, like cages for humans. An old man and an old woman were standing by the tracks, not going anywhere, just standing. They watched me approach but, as I passed, I realized they weren't watching at all, but looking through me, as if I was not there.

Halfway down a long street of mud, I saw a tall green minaret. I walked towards it, paused at the gate, and then went in. There was a little man on the door. He was startled to have a visitor, and one from the West, no less. I asked if I could see inside. 'Of course,' he said. 'Of course.'

I took off my shoes and stepped within. It was the first mosque I had been in. The walls were bare. The floors were carpeted. The windows contained tinted glass. There was an arrow on the ceiling, indicating Mecca. I spent a few minutes standing there. It was simple, humble even, but that was precisely why I liked it.

There was a room in the mosque with little wooden desks and chairs, surplus from a Soviet classroom. The little man explained that the mosque contained a school. Seventy years of Soviet rule had destroyed the Tatar people's knowledge of Islam, and now they had to start from scratch, to learn again. 'I am a student too,' he said. 'Even though I am old.'

By the door there was a wall-hanging, a huge rug that showed the giant mosque they were building in the Kremlin. 'It's a gift', he said, 'to us from the President. Not from Putin – from *our* President – Mintimir Shaimiyev.'

I like to read about the Kazan of old, of dreaming minarets and Asiatic bazaars, I do. But I'm glad it was destroyed.

If it existed today it would be a dilapidated heap, or a sterile heritage centre, an empty shell that existed for tourists only, insipid and dull, like Prague. But the obliterated Kazan can never be visited, except in our imaginations, and thus it can never disappoint. It has a mythic power, a dreamlike power. Through annihilation it has been transubstantiated. And the pitiful squalor of the real Kazan only adds to the beauty and power of the unreal one.

KALMYKIA

The author, with milk, in front of the Golden Gate, Elista

1

The summer came. I went to New York, hoping I'd find all manner of strangeness, freaks and weirdos. There were only yuppies and wine bars. I'd been fooled by the movies.

The best I managed was on Coney Island: bored, I went for a walk down a crap street away from the boardwalk. I saw a few old cars and some garages selling junk, and grew more bored. Then suddenly I came upon a white tent erected in the middle of the pavement. A black guy was sitting at a table with a little placard in front of him that read: 'World's Smallest Woman – $1'.

I gave him a dollar and entered. Directly behind him was a table, and sitting on that table was a tiny black woman, who stopped watching TV to smile at me. She had an enormous head, and a doll's body. With a miniature hand she indicated a sign: 'Hello, my name is Elizaveta. I come from Haiti. I do not speak English.' With the other she indicated a piece of paper giving her measurements. Then she smiled at me. She had big, bright eyes and a kind face. I smiled back.

We smiled at each other for a few moments more. I didn't really know what else to do. I decided to give her a dollar. I pulled it out of my wallet, and handed it to her. Her tiny hand quickly snatched it away, and made it disappear into her dress. She smiled, and nodded.

I smiled again, and left. I thanked the black guy at the table. He nodded.

2

Joe, meanwhile, took the Trans-Siberian to Lake Baikal, and then on to Mongolia, China, Kyrgyzstan and Uzbekistan.

While he was in Tashkent, some terrorists hijacked three aero-planes and flew them into the World Trade Center and the Pentagon, killing thousands of people. Uzbekistan, of course, is a Muslim country and borders Afghanistan. One of Joe's travelling companions, an expectant father, immediately left and returned to Moscow. However, there was little danger of violence to Joe and his friends from the Uzbeks. The authorities in that country torture Islamic militants and send them to the Gulag.

I myself had left America two weeks earlier, missing the catastrophe. As for Yosh, he had disappeared back into the void: nobody knew where he was.

3

Joe returned in October and we immediately began plotting a new adventure. Kazan had only whetted our appetite for black holes. Now we planned to push it much further. We bandied around several possibilities from among the European republics until we settled upon one that far, far out-stripped Tatarstan in obscurity and bizarreness. It was so obscure that a lot of Russians didn't even know where it was: the Republic of Kalmykia.

The Republic of Kalmykia is located in southern Russia, between the Stavropol and Astrakhan regions, to the north of Daghestan. It is flat, and mostly steppe - dry, empty land. Although it's the size of Scotland, its population stands at 300,000, less than that of Edinburgh. And of those, less than half are actually Kalmyk.

The Kalmyk are ethnic Mongols and their republic is the only one in Europe where Buddhism is recognized as a state religion. Isn't that remarkable? I was amazed to discover that so alien a place existed in my home continent, and even more amazed that I'd never heard of it. Surely it was good for at least one documentary on Channel 4, or one ten-minute segment on *Newsnight*? *Eurotrash*, even?

Apparently not.

4

If you look at Kalmykia on a map, you will see that it is almost entirely white. This whiteness is the cartographic expression of nothingness. I was fascinated by this emptiness. Once before, in Kazakhstan, I had seen the steppe, a vast sandy ocean of dry, dead land. It was beautiful and surreal, like a Martian landscape, like something from a dream. I wanted to see it again.

But I wanted to go there for deeper, almost metaphysical reasons. Kalmykia was a special type of place. It was a no-place, a non-state, with no representation in the Western imagination. It didn't appear in histories of Russia or the Soviet Union, except in the odd footnote, here and there. Imaginatively it didn't exist. And yet people lived in that no-place; they were born, struggled and died in it. At the time I had no idea where I was going in my life, and I was talking a lot about spiritual and metaphysical voids. This was my opportunity to visit a physical, literal one.

I wanted to see what *nowhere* looked like.

5

Remnants of history

The first Mongol invasion of Russia, which brought the Tatars to the Volga, is very famous. The second Mongol invasion of Russia, however, is almost totally unknown.

In the early seventeenth century, the Oirat, a small tribe

from Dzungaria in Western Mongolia, left their homeland and emigrated across Siberia to the steppes of the lower Volga. This was, and still is, a vast stretch of semi-desert in the south of Russia. The tribes already living there, eking out a dismal existence from the poor, arid land, were no match for this ferocious band of warrior nomads. They were quickly subjugated by the Oirat, who claimed the land for themselves.

Although this was a far smaller force than the original horde, the Russians nonetheless opted not to fight it. Instead the Oirat were offered a deal. In return for providing a defence against the Muslim tribes in the south, they would be granted dominion over all the lands they had recently occupied. From the southern Volga to the Ural mountains in the East, this was an enormous swath of territory that would leave them ample room for their nomadic lifestyle and village-burning ways. Perhaps the Russians did not consider this land especially valuable; perhaps the carnage of the 'Tartar yoke' was too near a memory for them to risk fighting it again. Either way, the Oirat were pleased by this offer and consented to its generous terms. In 1707 their khanate, which stretched to Europe's easternmost border, was officially established. For the next hundred and fifty years, Russia did not attempt to interfere with Oirat affairs, and they were, to all intents and purposes, autonomous.

By the middle of the eighteenth century, however, the Russian state had grown in strength and ambition. It was no longer willing to allow the potentially valuable pasture land of the steppe to be left to a mob of Mongolian savages, and still less willing to permit so unruly a force to roam unchecked over so much of Russia's territory. Catherine the Great decided to bring them to heel. She established a chain of huge wooden fortresses to encircle and enclose the tribe. Then, under the protection of the Russian army, she sent in Russian and German farmers to settle the land. Missionaries were dispatched to convert the Buddhist nomads to Orthodox Christianity. Finally, Russia began to intervene in the appointment of the tribal leadership.

The Oirat could countenance this treatment no longer. But they numbered only three hundred thousand, including women and children. They knew they would lose a war with the Russian empire. The elders, desperate to preserve their people's identity, resolved to leave the lower Volga and lead the tribe on a mass exodus east, back to their homeland of Dzungaria (now Sinkiang province in China), where it was said a beautiful and fertile land awaited the return of its lost children. The Emperor there had embraced Buddhism and was ready to welcome back his prodigal sons and daughters.

The elders decreed that the whole tribe should leave together, on the same night. Those on the west bank of the Volga would cross the frozen river to join those on the eastern side, and then they would all set out as one for home. But on the appointed night – 4 January 1771 – a violent storm blew up, wrecking the ice. The inhabitants of some fifteen thousand tents could not cross the river to join their kinsfolk. The elders abandoned them.

Those who were left behind became known as the 'Kalmyk', which means 'remnant'. And that remnant, once part of a band of proud conquerors, now lay conquered, and was subsumed within the Russian empire, where it remains, more or less, to this day, as the Republic of Kalmykia, a constituent republic of the Russian Federation.

The abandoned Kalmyk were administered by a Russian 'Guardian of the Kalmyk People'. They persisted in their nomadic lifestyle, and resisted pressure to convert to Orthodoxy. But now a tiny minority, they were just another obscure ethnic group among many spread across the Russian empire, the people that no one knew about then, or knows about now – like the Yevenk in the far east, or the Ubikh in the south.

As for the Oirat who did escape, ultimately they faced an even worse fate than the stranded Kalmyks. As they advanced through Europe and Asia they encountered evil upon evil. Hunger, disease and exposure claimed the lives of the young and the old, the weak and the strong. Russian, Kazakh and Kyrgyz forces staged raids that devastated the ranks of the once mighty warriors. In seeking to preserve their people, the elders instead brought them to the brink of destruction. By the time the tribe arrived in Dzungaria, only an exhausted and ravaged third of the original number was still alive.

6

Chess City

We were slow to get to Kalmykia. It took months. I blame the winter, and the brutal snow that smothered the country. It's hard to get motivated for an adventure when it's cold and dark all the time. However, the thought of the great wastes to the south did not leave me. In fact, as the endless dreary days rolled past and I gazed out the window at the slush and ice, at the back of my mind there was always the promise of the radical nothingness in Kalmykia. I became fairly obsessed, in fact.

Then Kalmykia began to come to me. That Christmas, Moscow's excruciatingly dull English-language paper the *Moscow Times* carried a long feature on a struggle in the world of chess. Amid a lot of stuff about Gary Kasparov's dispute with FIDE (the World Chess Federation) I found two surprising facts. First, the head of FIDE, Kirsan Ilumzhinov, was also the President of Kalmykia. They had a picture of him: he was a young guy, still in his thirties, very slim with a boyish grin. Most Russian leaders, on the other hand, are middle-aged slobs with faces like boiled meat.

Secondly, Ilumzhinov, a real chess fanatic, had been criticized for spending millions of dollars his republic could not afford on something called Chess City in Elista, the Kalmyk capital. Ilumzhinov had built it for the 1998 Chess Olympiad, which was held in Elista. Exactly what this Chess City was, or what it was for, the article did not explain. Nor was there a picture of this mysterious complex.

To me, however, it had the ring of one of those old-fashioned vanity projects indulged by an eccentric with too much power – like, for example, Peter the Great's collection of bottled babies, or Frederick William of Prussia's regiment of giants. That leader had his scouts travel Europe at great expense looking for guys big enough to join his ornamental regiment of very tall men, even once kidnapping a very tall Frenchman who didn't want to join.

For those inclined to admire such things, there are few things more beautiful or amusing than vast amounts of energy and money wasted over utterly eccentric and useless pursuits. Especially when done by a tyrant presiding over a country with a dirty, starving peasant populace. Usually we have to look to the past for this kind of diversion, but here, if I was lucky, was a modern instance.

By the end of March it was still cold but the snow had disappeared. Yosh, too, had returned, after spending the winter in Bangkok. It was time.

7

There was no rail link from Moscow to Elista, which meant we had to fly. There were two major drawbacks to this: (1) I was scared of dying; (2) I couldn't be arsed sorting out the tickets. I managed to shirk the job on to Joe's shoulders.

Joe went through the travel agents in the phone book one by one, asking about flights to Elista. Many had never heard of the place. One insisted that no such republic as Kalmykia existed. Someone else said it was in Kazakhstan. Then, after half an hour of summary dismissals, Joe found a woman willing to listen to him. She asked where he came from.

'England,' said Joe.

'Oh,' she said. 'That's exotic. You have a very sexy voice. Would you like to take me out this weekend?'

That's one of the nice things about Russia: every day something new and unexpected. Several calls later Joe at last found a travel agent that offered flights from Moscow twice a week, on Tuesdays and Saturdays.

He never took the amorous lady out, however.

8

The flights from Moscow's Domodedovo Airport left mainly for Siberia and Central Asia: former Gulag towns, like Karagandy, or industrial nightmare zones, like Magnitogorsk. The bizarre thing was that the airport itself was beautiful: you could almost believe you were in an airport in a *nice* country like Holland or Denmark. It was clean, air-conditioned, and almost efficient. What gave it away were the weather-beaten faces, the shuttle-trader bags, the clacking, guttural unknown tongues and alien gazes of men and women returning to earthly hells people in the West know little of. They were like invaders from another dimension.

A nice, modern bus took us from the departure gate towards a cluster of planes that huddled together on the edge of the airfield, like a council of giant Rocs from *The Adventures of Sinbad*. The first plane we saw was big, bright and relatively modern-looking. It had pretty insignia on the tailfin. This surprised me as I had read in the papers that Russian domestic carriers were rusty death traps almost as old as powered flight itself.

The second plane was also large and modern. I thought wistfully, 'That one looks quite nice.' But there were only about twenty of us, and it could have held over a hundred passengers. The third was slightly smaller, but still well maintained and seemingly comfortable, which was very reassuring. I began to wonder if there was nothing wrong with internal air travel in Russia. Perhaps the horror stories in the papers were merely clichés served up by lazy journalists. Or perhaps the truly deadly planes flew only from provincial city to provincial city, ferrying the insignificant poor to fiery deaths.

Then, however, the planes on the tarmac began to shrink, to grow older, and shabbier. I kept hoping our guide would stop and say, 'It's all right, this one's yours' – but there was always another plane beyond whatever rusty Meccano job we were approaching. And she just kept on going. The planes dwindled, they grew shrivelled, wizened, until I didn't think it was possible for two humans to fit in the cockpit of the things I was looking at. But still we kept on moving, and still they kept on shrinking. Finally we reached the last plane, an old VW camper van with wings. We stopped.

'This one's yours,' said the guide.

We entered through the rear.

9

A reconciliation with death

Our plane, a Yak 40, reminded me of the old flying machines you see being buffeted in storms in old black-and-white movies. In actual fact, it had been built in the 1980s. But the Soviet Union excelled at making things look old and tired.

The interiors were very curious. They seemed designed to make you feel uneasy. The cabin walls curved tight around us, and were painted a strange, unnatural green, the colour of leukaemia in the Soviet Union, of bald children who aren't going to get better. Sitting in my seat I felt very claustrophobic and thought about death, specifically my death, which I had so far successfully managed to avoid.

Suddenly, however, it seemed that death was very close. Perhaps, in fact, the Grim Reaper was sitting in the cockpit. I wondered if I was ready to meet my maker. A fiery airplane death would be relatively swift. The worst bit, undoubtedly, would be the screaming on the way down. I didn't think I'd like that. On the other hand, it would certainly solve some problems. I'd be liberated from thinking about my career for a start. I'd never need to cook again. And I wouldn't have to go back to work the following Monday. I'd end my days strong and healthy, en route to the great emptiness. Why, there was even a poetry to it! Maybe death was a sweet release after all, just like the ancients thought.

Take off was very rough, but I was expecting that. The plane lurched violently and we were almost thrown against the ceiling. It happened again as we passed through the clouds. That time I felt very nervous. But then I heard the other passengers laughing. Then I heard myself laughing, too. *Curious*, I thought. *My death never seemed funny before.*

10

The Kalmykia–Japan Friendship Society

The Kalmykia–Japan Friendship Society, though not the most

obscure association in the world, might rightly be considered one of the most obscure. As far as I am aware it only has one member, its president, a middle-aged lady named Svetlana, who cannot actually speak Japanese.

Nevertheless, she was sitting next to Yoshi on the flight to Elista. She was very excited, as she didn't actually get to meet Japanese people very often.

Now is that a good omen, or what?

11

No longer concerned by death, I slept like a baby while Svetlana and Yoshi were bonding. I awoke only when the plane dipped to land. I looked out the window and marvelled at what I saw: emptiness, like nothing I had ever seen. There were no trees or hills, no buildings or pylons or wires, there wasn't even the purple grass I'd seen in the Kazakh steppe. There was just dead white land as far as the eye could see and, above it, an infinite azure sky. It was astonishing.

The plane landed, remarkably smoothly, and we disembarked. I got off first, and took a long look around. Everything was dead, beautifully dead. No doubt this sounds very nihilistic, but this was what I had come for. This was the perfect expression of the void. This was my version of Wordsworth's 'Daffodils'. I wanted to get back on the plane and return to Moscow. I had seen what I'd come for: nothing. There was really no point in going on. Life, however, demands that you go on. Joe and Yosh joined me on the tarmac.

'You wouldn't think you were still in Russia,' said Joe. 'It's amazing.'

'You might not even think you were still on earth,' I said.

Behind us, hovering on the edge of this great empty field, was a row of ancient propeller planes. I had seen their sort before, in museums. These, however, were waiting to be flown. They were the Kalmyk fleet. Suddenly I understood why I kept reading about plane crashes in Russian newspapers.

Behind the planes was Elista International Airport. It was little more than a shed. Well, OK: a shed with a Buddhist pagoda built on the roof. Although it was Saturday afternoon, all the doors were padlocked and there was nobody around. Only the toilet was open. It was a wooden outhouse built over a smelly hole.

Three flags rustled in the wind. First, the Russian tricolour, then the Kalmyk flag (a white lily in a blue circle on a yellow background) and finally the FIDE flag (a blue knight chesspiece on a white background). I remembered Ilumzhinov's mysterious vanity project, Chess City: it was out there, waiting for me.

Four taxis were waiting in front of the flags. They quickly filled up and vanished into their own clouds of dust. We might have been stuck there until the next flight from Moscow, had not Yoshi been sitting next to Svetlana on the plane. The President of the Kalmykia–Japan Friendship Society informed us rather imperiously that she had a personal driver who would take us into town. The 'driver', in fact, was her husband, a little man with a gentle smile.

12

As we drove through the steppe Svetlana planned our stay for us. She spoke good English and I liked the way she used my language. I was struck by the way she seemed to swirl words around inside her mouth, almost as if tasting them. Sometimes, when pronouncing a particularly long one like *substantial* (which she had a particular fondness for), her eyes would flash and her tongue would briefly appear, flickering across her lips.

'Well,' she said. 'We need to find a place for you to stay.' She turned to her husband. 'What about your Aunt Luda's? She's got a spare room. They could stay there for free.'

It was remarkable. She had managed to intuit that we were cheap bastards.

'It's only one room, Sveta,' he replied. 'It's rather small for the young men.'

Damn, I thought.

'Then what about your brother? He could move in with us for a few days. They could have his flat.'

'I'd have to talk to him first . . .'

'Well, talk to him.'

'Why don't we take them to a hotel? For the first night at least?'

Svetlana pondered. 'Maybe that's not a bad idea,' she said.

Svetlana turned to us and explained the plan. Then she began asking questions.

'Now . . . what is the purpose of your visit to Elista?'

'Oh, just tourism,' said Joe.

I expected scepticism. As with Tatarstan, it had been difficult to persuade people we were going to Kalmykia purely for tourism. When we bought the plane tickets, the travel agent asked if we were journalists. A businessman on the plane had watched us closely and with great suspicion. Svetlana, however, was delighted.

'Ah! Tourism! Excellent, excellent! Well, we'll need to work out some kind of itinerary for you.' She turned to her husband. 'What is there for them to see?'

'Er . . .' he said, thinking. 'Chess City.'

'Ah yes, Chess City, you must see Chess City.'

I considered asking for more information, but decided not

to. I did not want to deprive myself yet of so delicious a mystery.

'What else?' she asked her husband.

'Er . . .' he said. 'Er . . .'

'Never mind,' said Svetlana. 'We'll think of things. Now, Yoshi, maybe you could come to our school and give a talk to some of the children about Japan. How long will you be staying in Elista?'

'Only one or two days,' said Yoshi.

'Hmm? What's that?'

'Only one, two days.'

Svetlana was silent. I could feel her shock, her disappointment. Suddenly all her efforts at promoting Kalmyk–Japan friendship had fallen through.

I felt guilty.

You are now entering Elista. Or maybe leaving. Doesn't make much difference, really.

13

Mirage City

As we drove, objects would occasionally emerge out of the nothingness around us – a telephone pole here, a concrete bunker there, an abandoned factory building there – the usual detritus of the Russian road. Then, after about half an hour, Elista itself reared up out of nowhere, a city of dust and concrete.

None of the buildings was very high, or very old. And we could see nothing that dated from before the Second World War: it was entirely Soviet. But in spite of that, the streets had a certain shabby charm. The blocks of flats had been painted in bright, cheerful tones – pink and green and blue – and featured ethnic designs moulded into the concrete, to make them less faceless.

This was not a city where people rushed to go anywhere. There were hardly any cars. In fact, there were hardly any people. It was just a collection of concrete blocks sitting in the desert, washed out and growing steadily more decrepit. Although it was 2002, they still had huge chess murals from the 1998 Chess Olympiad painted on the sides of buildings. It felt like I was in a mirage that had forgotten to disappear.

Joe nudged Yoshi. 'Ulaan Bataar,' he said, indicating the city's stumpy concrete obelisks. Yoshi nodded in agreement. I struck the capital of Mongolia off my 'places to visit' list. I had always imagined it to be an ancient and beautiful city of mystery. Evidently it too was a pile of Soviet crap.

A broad road took us straight to the centre of town. I caught a brief glimpse of the youthful President on a billboard, pictured alongside the Dalai Lama.

14

The sparkling destiny of Kirsan Ilumzhinov

I

> I have been on a UFO. The extraterrestrials put a yellow
> space suit on me. They gave me a tour of the spaceship
> and showed me the command centre. I felt very comfort-
> able with them.
>
> Kirsan Ilumzhinov, 2001

Elected at the age of thirty, Ilumzhinov was the first leader of
post-Communist Kalmykia and the youngest president of a
'sovereign state' (Kalmykia uses the same language in its constitution as Tatarstan) in the world. A former businessman
and self-proclaimed millionaire, one of Ilumzhinov's first acts
as President was to invite the Dalai Lama to leave exile in
India and move to Elista. He explained that the great religious
leader's arrival in Kalmykia 'would have strongly stabilized
the political situation in the republic. And, as is well known,
political stability is the milk of economic growth.'

If inviting the Dalai Lama to live in your semi-desert wasteland strikes you as a strange way of stimulating economic
growth, you are not alone. Ilumzhinov is a very strange politi-
cian with many strange ideas. But that, at least, makes him
interesting. Consider the following text from his autobiography, *The President's Crown of Thorns*. Here he explains that
he was born in 1962, the Year of the Tiger, and quotes an
ancient Kalmyk prophecy relating to that year:

> And the days will come when the souls of the believers
> will dwindle to the size of an elbow and man himself will
> become as faint-hearted and timorous as a hare, and the

lustre of Buddha's great and pure teaching will grow dim. Then the people will indulge in drinking and greed, and the worthless will rule the world. Then he will emerge, the Tiger, the powerful protector of the earth and the Lord of all oriental lands. The earth will be shaken by his horrible roar and the worthless and miserable rulers will scatter in fear, there will be no more lies and the minds of the stray will regain clarity. Those born in the Year of the Tiger will be summoned to govern them and bring nobility to their people.

Now I wonder who could he be talking about?

II

Ilumzhinov's autobiography is a marvellously ambiguous text. Although it's difficult to believe a word he says, his style is so naive and his thoughts so strange that it's also difficult to believe he is lying.

For example, he indulges in all the usual 'I never wanted to be president' nonsense and claims that he became a millionaire in the Soviet Union without breaking any laws, which is rather like claiming to have had sex without losing your virginity. Then he talks a lot about how much cash he gave to charity. It's easy to dismiss all this as self-aggrandizing claptrap.

He explains his penchant for photo ops with, variously, the Dalai Lama, the Patriarch of Russia, and Pope John Paul II as arising from a desire to raise the profile of the Kalmyk nation. This may be true, but it is also easy to see them as the actions of a vain, fame-hungry individual, which Ilumzhinov, like most of us, almost certainly is.

Simultaneously, however, he loves to indulge in poetic flights, and dabbles in history and mysticism. He rabbits on

Uri Geller-style about subjects as varied as ESP, the afterlife, zombification, drugs, chiromancy, theosophy, UFOs, clairvoyance and bio energy with great sincerity. He talks at length about the universal moral law, the judgment that comes after death, the unity of all religions. He unfolds before us a mystic vision of cosmic unity he had while lying on his back looking at the sky, and explains that before standing for president of Kalmykia he flew to Bulgaria to consult with an old mystic called 'Vanga'. Vanga looked into his eyes and saw the suffering his people had undergone. Then she gave him her blessing: he was the one to lead his nation to greatness.

Ilumzhinov paints himself as an innocent, steering a spiritual path in the midst of much corruption and lies. A man motivated only by love for the poor and downtrodden, the insulted and the injured. He admits to mistakes, but claims he always does his best: 'I have been betrayed, deceived and conned by people because of my gullibility and faith.'

III

He has his detractors, however, who don't consider him gullible at all but rather believe he is a cunning, tyrannical crook. These include most of Russia's political liberals and democratic reformers. They point to his failure to attract any foreign investment whatsoever to Kalmykia, his penchant for spending large sums of cash on vanity projects (aside from sinking millions into Chess City, Ilumzhinov spends a third of the state budget on Elista's football team), the relentless decline of Kalmykia's economy, nepotism, wide-scale election fraud and the suppression of all opposing voices in the media.

In addition to these pleasant phenomena, Elista has also witnessed the usual onslaught of car bombs, shootings and death threats that mark Russian political life. But Kalmykia is especially notorious. The most infamous incident in

Ilumzhinov's reign came in 1998 when the corpse of Larissa Yudina, a journalist for an anti-Ilumzhinov newspaper was found face down in a pool of water on the outskirts of Elista. She'd had her head smashed in. Some of Ilumzhinov's former aides were later arrested and gaoled for the murder. When Ilumzhinov was pressed about it on Russian TV, he replied in typically eccentric style by ignoring the question entirely and declaring he would run for the Russian presidency in 2000.*

Attempts to paint Ilumzhinov as a common crook don't work for me, however. At the very least, he is an uncommon one. As much as he enjoys power and seeks celebrity, he is also a master provocateur. For example, upon taking control of FIDE he proposed holding the 1997 Chess World Championship in Baghdad – this at the height of sanctions.

Indeed, one of my favourite Ilumzhinov comments concerns Saddam Hussein, whom he met several times before the tyrant was deposed and found hiding in a dirty hole. Of the murderous dictator who produced a copy of the Koran written in his own blood, he said, 'I found him very pleasant. He is a normal man.'

While I was in Kalmykia, however, I didn't concern myself much with politics. In fact, regardless of whether Ilumzhinov was an evil bastard or not, I wanted to meet him. Tourists were rarer than black swans in Elista, so Joe and I hoped we'd be able to present ourselves to Ilumzhinov as envoys from our homelands. We figured we could show him that word of the Kalmyk nation was getting out and now Western people wanted to visit Elista for their holidays. He'd like that. We'd be like Marco Polo coming to Kubla Khan.

On my journey I didn't want to think of the evil in the world; it was too boring. Why visit a place only so that you

* He didn't, by the way.

can denounce it? How puritanical, how dreary. How easy. Why not look for the beauty instead?

I wanted to be innocent. I was willing to let Elista reveal what it wished to reveal.

Chess, compulsory in Kalmyk schools, unites the races.

15

Svetlana took us into the hotel and helped book our rooms. She was a forceful and competent woman and within a minute we had beds for a couple of nights. Then she bade us farewell.

As she left I had mixed feelings. Partly I was relieved, as I was unnerved by her overbearing helpfulness. But, on the other hand, I knew that I had failed to grasp the olive branch of friendship that had been held out to me. A door had opened, briefly, and then closed again. Whatever lay beyond it, I would never know.

I was cheered up by the Hotel Elista, however, as it was a crumbling heap. I like dilapidated hotels. They have a special, unique atmosphere of melancholia. They are also very cheap. In this one there was no hot water and electric cables lay exposed in the corridor. There were also a couple of dead fridges cluttering the place up. Much to my surprise, however, we had BBC World in our rooms. BBC World, of course, is crap but nevertheless soothing when you are stranded far from civilization. We relaxed for a while, watching a remarkable *Horizon* documentary on cot death. After that I proposed to Joe and Yosh that we get out and look around.

16

As soon as we stepped outside, however, I felt a slight, almost imperceptible shift in reality. Time slowed down. Everything got warped.

What had happened? I don't know. It was something impossible to pin down. There was a bizarre gold clock outside the hotel: it just didn't look right. Its jagged edges were too jagged. Its gold was not the gold I knew. Then a child ran up to Joe, hand outstretched, begging for money: he seemed angry and hostile. It was still light: I had expected it to be dark . . . These details threw themselves at me. They felt alien, jagged and strange. My senses were heightened too, becoming almost unbearably acute. It was as if I could see everything from every angle simultaneously, like Ray Milland at the end of *The Man with X-Ray Eyes*. The dead city was glowing, shifting, sliding all around me.

I was not alone either. Joe and Yosh felt pretty nervous too.

We crossed the street to the Avenue of Heroes. The Avenue of Heroes was a narrow stretch of grass sliced in two, lengthwise, by a concrete path. It was lined with trees, which in turn were full of huge, beady-eyed black crows. They squatted in their nests, screeching incessantly. It was a brutal cacophony.

I couldn't hear any of the usual city sounds. There was no hum and roar of traffic, no music, there were no fragments of other people's conversations. There was only the screech of the crows, filling the air. It was disturbing.

'You're fucked,' the crows cried. *'You're all alone and nobody knows where you are. Svetlana's left you! You're really fucked!'*

Attempting to assert some form of control over the environment I got out the map. I saw a statue marked nearby. We followed the map to the monument to *Jangar*, the folk epic of the Kalmyk people. A huge bronze bard sat on a plinth, arm raised in readiness to strike the strings of his Mongol lute and begin his declamation. It was impressive. But we were attracting attention. The city's youth, out drinking for the night on the park's benches, sniggered and whispered as we walked by. 'Hey! English!' they whispered. 'Hey, America! OK? Fuck! Hello! How are you! Fucking English! Hello!'

I stood, blinking at the monument for a minute or so. 'Fuck! Hello! How are you?' came the whispers. 'You're fucked,' said the crows. I told myself there was no real threat. The locals were just curious. But in the morning I had been in Moscow and now I was stranded somewhere in a desert. Our failure to plan anything had left me delirious and disoriented. Twenty-four hours earlier I hadn't even seen a map of Elista. Joe, meanwhile, was making me worse. He had once spent an entire night unconscious in an icy puddle courtesy of provincial Russian hospitality. His paranoia was leaking into mine.

It was no good: we had to get away. We climbed a hill to escape and walked under trees for greater camouflage. But there were people up there too, men sitting next to men, men with girls on their laps, all of them drinking. 'Shit!' they said. 'English! Hello! How are you? You like *geerls*?'

Paranoia strikes deep. I was on the verge of panic.

17

I realized suddenly that I was hungry. *'That's what I need,'* I thought. *'To eat something. That'll calm my nerves.'* There was a Chinese restaurant marked on the map, but when we reached it we found that all the doors were padlocked, the windows were filthy, and there was nothing inside save abandoned tables, dust and cobwebs. Svetlana had given us directions for the Sputnik Café, where she guaranteed us we could eat something 'substantial' – but I couldn't remember them. The map had a few other places to eat marked on it, but they were far from where we were standing, and my nerves were so jangled it was difficult to read.

We walked on. We passed the shrine to the Buddha Shakyamuni, a white cross-legged statue in a golden robe that fluttered in the April breeze. We walked through a huge Mongolian gateway, passing under an enormous set of heavily swinging chimes. These Asian monuments, in the middle of a Soviet town at dusk, were beautiful and surreal. But we couldn't stop to appreciate them.

We saw Lenin, standing, one hand in his pocket, facing the white-concrete Kalmyk Parliament. Then we stumbled upon a statue of Pushkin alone by some trees. There were no benches there, and, consequently, no one around. I pulled out the map.

Apparently I was standing in front of the Café Sputnik: but

I couldn't see it. The map was five years old. Perhaps the café had been demolished. But there wasn't even the shell of a building or a vacant lot to suggest anything had been there in the first place. There was simply nothing.

It made no sense. The total non-existence of any restaurants whatsoever in the city centre was hard to accept. Even for Russia, this was excessive. I yearned for a McDonald's.

18

The hunger was now roaring away inside me. I put the map away. It was no use. Maybe it was a fantasy map, drawn up by somebody who had never seen the city. How else could I account for all the buildings that weren't there? We had no choice but to keep walking until we found a place to eat. As a last resort there was a restaurant in the hotel, but it was a Mafia-style hang-out, full of smoke, and flat-headed thugs, and serpentine prostitutes. I didn't want to go there.

At that point, as we turned back towards the Avenue of Heroes and the crowds of whisperers, two men stepped out from behind some bushes and stood in front of us, blocking the path. One was Kalmyk; the other was Russian. It was obvious that they weren't going to move. *Great*, I thought.

I assessed the situation. They weren't huge. And there were, after all, three of us. But it looked bad. It was getting dark, and I don't know how to fight. I spent the long six seconds walking towards them mentally preparing myself to kick one in the cock and then run for it. *Will they step aside?* I thought. *Or will they have a go?*

They went for their pockets. *Shit*, I thought. *They're having a go.* What did they have in there? Knives? Chains?

Irritating interlude to build suspense

Some time later, relaxing on the sofa in my flat in Moscow, I had a brilliant idea for what I could do with my life. I could start my own Scotland–Kalmykia Friendship Society and organize exchanges between schools, and maybe bring over Kalmyk folk ensembles to the Edinburgh Festival, that sort of thing. Then I realised I could expand it further and create a society devoted to friendship with all the Asian peoples of the former Soviet Union. I could travel to Uzbekistan, Kyrgyzstan and Siberia scouting for talented groups to bring over to the UK. I'd get to meet interesting people and eat a lot of free meals. Best of all, I wouldn't have to worry about making a profit. I could apply for lots of grants from worthy organizations and live high on the hog at the expense of the European taxpayer! Why it was brilliant!

I never got round to doing it, though. You know how it is.

Interlude over.

The hands left the pockets. They didn't have weapons. They had little books. The Russian guy handed me one. I read the title. It said: *The Way to God.*

Then they attempted to convert us. Joe said he didn't understand Russian, but the Kalmyk evangelist was unconcerned. 'It will speak to your soul,' he explained. He offered his hand. I shook it. I was pleased that a stranger wanted to save my soul. It was a positive omen, like meeting Sveta on the plane. There was a moral in there, somewhere.

I turned and saw a shack made out of corrugated iron and concrete: the Café Sputnik.

19

The little girl

We sat in the Sputnik Café eating some seriously shitty food. Even though I was starving it was difficult to muster up much relish for the meal in front of me. The meat balls were cold and full of gristle and very hard to swallow, but they were by no means the worst thing. The worst thing was the 'special Kalmyk tea', which was a lukewarm mixture of grease, tea and salt. That was like drinking a cup of Bernard Manning's sweat.

A Kalmyk woman came in with her daughter, who was about eleven years old. The girl was very slim and had a long, long plait that reached all the way down her back. They sat facing away from us, but as soon as the girl heard us speaking English, she whipped round, almost in fright. But she was shy, and quickly turned away again. She whispered something to her mother, indicating us with a slight turn of her head. Her mother nodded, but didn't look up. For the rest of our stay the girl would intermittently look round, sneak a peek, and then turn away again.

'Look at that little girl, Joe,' I said.

'What?' said Joe.

'Over there. Next to her mother. She's watching us.'

Joe looked. 'Oh yeah,' he said.

'She's watching us.'

'Hm.'

'She's never seen foreigners before.'

'Probably.'

'We're the first foreigners she's ever seen.'

Joe nodded. He was thinking.

'Just imagine her world, Joe: every Saturday she comes here with her mum, to the Sputnik Café.'

'Yeah.'

'And that's her special treat, Joe. Her Saturday trip to the Sputnik Café. That's all she has.'

I was extemporizing from my own childhood in Dunfermline. As a boy, when I was sick, my mother would take me to Littlewoods café for a 'drink and doughring'. This was a rare treat for the opportunity it presented to have my mum to myself for a while. As one of four children, such occasions were rare.

'I suppose.'

'And her mother would like to give her more, Joe, but she can't. She's poor. She's dirt poor. It's a daily battle just to keep her daughter clothed and fed.'

'Hmm,' Joe grunted.

'And just think of everything we have Joe, everything we take for granted. We can travel the world, we can come to Kalmykia. And then we can leave.'

'Yes . . .'

'But she can't leave. She can never leave.'

'Hm.'

'She watches Moscow on TV and sees the adverts for clothes, for shops, for McDonald's . . . but everything you and I take for granted is an unrealizable fantasy for her.'

'Yes . . .'

'Completely unrealizable. We eat in McDonald's all the time, and we think it's shit. But even that is an unattainable dream for her.'

'You're right . . .'

'I mean, that's the most she can realistically hope for: that maybe, one day, she'll have enough money to go to Moscow. To go to Moscow and when she gets there, eat in McDonald's.'

'You're right.'

'And us – three foreigners in the Sputnik Café, we are some-thing strange and mysterious for her. Something magical.

She'll go to school on Monday and tell her friends all about it: "There were three foreigners in the Sputnik Café!" And when she's older, and maybe has a daughter of her own, there'll be times when she'll be doing something, cleaning the house, perhaps, and suddenly, when she's looking up from her work, we'll come to her. She'll remember us, and she'll wonder who we were, and where we had come from, and what we were doing . . . As long as she doesn't die first, of course.'

I was quite carried away by my depiction of the girl's inner life. It was becoming utterly real for me. And as I spoke she would continue to turn back and peek at us, then turn away again when I met her eye.

Joe, meanwhile, was looking deeply melancholy. He is very sensitive to stories. As for Yoshi, he was inscrutable. He could have been thinking about his best blow-job ever, for all I knew. I couldn't tell if he was even listening to me.

We got up to go. The girl watched as we left. I was leaving her for ever, and it hurt. In a matter of minutes I had become involved. She was already haunting me, as I, in my small way, was about to haunt her. I wanted to say something to her, or give her some gift from my homeland. But I had nothing, neither words nor tokens. We walked out of the door and left her for ever, she who would be the keeper of our memory in the void.

'Goodbye, little girl,' I said, once outside.

The End.

20

Nine Kalmyk proverbs

Three infinities collide in the steppe: the infinity of the steppe itself, the infinity of the sky and the infinity of the human soul.

Never catch a panther by the tail, but if you do, don't let go.
If you play with a knife you will eventually get hurt.
The light is born of the darkness.
Boiled meat will never be raw again.
The infinity of the soul is the same as the infinity of space.
When the strong exert themselves they grow even stronger,
but when the weak do the same they break their backs.
The juiciest apple will be eaten by worms.
Oops! . . . I did it again.

21

Secret wars

There is a war memorial in the centre of Elista: huge Mongol heads rear out of red rock, grim and determined in the face of death. They face the eternal flame, which flickers away, compulsory for every city in Russia. Beyond that, three huge aluminium prongs stick out of the earth like a giant canteen fork, poking at the clouds. It all faces an ugly patch of flat grass that leads to some wooden shacks. Goats graze on the grass.

We are not accustomed to thinking of Mongols fighting in Europe. But they did; as did many other Asians, hauled by Stalin from the steppes of Asia, from tending their sheep, from their fires of dried dung, to face bullets and shells in the war zone: Uzbeks, Kazaks, Tatars and many others, all given uniforms and arms and sent to die in the trenches of Europe.

There's a story in Michael Burleigh's *The Third Reich* about a Tatar conscript who couldn't speak Russian. Sick of the trenches, sick of being shot at, sick of being hungry and barked at by his commanding officers, he decided to defect to the enemy. It couldn't be any worse than the life he was enduring fighting for Stalin and the Soviet Union. So one night he crept out of his trench, and began crawling through no man's land, towards the Germans. It was dark out there, however, and he got disoriented. Confused. Bewildered. What direction was he going in? Was he ever going to get there? Then after what seemed like an eternity, he at last found the German trenches. He walked directly to the officers' quarters and gave himself up.

The only problem was that he wasn't in the German trenches. He had gone round in a circle and surrendered to his own army.

They shot him, of course.

22

In the summer of 1942 most of the republic was controlled by the Nazis. For many Kalmyks, however, this was not an unwelcome occupation. Over twenty years of brutal assaults on their religion and lifestyle had bred in a generation a great hatred for the Soviets. And the government's contemptuous treatment of the Kalmyk herders had worsened during the war. Just before the Nazi invasion, secret police armed with rifles and cold hearts had forcibly requisitioned 2 million cattle. The Kalmyks formed illegal guerrilla squads to prevent this happening again.

Once in control, the Germans implemented some popular moves. They encouraged the Kalmyk rich in Elista to share their wealth and feed their poorer compatriots. They also introduced limited democracy, allowing the Kalmyks to hold mayoral elections in their settlements. Finally, collectivization was immediately abolished and individuals were allowed to own as much livestock as they wished.

This, of course, was not because the Nazis sympathized with Kalmyk herders. Although Hitler had originally been opposed to using 'inferior' Soviet races in his armies, the German army was overstretched in Russia and badly needed reinforcements. The Nazis knew that the small races of the Soviet Union hated their masters in Moscow, and turned this hatred to their own advantage. They formed several collaborative regiments from among the peoples of the Soviet Union: Armenians, Azeris, Georgians, North Caucasians, Turkestanis and Volga Tatars all fought for the Germans. Later in the war Latvians, Estonians and Ukrainians also provided Hitler with soldiers. In fact, the Latvians and Ukrainians went so far as to turn the Zyclon-B taps in death camps in the latter stages of the war. The Kalmyks, meanwhile, supplied the Nazis with a six-thousand-strong cavalry corps.

Their value to their new masters lay in intelligence gathering and detecting acts of sabotage. Kalmyk scouts would check railway lines for loosened or missing ties and concealed explosive charges. They would then notify the German authorities, averting casualties and disruptions to the supplies heading to the front.

Not all Kalmyks, however, went over to the Nazis. Many remained faithful to Stalin and their Soviet motherland. In total, eight thousand Kalmyks were awarded various orders and medals for their patriotic service, while twenty-one men were awarded the highest accolade of 'Hero of the Soviet Union'.

The Nazis did not remain in power for long. In January of 1943 the Soviet army 'liberated' the territory of the republic. Stalin then ordered the entire population deported for collaborating with the enemy. The Kalmyk Autonomous Republic was abolished and a hundred and seventy thousand men, women and children were herded into cattle wagons and sent to Siberia.

23

That kind of thing happens all the time, of course. We are surrounded by atrocities, genocides, extinctions. They are so many that only the really big ones grab our attention. We all live on territory that was grabbed by someone's sword, however long ago. Someone else died so that our ancestors might live. How many people, nations, have slipped unnoticed from the face of the earth? Exile and murder are banal, they are what nations are built on.

The Kalmyks did not die out, however, though they suffered. One story from their suffering: they lived in shabby barracks, deep in the forest, surrounded by the cold, the darkness and ever present death. Twice a month they had to present themselves to the local KGB commandant. They had to walk ten to fifteen kilometres in all weather, even deep in the winter, when it was forty degrees below zero. If they did not march, they would be considered criminals and shot. And so, once a month, the whole people picked themselves up and walked, the healthy ones dragging the sick and the dying on sledges through thick Siberian forest so that they too could be registered. Even the dead they had to bring with them: Stalinist bureaucracy left no stone unturned. The death of every exile required certification.

So the Kalmyks walked through the forest and, as they walked, the wolves followed them. The wolves were brazen. They walked right alongside the exiled people, eyeing them up, watching the weak, waiting for one to fall. And the Kalmyks could not defend themselves against the wolves. They were enemies of the state, forbidden to carry weapons. To be caught with a gun, an axe, or even a knife meant instant execution.

The march through the forest was not the only ordeal, of

course. No: once that was over, the Kalmyks had to spend hours standing in front of the commandant's house. He was a busy man, after all. In the summer it wasn't so bad. There was just the heat, and the flies to contend with. But in the winter, in the cold . . . people couldn't take it. They died just waiting. By the time their turn came to be checked off, they were no more. Their names were crossed out, a life concluded with one swift stroke of a grim bureaucrat's pencil. And lives began in the same way. For even in hell, men and women don't give up. They come together, and children are born.

After registration it began again: the long tread through the forest, the long march to a home that was not home. The wolves kept watch, their eyes glowing yellow in the Siberian night.

The Kalmyks spent twelve years in Siberia, marching back and forth, back and forth, and dying. Then Stalin died. Khrushchev, his successor, was less cruel. He permitted them to return home. In 1955, after twelve years in exile, six thousand ravaged souls found themselves standing once more in the land their forefathers had conquered and reigned proudly over.

24

Unseen memorials for the unknown tragedy

I heard that in the villages today there are old people, with faces like tanned leather, cracked and brown from years spent herding sheep in the steppe winds who live in dread of another war. When visitors from the outside world arrive at their settlements they ask: *Will there be another war? Will there?* They fear another deportation. You could not go through that twice and survive.

The deportation left a wound that is still very raw, and may never heal. In Elista there is a monument to its victims by the Russian artist Ernst Neizvestny. His surname means 'unknown' – a name given by Soviet authorities to war orphans whose parents were untraceable and of whom no records remained. I never saw this monument.

There are other memorials, however. In Chess City I saw a sculpture of a little man carved out of a tree. He was huddled up, shivering with cold. It was called *Exile*. In the State Concert Hall I heard the State Ensemble of National Instruments play Arkady Mandjaev's Second Symphony, *Siberia*. It was a sombre, twenty-minute dirge: a minute for each member of the audience. They bowed their heads appreciatively, but their applause was restrained. It was clear that nobody liked this music. But the applause was sincere. The symphony's necessity at least was recognized, if not its worth.

The strange thing is that the Kalmyks do not hate Russia for what was done to them. The Kalmyk Embassy in Moscow proudly lists the figures for those who fought for the Soviet Union. Ilumzhinov, in his memoir, does likewise. *How many more there would have been*, they say, *if only Russia had trusted us!* No, the Kalmyks do not hate Russia. But they cannot understand. After centuries of fighting alongside the Imperial and then the Soviet armies, to be treated thus, because of a few traitors – why?

Why?

25

The way to Chess City

After the Sputnik Café debacle, we spent the following morning attempting to locate food sources. There was a decent-looking place across the road from the Kalmyk Parliament, but when I stepped inside I was told it was shut. Eventually we found a bistro behind the hotel, next to a flea market. It was very greasy and gypsy children kept running in to beg from us. But it was the best option available. I also found that after eating I was less paranoid. The locals continued to stare, but it bothered me less.

I decided to have a stab at finding Chess City. There were several problems, however: (1) It wasn't marked on the map, and (2) I didn't know what it was. It would have been easy to get in a taxi and ask the driver to take us there, of course. But I prefer to do things the hard way. Elista was so devoid of features I thought it would leap out at us.

Chess City #1 was a large glass building on top of a hill in the city centre. It was large and relatively modern, and didn't look like any of the city's other buildings. Yet it was little more than a lead-grey glass box in terms of design and it had an air of neglect I knew would not be permitted for a palace devoted to Ilumzhinov's passion. Yoshi tried the door, but it was locked.

Chess City #2 was a little shed with a plaque on it that said CHESS, but I doubted it could be said to constitute a city, even in Kalmykia.

The map had symbols marking the state museum and the state theatre nearby. I thought Chess City #3 might be there, as it would surely be at home among such monumental state institutions.

We followed the map, and within minutes were standing next to a large pile of rubble and a half-ruined structure. This was the State Theatre. Nearby there was a concrete sphinx sitting on a piece of wasteland, its base wrapped in newspaper, and a strange pole topped with a little Mongolian roof. There were a few builders hanging around the ruins, smoking fags.

They stared uneasily at us. Until our arrival they had been the only animate objects in this part of the city.

There was a concrete bunker on the edge of the complex. It looked like a storage shed for workers' tools, or maybe a house for the power generator. But I had a funny feeling about it. And sure enough, next to the door I found a plaque, which read: STATE MUSEUM OF KALMYKIA. It was tiny and it had no windows. It was locked and bolted, too.

Chess City #4 was a fleeting phantom, one I never had faith in. Not far from the ruins of the theatre I saw a relatively new building. But it was too small; it looked like the type of new home you find on the outskirts of British cities.

I suspected an official connection however, as it was surrounded by a big fence and there were crap contemporary sculptures standing in the garden. For a second I wondered if it was the president's residence. But it was too small for that. Russian leaders like to treat themselves when they build their own pads. Besides, the view was hardly presidential: a dismal valley dotted with lots of dilapidated wooden shacks. I couldn't imagine Ilumzhinov would want to look at that when he got up in the morning.

At 3 o'clock on a Sunday afternoon I temporarily abandoned the search for Chess City.

I walked around in this strange nothing zone staring at blocks of flats for a while. Some Teletubbies painted on a wall provided a momentary distraction. I went closer. They didn't have any faces. Then I spotted a man eating out of a bin.

I was starting to get excited. Elista was even emptier than I had hoped.

The State Museum of Kalmykia

26

The true meaning of our lives

Joe and Yosh, however, were not at all amused. In fact, they were mildly depressed. They were talking about cutting our stay short and leaving.

No! I thought. *That must not happen!* There was still a lot of nothing I wanted to see, still a lot of boredom I longed to experience. *This is reality*, I thought in my excitement. *This place reveals the true meaning of our lives! We're all just floating around in a void, surrounded by crap, looking for ways to pass the time, man.* We had only scratched the surface of Elista's vast emptiness!

I saw, however, that if I was to persuade Joe and Yosh to stay, I had to find something *substantial* for them. They weren't satisfied with my anti-goals. They did not share my delight in the locked door. No, they needed a real goal, something to aim for. But what could possibly constitute a 'real' goal in Elista?

I saw a poster for Mariah Carey's movie, *Glitter,* stuck to the wooden fence around a building site. *Hmm*, I thought. *Could this do the trick?* Film fans will recall that the movie tanked at the box office, and was followed by Mariah's own nervous breakdown. In its miserable afterlife, *Glitter* had found its way to the Kalmyk steppe.

I thought I could persuade them to look upon it as a kind of joke: Ha ha . . . let's go and see the worst movie in the world while we're in the biggest void in the world, it'll be really funny. Come on, guys!

There was a problem, however. *Glitter* had played for only three days. The movie had already gone. The Mariah I was looking at was one of several old Mariahs posted around town, slowly rotting. Someone had drawn a cock jizzing into her mouth. *Poor Mariah*, I thought. She still had her trademark psychotic grimace, that fearful *I-am-pretty-please-love-me* look in her eyes. The agony of her failure lived on.

So *Glitter* clearly wasn't going to do it. Joe and Yosh split off from me and smoked together. They were talking. I knew I was facing a mutiny soon, if I didn't come up with something. By this point we had drifted to the square in front of the Parliament. Just then I spotted some pictures of Spider Man and the Teenage Mutant Ninja Turtles stuck to the wall of the National Library. Underneath them the legend read: EXCITING DISNEY SHOW!!! Yeah! We could do that! I was about to call Joe and Yosh over, but then I noticed it was scheduled for weeks in the future.

'What are we going to do?' asked Joe. There was a hint of threat in his voice. 'I'll think of something,' I replied. I got out the map and led them to the Russian-language theatre on Gorky Street. There was nothing worth watching on and I wouldn't have been able to understand it anyway. But I did find something interesting in the foyer. They ran a sideline in developing photos, and had chosen a very unusual picture to demonstrate the different sizes of print available. Rather than a picture of a wedding, or a happy child, as is the norm, they had two huge pitbulls tearing each other's throats out. Just in case you thought you were hallucinating, the image was repeated again, in an even larger format. Clearly there were some diversions available in Kalmykia. But you had to know where to find them.

The pitbulls cheered Joe up for a minute. But I knew it was only temporary. And they hadn't done anything for Yosh. We stepped outside and started drifting towards the hotel. Suddenly I saw a hand-painted poster for a Kalmyk Rock OPERA, hanging by the side of the road. It was clearly the only thing on in the whole city. Immediately I proposed it to Joe and Yoshi.

They were dubious. 'What's it about?' asked Joe.

'I don't know,' I replied. 'But it's either that or an evening of drinking in the park with the local teenagers.'

Faced with this choice they agreed. I left them in a bar and quickly ran off to get the tickets before they could change their minds.

27

Meanwhile, outside the city, the desert was spreading.

For the last fifty years in Kalmykia, sand has been encroaching on the land. The sand was always there, beneath the black earth of the steppe. When it lay undisturbed, it did no damage. But then the all-knowing authorities in Moscow ordered that the land should be ploughed to grow cereal. There were many mouths to be fed in the Soviet Union, after all.

The Kalmyk elders protested: it was madness, they said. For centuries they had lived in harmony with the steppe, because they understood it. They had grazed their animals on it, yes, but they had always shown restraint. They had not interfered with the delicate balance. They knew how precarious their existence was.

Moscow knew better. Moscow insisted. Great machines came and ploughed the land. And the sand was exposed. And the sand began to spread. Rare plants and herbs disappeared. Animals that had roamed the steppe for centuries, millennia, died in large numbers. Piles of saiga antelope carcasses mounted in irrigation canals. The stench of their decomposing carcasses drifted along on the steppe wind. Their skulls and foot-long horns littered the steppe.

For how long will the Kalmyks be able to cling to their homeland? Kalmykia will soon become Europe's first desert. Will abandoned cities sit half submerged in the sand? Will there be lost zones: squat concrete towers with shattered windows, children's dolls, the odd shoe lying on the surface, the upper pagoda of a temple visible? Whispers on the wind of struggles and a people that nobody recalls?

Hm. Actually, it might be quite beautiful. In a desolate, Fall-of-the-Roman-Empire kind of way.

28

En route to the theatre I passed a billboard featuring a giant photo of Ilumzhinov standing alongside the Patriarch of the Orthodox Church, another shot from his scrapbook of encounters with the famous. Then, not far from these Titans of earthly and spiritual power, I saw one of God's frailer creatures: a mentally handicapped girl wearing a shawl. She was standing outside a wooden hut, staring at the road. Chickens were in the yard.

I mention her, dear reader, because after five years of living in Russia, she was the first person with Down's syndrome I had ever seen. Usually the Russian authorities lock the handicapped up in asylums. Sometimes they tie them to their beds. Death by curable diseases or malnutrition is not uncommon. She was one of the lucky ones. I had little time to meditate upon her fate, however. I ran on to the Jangar Theatre, the venue for the rock opera.

The Jangar was an old, dirty concrete cube that demonstrated the curious taste designers of the Brezhnev era had for decorating in the colours of dirt and faeces. This is something I've noticed in many Soviet towns. The exterior and lobby of the Jangar, for example, were done in a brown that made you feel unclean just to look at it

I entered the theatre and stepped up to the *kassa* and asked if they had any seats for that night's performance. She pointed at a huge Kalmyk woman sitting at a table by the door. 'Ask her,' she said.

I went up to the woman.

'Hello,' I said. 'Do you have any tickets for tonight?'

She looked me up and down in disgust.

'Who are you?' she asked.

'I'm a tourist,' I replied.

She sniffed. 'What do you want?'

'Do you have any tickets for tonight?' I repeated.

She paused. Breathed in. Breathed out. Looked at the large pile of tickets to her left. 'No.'

'Are you sure?' I asked.

She turned her back to me.

I knew she was lying, so I sat down on a bench, directly behind her. About ten minutes later she turned and saw that I hadn't gone away. She asked, 'How many do you need?'

'Three,' I replied.

She counted out three tickets from the pile.

There is some moral or truth about Russia in my interaction with the lying woman. I don't know what it is.

President Kirsan Ilumzhinov of Kalmykia and Alexei II, Patriarch of Moscow and All Russia. Next to a road. Near some shacks.

29

Dzhangar [*sic*]

The Tatars have a large literature of unread books. The Mongols also have a great wealth of poetry, religious writing and epics unknown outside Mongolia. Among them are *The*

Secret History of the Mongols, *Gesenada* and *Jangar*. Probably it is better not to read them. What book, after all, could live up to the title *The Secret History of the Mongols*? None. I bet if you cracked it open you'd just find long lists of names, descriptions of battles and probably some hoary old bullshit about flying mountains. No: better to leave that one alone.

Of these three epics, the Kalmyks brought only one with them: *Jangar*. It strikes me that if your culture has only one book, then it had better be fucking good. The Kalmyks meanwhile stick the name 'Jangar' on everything: streets, cinemas, folk ensembles. It's all they have: the cornerstone, with a dimly remembered Buddhism, of their identity.

Sometimes I like to spell *Jangar* with a 'D' as '*Djangar*'. It is also possible to spell it as '*Dzhangar*'. It takes five days to recite the whole song-cycle. There are sixty-eight happy songs and a hundred and eight miserable ones. The story, meanwhile, is the usual mythological stuff about a Golden Age, and twelve, fearless warriors and their leader, Jangar, who guard their magical homeland of Bumba from terrible enemies, such as Mangus, the evil monster.

I once saw parts of this epic performed in Moscow, in a club called Dom, which specialized in ethnic music and avant-garde performance. It was on a Wednesday night, and about nine people turned up. A little guy came on stage, strummed his *dombr* and groaned for about an hour. He was a throat singer, which meant he could produce two voices simultaneously, one of them a high-pitched whistle, the other a low drone.

During his performance a cellphone went off. He looked around, annoyed. Then he realized it was his. He interrupted his groaning to answer it. Then he resumed. After about forty-five minutes he stopped playing. 'Are any of you actually enjoying this?' he asked.

The people in the audience looked at each other. Somebody mumbled yes, and he continued for about another twenty minutes.

30

I thought it might be quite interesting if I could put an excerpt from *Jangar* in this book. Give the reader a sense of the Kalmyk mind, that sort of thing. The problem was that (a) I didn't have a copy of it, (b) I didn't know where I could get one, and (c) I wouldn't be able to understand it even if I did. Not because I can't speak Kalmyk, though of course I can't – I assumed there would be Russian-language versions of the *epos* floating around. The Soviet Union patronized its ethnic peoples by translating their folktales into Russian and distributing them all over the place: that was the consolation for being forbidden to study your own religion and language and culture. But even if I did find a Russian-language version I wouldn't be able to understand it. I'm just not up to poetry, you see.

So I did some web surfing and found a forum called www.elista.org: 'Where Kalmykia Gets Together on the Web'. It was visited by Kalmyks and also Mongols interested in the fate of their western brethren. Most of it was bollocks about pop music, though there was some tortuously pedantic stuff about language and history too. I posted a message: 'A Scotttish Journalist Asks For Help' where I appealed to the patriotism of the Kalmyks. I explained I was researching a book on Russia's ethnic republics and that Kalmykia was one of those I had selected. I think I hinted it was my favourite republic too, in a shameless attempt to curry favour. Then I asked if anyone could help me track down an edition of *Djangar* and translate it into English. I wanted to 'introduce their national epic to the English speaking world for the first time'. I didn't mention that the working title of my book was 'Bad Places'.

I'd tried similar things before when writing about gangs in Tatarstan, and with good results. However, the Kalmyks were slow to rise to the patriotic challenge. A few days passed. I didn't receive any emails. I went back to the forum to check up on my question. It was languishing in obscurity. About forty people had looked at it, but only one had posted a reply. The rest had washed their hands of me and my request. The reply, meanwhile, was a link leading me to a site where *Jangar* was on display. I followed the link but there was no way I could read the thing.

So I wrote to the guy who had posted the link. It turned out he was a Kalmyk grad student studying law in Boston. He had a Russian name – Vyacheslav – and was really excited that someone was trying to bring his nation to the attention of the world. He was willing to translate a section of *Jangar* for me.

We discussed which bit would work best. Then he asked me to give him three weeks. That was fine. I liked the thought that somewhere in America there was a specialist working furiously at translating something for my book. It made the project feel really international. I looked forward to adding his cool Mongol surname to the acknowledgements section.

So three weeks passed. I celebrated Christmas and New Year. The world moved on. Beagle 2, the British-designed Martian probe, fell down a hole and disappeared. A letter of Princess Diana's was unearthed wherein she expressed her fears that Prince Charles was going to arrange for her to die in a car crash. Tony Blair faced rebellion over tuition fees and the blackening of his name in the Hutton Report. Michael Jackson was arraigned in court on charges of paedophilia.

Then at last I received a letter from Vyacheslav; attached was the document I'd been waiting for.

Excitedly, I clicked on the icon to download it. I was curious to read some of the story, at last, to see if it was actually any good. I also wanted to check the quality of Vyacheslav's English. I had already started work on the next section and hoped I wouldn't have to do much rewriting. A stream of electrons surged through cyberspace bringing his work to my computer. The saga of the Kalmyks, their One Great Book, soon I would see it and prepare to release it into the world at large, to give them their moment of glory! Look world, I would declare, this, this is a nation!

Except that . . . Vyacheslav's 'translation' was a single sheet of A4 he had clearly copied from elsewhere. Hm. I wrote to him: 'Hey, Vyacheslav, I think there's been a mix-up. This is just a brief note. Where's the stuff you translated?' The response came two days later. It was rather curt. 'I didn't literally translate *Djangar*. I edited and summarized it. Best regards, Vyacheslav.' Yes, well. He didn't half summarize it. It takes five days or so to recite the whole song. It takes about five seconds to read Vyacheslav's version.

It was Christmas and New Year, I suppose. I'm sure he'd been invited to a lot of parties. Also, translating is hard work and he probably had no idea what he'd committed to until he started toiling over it. Lastly, and perhaps most importantly, I wasn't paying him for his time – a law student, and in America no less. No, I was asking him to do it out of love for his native land. That doesn't pay the bills.

Anyway, this is what I have to offer you. A Kalmyk's interpretation of his culture's great book.

Enjoy.

31

Djangar – majestic Kalmyk epic

The Kalmyk people possess a wonderful heroic legend about a great hero Djangar. Songs about Djangar are the most favourite and widespread in Kalmyk folklore and are called epic. These songs mainly glorify blooming country called Bumba and its epic hero, defender and chief leader – Djangar. The country of Bumba, where the main characters of the poem live, is the country of immortality and eternal youth, the country where its inhabitants live in prosperity and happiness.

Djangar also describes the relationships which existed among Kalmyk people in XV century. That was the time when Kalmyk (Oirat) State was established on the basis of unification of four Oirat tribes. It is very likely that it was that time when *Djangar* was composed. However, only in 1804–1805 Professor Bergman published two songs from *Djangar* epic in German language. It is still unknown who recorded and translated these songs from Kalmyk into German.

The main idea of *Djangar* epic is the protection of the country of Bumba. All songs depict specific episodes of struggle of Djangar and his warriors with foreign invaders who are trying to intrude the country of Bumba. It is necessary to emphasize that all of these wars with invaders are defensive in nature and their aim is to protect the honour and freedom of Bumba from intruders.

For instance, in the fifth song, 'On Duel of Hongor – Crimson Lion with the Horrible Dogshon Mangna-Khan, Who Has a Gigantic Manzan Horse', Hongor's feats are described where he was not afraid to take a stand alone against Dogshon Mangna-Khan who intended to subdue and destroy Bumba.

In the sixth song, 'On Glorifying Deeds of Savr – Heavy Hand', brothers-heroes Savr and Hongor are fighting for honour and property of Djangar against Zambala-Khan, who stole countless amount of horses that belonged to Djangar.

Also, *Djangar* played an inspirational role for the whole Kalmyk people which is proved by the Kalmyk history. Kalmyk warriors, who participated in movements of Pugatchev and Razin, in military forces of Peter the First against Swedish intruders, against invasion of Napoleon in 1812, in World War II fighting with German intruders, always remembered about the great deeds of Djangar and his twelve warriors. *Djangar* always inspired Kalmyks for the struggle for the life which is full of happiness, the life which existed in wonderful country of Bumba.

Finally, *Djangar* incorporated the description of everyday life of Kalmyk people, its customs and traditions and thereby became an inalienable part of Kalmyk cultural treasury.

32

We will rock you

I

After getting the tickets I spent an hour or so lurking in Elista's Central Park of Culture and Rest. I wanted to absorb more of the city's remarkable atmosphere of locked doors and abandoned buildings. I was distracted, however, by a young couple snogging brazenly in front of me, hands in each other's pants. Also, a goat came close to me and made me nervous. I was worried it might bite me. Then I imagined I could feel ants crawling up my leg and I couldn't concentrate at all. So I went to meet Joe and Yosh, who were drinking in a bar to blot out their miserable surroundings.

II

Squeezed into my seat at the back of the Jangar Theatre I watched the crowd file in. Most of the people were Kalmyk. There was a real air of excitement, of anticipation, as if they were at a premiere of something important. The huge guy sitting next to me in a cowboy hat was reading the programme, sounding words out loud in English:

'The . . . life . . . young . . .' And then, in Russian, 'What the fuck? I can't understand this! Where's the Russian?'

I looked at the programme myself. It was odd: the synopsis on the back was in English. It was quite fluid and even contained the phrase 'grey eminence', which impressed me no end. There was no similar synopsis in Russian, however.

I thought of Elista's 'international' airport and the BBC World on the hotel TV. The regular updates on the Queen Mother's corpse. The pictures hanging around town of Ilumzhinov standing next to the Dalai Lama and the Patriarch.

Kalmykia was a place trembling with anxiety. Nobody knew about it. Nobody had seen it. It consisted mostly of emptiness. It could be erased quietly and hardly anybody would notice. In fact, it had already been erased once and nobody had noticed.

The world beyond the steppe they knew only through the pictures they saw on old Soviet TVs, from the voices they heard crackling on the radio, messages that might as well be from another star. The synopsis was in English to demonstrate that Kalmykia too was a part of the global English-speaking community. Whether anybody understood it or not was beside the point.

A little grey-haired man emerged from behind the stage curtain. He introduced the show: it was a production of the Kalmyk Republic Youth Theatre, he explained, and they had worked long and hard at putting it together. Then suddenly he started talking about something else. 'Tonight's performance wouldn't have been possible without the gracious assistance of Kirsan Ilumzhinov, our President, and we are very grateful to him. Please stand and show your appreciation for a few moments.'

I had never applauded a president at a musical before, but the audience thought nothing of it. They dutifully stood and clapped. We joined in.

I remembered my hope of meeting Ilumzhinov. The problem was: how to get to him? I didn't even know if Ilumzhinov was in Kalmykia at that moment. Clapping felt like an incantation. Maybe after the show he'd materialize in the foyer and then we'd talk to him.

IV

The hall darkened. The audience grew hushed. The curtain parted.

The stage was decorated with various pipes and bits of metal. Suddenly the performers came charging on, about twenty of them, stamping their feet and banging dustbin lids.

The synopsis had primed me for a tale of lost youth on the city's mean streets. Nothing to do, nowhere to go, no future to look forward to, the denizens of a grim housing scheme formed a gang, a wolf pack roaming their bleak urban desert: a little like my film, *Gangs of Kazan*.

In the first act, the gang pushed each other around, and generally acted hard. The leader had two bitches vying for his attention. There was a catfight, and they pulled each other's hair and screamed a lot. Then a beautiful innocent came on and sang a song about how much she loved the stars. The gang leader saw her and fell in love. He invited her to meet his cohorts, who all did a routine introducing themselves. Being innocent, she didn't recognize them as street trash and thought it was all exciting and wonderful.

Then she was left alone with the leader's lieutenant. He was a really fat guy who appeared to be wearing lady's eyeliner. Why she fell in love with him I couldn't understand, although he did have a good voice. They sang a few songs together, about leaving the gang behind and watching the stars together. But – oh no! – they were spotted and grassed on by the 'grey eminence'.

Then it all got very tragic. The innocent girl was gang-raped and her fat love got stabbed to death. At the end, she was left, broken and alone in the centre of a darkened stage. The curtain closed.

The audience, briefly, was silent, hushed by this unexpectedly bleak conclusion. And then it erupted: first into applause, and then a standing ovation that went on and on and on.

v

I myself was shocked. I had gone expecting (*nay, hoping for*) an atrocity, a school bus crash. It seemed too much to hope for something good, so I was primed for the pleasures of the bad. But in fact I had found genuine quality. The Republican Youth Theatre of Kalmykia really knew how to put on an all-singing, all-dancing extravaganza.

But there was more to it than that. The power of the play was enhanced by the fact that these gifted young people were performing for a tiny audience in the middle of the void. Practically no one could see them. And what were their chances of ever making it anywhere? The odds against that were astronomically high. But in spite of that, or perhaps because of it, they had given everything to their roles. I had rarely seen a group of performers infuse a show with so much of their own vital essence. This musical was their cry against the void, against the silence of the world's response to their existence. This was the Kalmyk response to the deportation, to World War II, to centuries spent abandoned in the desert: an all-singing, all-dancing declaration of existence.

The crowd was proud. That their tiny republic could produce such music, such beauty! It validated their existence too. Having spent two days wandering around in a genuine urban wasteland, walking from ruin to ruin, from ghost institution to ghost institution, it was as if the theatre throbbed with all the life we hadn't seen, that had been hiding from us.

The old man returned and told us that the troupe was travelling to Rostov-on-Don to participate in an international theatre festival there. Exactly how international a festival in Rostov-on-Don could be is questionable, but clearly this was their only opportunity to shout at the world and declare their reality. I felt nervous. I wanted badly for them to do well, to be recognized and rewarded for their gifts, although what form this reward could take I did not know. I suppose it could only be to leave Kalmykia and go to Moscow, where 'real' people live.

And this was probably exactly what they wanted.

VI

We went out to collect our coats. There was a long queue. Standing in front of us was a blonde Kalmyk girl. I had noticed her earlier, outside the theatre, where I had been struck by her radical look. She was listening to our conversation intently. Eventually curiosity overwhelmed her and she turned round. She asked us about the play and the usual stuff about where we came from. Then she paused. She was thinking.

'I am a student in the English Department at the State University of Kalmykia,' she said.

'Your English is very good,' I said.

'There is a man from Ireland there.'

'Really?' I was surprised.

'Yes. His name is Brian Kennedy.'

'Hm,' I said.

She paused. 'Do you . . . *know him*?'

'Er . . . no, no I don't.'

She paused. 'He is a good man,' she said. 'He has given books to our library. And CDs. We don't have many modern books, because' – she paused – 'our republic is very poor.'

'Yes,' I said. 'He sounds like a very good man.'

'He has a wife and two children, a boy and a girl.'

'Really?'

'Yes . . . But I do not know where they are.'

'Ah,' I said.

'He is going to leave us at the end of the year . . .'

She looked doleful, for a moment. Then: 'Goodbye.'

Suddenly she bowed her head and charged out the door.

I was disappointed, to say the least, that this Irishman had beaten us to Elista. That he had seen the Golden Gate, the Buddha Shakyamuni, before us! The bastard! Suddenly the pall of reality fell over me. I realized we were never going to meet the President: not if there was a foreigner working as a language *assistant* in the university. He had already debased our currency as a piece of exotica. He had ruined my chance to be the President's talking monkey. How dare he!

VII

On the way out we met the director of the ensemble, who was standing by the door, canvassing for opinions. He was incredibly excited to discover some foreigners in his theatre. So excited, in fact, that he brought the two leading men, Igor and Kolya, out from backstage to introduce us. We shook hands, and then stood smiling awkwardly for a few moments. I had never been received like royalty before and couldn't think of anything to say. 'Hello . . .' I said. 'My name's Daniel.' They nodded sagely. I said it again. 'Daniel, that's my name. You were very . . . uh . . . good.' I wished them success for Rostov-on-Don.

Meanwhile, the doors to the hall were still open. Out of the corner of my eye, I was watching the stage. The lead actress, the girl who had been gang-raped, was still there. She was standing alone, gazing out, almost in a trance, on to the empty seats. She looked intensely sad. I wondered what she was thinking about. The futility of it all? That all the talent in the world won't get you anywhere if you live in a void?

I shook hands with Igor and Kolya one last time and then left. I was on a high, but simultaneously I was convinced I had failed. Yet again, as with Svetlana, a gateway to another world had opened: it was in the director's enthusiasm, in the sadness of the actress, in the shy inquisition of the blonde girl. It had flickered in front of me and then vanished.

We went back to the hotel.

33

An interesting point regarding those peoples of the former Soviet Union whose names begin with a 'K': sometimes there is more than one way to spell those names. *Kalmyk*, for example, is sometimes written *Kalmuck*, just as *Kyrgyz* can also be written *Kirghiz* and I have seen *Kazakh* spelt *Kazak*. There is also a group of baptized Tatars called the *Krashen* or *Kreshen*.

This signifies that no one in the English-speaking world gives a fuck.

The Secret History of the World #23,470

Yoshi wanted to take some photos of Elista's market. I think he had some *National Geographic*-style pictures in mind – you know, poor people in colourful headscarves with gold teeth hawking strange fruits and spices, their bony-ribbed off-spring just waiting to find a camera they can smile at: the charming poor.

Instead we walked through a dust cloud into a *mélange* of tents and tables. Old women were hawking bottles of milk, bits of meat, and jars of unidentifiable pickles and preserves. A Kalmyk girl was selling cheap Chinese robots and toy snakes. A Tatar was hawking shapeless, poorly made dresses and lots of black socks.

Near by there was a covered bazaar. Yoshi led us inside, still hoping for some photographs. But it was a large, foul-smelling concrete shed. People were selling a few skinned animals, piles of entrails, jars of spice. Yoshi didn't take any pictures. 'This . . . bullshit,' he said.

There was one beautiful thing, however: directly across from a pile of meat, a stall selling incense and colourful Buddhist *tangka*s, devotional paintings. What a magnificent juxtaposition! The *tangka*s, meanwhile, were not original paintings, but cheapo reproductions of Tibetan ones. That, however, only made the scene more beautiful.

35

The Palmov Museum

In Kalmykia you can visit the Palmov Museum of Local Lore.

This inauspicious building contains no fewer than 56,500 items relating to Kalmyk history and culture in its basement. That's 56,500 items. Folk crafts; holy relics; old clothes and bones. Bits of jewellery. All of it in boxes, with labels, covered in dust. And one or two specialists labouring away, categorizing, classifying, interpreting and reinterpreting, but receiving next to nothing for their efforts. And in their heads all manner of information relating to old clothes, rites and rituals, information that will be shared with nobody.

Theirs is a lonely calling. These fragments they have shored against Kalmykia's ruin: snatched from the sands of the steppe, in order to stop the wind of nothingness, the wind of forgetting from blowing it and an entire people away into oblivion. It is a wind that has erased far greater tribes, nations, cultures.

Sad Teletubbies.

Dirty police bastards

I

It happened in the bus station, as we were hailing a taxi. No sooner had we sat down than there was a knock on the passenger window. I turned round and saw a policeman, a piggy bastard with an impertinent grin and beady eyes, and a spidery little moustache growing in spurts from his blubbery top lip.

'Good afternoon, gentlemen,' he said, smiling and saluting.

'Good afternoon,' I replied.

'Documents, please.'

We handed them over.

He studied them slowly. Probably he couldn't read the Roman alphabet. Then he asked the usual questions: where were we going, what were we doing? He found it difficult to believe that we were tourists. There were no tourists in Elista. He pointed a grubby sausage-finger at me:

'You,' he said. 'Come into the station.'

II

The function of the police in Russia is not to uphold law and order, but rather to stress the arbitrary nature of power in the country, and remind you that at any time, and for nothing, you can be thrown in a cell or worse. They routinely harass, beat and extort dubious 'fines' both from Russian citizens and from foreigners, ostensibly for infractions of the law, but mainly because they can. A common nickname for them is *musir* – 'trash'. They are not very nice.

The police station in Elista's bus station was very small, consisting of an office and a waiting room only. I was left standing in the entrance while Fat Cop's superior, a grave man seated behind a glass screen, examined our documents. Suddenly I remembered I had hidden $150 between my passport and the passport holder.

I was scared that the cleaners in the hotel might steal my cash, you see. So I had placed it in the location where it was most likely to be found by the police, who were far more likely to steal it in the first place. Ah! My cunning was boundless. I looked down at the veiny hands holding my documents and saw the edges of my bills poking out from behind the passport cover. Had he noticed them?

Grave Cop asked me the same questions Fat Cop had, and then asked them again, and again. My answers did not change. Then he picked up the phone and dialled a number. I couldn't understand the ensuing conversation, but somewhere amid the stream of Russian I heard the letters FSB. Startled, I listened more closely, to see I wasn't mistaken. He said it again, FSB.*

For a moment I saw myself stripped and beaten in a concrete cell on the verge of the desert, injected with a truth serum, about to receive a visit from Mr Rubber Glove. Then I calmed down. Why would the FSB be interested in us? We were nobodies. Furthermore, he was taking it to a level where petty extortion would be more difficult on his part. It was actually good that he had called them.

At this point Yoshi appeared in the doorway. 'It not good to be alone with police,' he said.

He was speaking from experience. He had been harassed by the Moscow police countless times. They don't like Asians in Moscow. When Grave Cop saw Yoshi he indicated to Fat Boy to bring us inside the station. We were ushered into a little waiting room, which consisted of a table, some chairs and a 'cage'.

The cage is the tiny gaol cell located in every bus, train and

* The FSB is the successor of the notorious KGB.

metro station in Russia. Usually they are occupied by drunks and dark-skinned people who have been stopped in the street without the correct documents. Often they have mysterious marks on their faces, bruises and lumps and cuts. I had never been inside a cage. This one, however, was tantalizingly vacant – just waiting for some new guests. Fat Cop was sent to fetch Joe.

Grave Cop ran through his set of questions yet again. I answered patiently and politely, meanwhile trying to keep my eye on my passport to see if he was attempting a sleight of hand on the money. Not that I could have stopped him, of course.

Joe arrived, red-faced, nervously twisting his moustache. He sat down between Yoshi and me. He too had had a few nasty run-ins with the police in Moscow, including a spell in the cage. Our current situation was more intimidating, however. If anything happened, there was no one to call. And we didn't know the Kalmyk police. We didn't know what they were capable of.

'They can't do anything to us,' said Joe. 'We haven't committed any crimes.'

'Stay calm, Joe,' I replied. 'The cops are like dogs; they only pounce if they sense fear.'

We sat there for another five minutes, while the Grave Cop typed on his computer and Fat Boy hung around in the background, watching us, waiting to see what was going to happen.

III

Grave Cop stopped typing. Leaning over, he opened a drawer in his desk. He rummaged around for a few moments, sorting through papers, and then pulled out a compact, black revolver. I blinked: had I really seen a gun?

He held it up to the light, as if he was admiring it, or perhaps allowing us to do so, intentionally instilling fear. He checked it was loaded and then stood up. He nodded to Fat Boy, who quickly went outside, closing the door behind him.

'What the fuck is this?' whispered Joe.

'I've got no idea,' I said. 'But it's weird.'

The cop walked towards us. He stopped by the little table, and very solemnly, spoke: 'Get down on your knees.'

'What did he say?' asked Joe.

'I think he told us to get down on our knees,' I said.

'*What?*'

'Excuse me?' I said, to the cop.

The cop stared at me, icily.

'I don't understand,' I said.

'You've understood everything else so far very well. Get down on your knees. Now.'

'What did he say?' asked Joe.

'He . . . er . . . he told us to get on our knees again.'

'He can't make us do that . . .'

The cop was staring at us, teeth clenched. Barely suppressed rage flashed in his eyes. He levelled the gun at my face. 'You understand,' he said.

'Maybe we get down on knees,' suggested Yoshi.

'OK,' I said.

I slipped out of my seat and knelt on the floor. Joe and Yoshi did likewise.

'Good,' said the cop. 'Good.' He smiled briefly.

We studied the floor.

'Look up,' he barked. 'Look at me.'

We looked up, obedient as dogs.

Slowly, he extended the barrel of the revolver towards me.

'Now,' he said. 'You. I want you to . . .'

This time I really didn't understand what he had said. But I didn't want to make him mad.

'Excuse me?' I said, trying hard to sound sincere.

He watched me. Clenched his jaws, briefly. Paused.

'I said I want you to . . .' He repeated the same unknown word.

I stood there on my knees, trying to guess what he wanted. It was very awkward.

'I think he wants you to suck it, man,' whispered Joe.

'What?' I said. 'Fuck off.' But when I looked up at the cop, he was nodding.

'Right,' he said in English, nodding. 'I vant you to sack eet.'

I paused.

'Is this some kind of joke?' I asked.

He shot Yoshi in the face. 'Fuck!' I yelled, diving for cover, as brains spattered against my jacket. I heard Joe screaming. I looked up and caught a glimpse of Yoshi's faceless corpse leaning against him. It was pouring blood on to his shoulder, down his arm, into his hair. 'Get it off me! Get it off me, man!' Joe was soaked in Yoshi's blood. Then the cop indicated me with the barrel of his revolver.

'You,' he said. 'Suck eet. Or die.'

'How about I squeal like a pig instead?'

IV

Actually, I made all that up. He didn't pull out a gun. He didn't do anything, except give us our documents back, wish us a pleasant day and then let us go. He even checked that our taxi-driver wasn't ripping us off. He was an honest man. But I figured that was a little anti-climactic.

We were stopped repeatedly by the police in southern Russia. There was, after all, a war on, although it was hard to imagine the violence in Chechnya when surrounded by the peace of the steppe. After leaving Elista we travelled to Astrakhan where we were detained in a police station inside that city's Kremlin for half an hour. Two days after that the police raided our hotel room in Volgograd at midnight to check our documents. And then on the way back up to Moscow the police entered our carriage on the train and interrogated us for twenty minutes.

v

Fat Cop led us back to the taxi rank, all smiles and friendly questions.

'Do you like Elista?' he asked.

'Oh yes,' I said. 'It's very beautiful.'

'Have you been to Chess City?'

'It's hard to find,' I said. 'We looked all day yesterday and couldn't find it.'

'Ah!' he explained. 'That's because it isn't actually in Elista. It's in the steppe. You need to take a taxi there.'

'Is it actually a city?' I asked.

'Oh yes,' he said. 'It has streets, houses, offices . . . and the Palace of Chess. It's very beautiful,' he assured me. 'Very beautiful.'

Once more the mirage of Chess City flickered before my eyes. I had to go there . . . I had to see it . . .

37

Twelve facts about the Queen Mother

Did I mention that while we were in Elista the Queen Mother died? It happened on our first night, in fact. I was sitting with Joe in our room watching TV. Jeremy Clarkson was pratting on about cars when suddenly the broadcast was interrupted and Peter Sissons's very solemn head filled the screen. 'The Queen Mother has died, peacefully, in her home, at Sandringham. She was a hundred and one.'

It was quite surreal, I should say, to find oneself in a hotel room in the middle of nowhere listening to news like this. Furthermore, as there was nothing else to do, we watched the BBC's coverage for four hours, watching reports and listening to the same eulogies over and over again as the steppe wind blew outside our window. Here is what I learned about Her Majesty:

1   She was a hundred and one.
2   She had died.
3   Her life spanned a century.
4   She was placed in her coffin within hours of her death.
5   Her husband had died fifty years earlier.
6   She had called him 'Bertie'.
7   She had been 'born a commoner'.
8   In a palace.
9   In Scotland (now that was surprising).
10 She did something good in World War II like refusing to be evacuated and thus raising the people's spirits.
11 She liked Canada.
12 One of her most faithful admirers liked to dress as a clown.

Actually, she didn't seem to have done much with her hundred and one years. No one had anything to say; no one had any specific memories. It was very strange. The BBC is rubbish. They had years to prepare for the old dear's death and that was the best they could do. The government should scrap it and replace it with cartoons.

38

Temple of the void

Dead fox in the temple

And so the days rolled on and into one another. We drifted around, wandering from locked building to locked building, trying to entertain ourselves, trying to divert ourselves with small goals set against a backdrop of nothingness.

There was a new Buddhist temple near Elista, and Joe was pressing hard for us to visit it. Like I said at the beginning, he was into the Golden Horde, the Mystical East and all that. I myself have almost zero interest in Eastern religion and philosophy but saw no reason not to visit the temple. It would pass the time. Furthermore, Joe said that Kalmyk Buddhism allegedly contained elements of ancient shamanism and this did intrigue me. I agreed to go along. I thought an encounter with a Buddhist shaman might provide me with a few stories.

The temple was located in the steppe, at the top of a small plateau. Surrounded by dead earth, it seemed to hover like a red-and-white cube on the border between land and sky, right at the point where the yellow met the azure. This was where Ilumzhinov had invited the Dalai Lama to live. The Dalai Lama would have been lonely. Apart from a weird mutant dog thing with stumpy legs, there were no signs of life.

I walked around, studying the murals around the doors and inspecting the prayer wheels. It was all very nice, but I felt like it was what I was *supposed* to appreciate, like it was meant to be good for me somehow and I couldn't help but kick against it. I could see in my mind's eye a pious entry in the *Lonely Planet* informing me of the significance of the different murals, and instructing me to feel edified by the resurrection of Kalmykia's heritage, as the republic threw off years of Russian colonial oppression (*yawn*). It had to be in my mind's eye, however, as the *Lonely Planet* doesn't have an entry on Kalmykia.

It was locked and abandoned, of course. Unable to get in, I wandered round the back. I'd been round the back of many monuments in Russia and found some interesting things: piles of scrap metal, logs, bits of the monument that had fallen off and been dismantled. Behind the monument to Mother Russia at the mass grave in St Petersburg I found some surplus railings. Behind the Museum of the Armed Forces in Moscow there were rows and rows of tanks and aircraft. Best of all, behind the Museum of the Great Patriotic War in Moscow I found a man with blue skin. It comes as a result of drinking the wrong type of paint-stripper, I'm told. He was rather shy and ducked under some trees to escape my curious gaze.

There was nothing behind the temple, however: just a big, blank wall. Perhaps it was too new to have accumulated any detritus. Or perhaps there was none to accumulate in the void. I decided to walk over to another Buddhist structure, which stood about fifty metres behind it. It was a little glass house, with a pagoda-style roof. It intrigued me.

There was a strange form, a black blob lying on the ground by the steps leading up to the door. As I drew nearer I began to make out more details. It was shaggy, about the size of a dog. What could it be? An unusual welcome mat? A fur robe, abandoned by one of the monks?

No, it was a dead fox! I was enormously pleased. I like dead animals, and have a collection of photos of dead birds, cats, rats, pigs, dogs, etc. This one was relatively fresh, the corpse only about a day or two old. The fur was slightly matted, and its eyes and mouth were wide open as if it had died from a terrible shock. Now there was a mystery: what had happened to it? How had it met its end? And more to the point: what was it going to be reincarnated as? There were no marks or wounds on the body. Perhaps it had walked around the temple anti-clockwise and an angry Buddha had struck it down. That's a sin, or so I'm told.

But the greater mystery was what it was doing there in the first place. Hadn't the monks seen it? Why hadn't they carried it away? Were they that lazy? Then I wondered if there were any monks at all in the complex. Maybe Ilumzhinov had just built it to show off. I remembered a story I had heard years earlier – that the Soviet government once built a huge Buddhist temple in the east to demonstrate their religious tolerance to the outside world. It was only ever opened when tour parties came to town. And the monks were not monks at all but KGB officers in robes.

The glass house was also locked, but I peered inside. It was completely empty, except for a framed photo of the Dalai Lama leaning against the back wall, and, near the door, an ashtray containing a few twisted fag ends. I felt there was some incongruity.

I lay down beside the fox to see what it had been looking at when it died: the back of the temple. Then I returned to the front steps to find Yoshi and tell him of my discovery.

Yoshi didn't care. I couldn't persuade him to have a look either. But while I'd been examining the fox, two young Kalmyks had materialized from the emptiness and unlocked the doors to the temple. Whether they were shamans or not I can't say, as they didn't speak a word to us. Nevertheless, I went in and looked around, to fulfil my duty as a good, culturally sensitive visitor. It was pretty. I left. Yoshi, waiting outside, offered to take me back in with Joe and explain some of the murals. I declined.

I preferred to sit on a bench and observe the emptiness. That, and not Buddhism, was what I had come for.

39

Clans of the Desert

Our taxi-driver had abandoned us while we were in the temple, so we began trudging back along the dusty road that led to Elista. This being Kalmykia, it was deserted and so it took a while for a bus to pass and pick us up. Out there on the road, however, I had an idea for a movie, a rather experimental one, perhaps, but nevertheless interesting.

There are two tribes of Mongols in the Kalmyk steppe but they ride motorbikes, and fight with guns and chainsaws. The film begins with some scenes of rape and pillaging, then the leader of Tribe A abducts the most beautiful girl from Tribe B amid smoke, fire and sawn-off limbs. She is the daughter of the clan chief. Tribe B assembles its mightiest warriors and sends them into the steppe on Harleys to bring her back. They ride off, disappear into dust.

The champions of Tribe B go looking for the main camp of Tribe A. They stumble upon little gatherings of yurts on their way. Lots of innocent people die horribly, including old men, women and children. Word gets back to the leader of Tribe A that his enemies are terrorizing his people. Love has made him philosophical and he pauses to regret the chain of events he set in motion by kidnapping the Beautiful Girl. He says that this war, like all wars, is a grain of sand in the desert. He sees that he has no choice, however, and sends out his best warriors to take on those of Tribe B.

War ensues. Carnage rules. Amid the roar of motorbike engines heads explode, limbs fly, stomachs are torn open. The heroes die off, one by one, *Magnificent Seven* style.

Everything is harsh, stark, and yet beautiful. The camera lingers slowly on the vast empty steppe, the infinite blue sky. A shaman shakes his stick at a pile of rocks and water flows forth. The saiga graze peacefully, as oblivious and alien as the sky and land. The faces of the actors are especially important – they should all be ragged, rugged, craggy, wind-damaged, brutal. These are the faces of people who have spent a lifetime in the open, in the steppe winds. Though violent as beasts, they look impossibly wise, ancient. The Beautiful Girl, however, has soft creamy skin. It's a miracle. It almost shines.

The battle ends, and Tribe B, though decimated, is triumphant. Unfortunately, the Beautiful Girl has fallen in love with her captor. She pleads for his life. Her pleas are ignored, and his limbs and neck are tied to five motorbikes driving off in different directions. The Beautiful Girl is made to watch as a punishment. He dies rather messily. However, in a bizarre twist which makes absolutely no sense, a bluejay suddenly erupts from his dead entrails and flies off. The girl magically transforms into a dove and follows him.

The music comes mainly from wind and the croaking of a

solitary bard with a *dombr*. The film is mostly silent, but when the actors do speak they speak in an invented language of harsh, guttural noises.

40

After my trip to Kalmykia I was so fascinated by the republic I spent a lot of time trying to find out more about this lost tribe and its history. It wasn't easy. Information was thin on the ground. Here, in fact, are all the references to Kalmyks in books and magazines I managed to collect in two years of searching:

1   Lenin's maternal grandmother was Kalmyk. This was not a well-known fact in Soviet times, and still isn't. Indeed, the Lenin monument in Elista is aggressively European-looking.
2   Pushkin, the Russian national poet, mentioned the 'Kalmyk steppe' in a poem. He didn't mention the people who lived in it, however.
3   At the end of the nineteenth century the father of the avant-garde poet Velimir Khlebnikov* was appointed

---

* A sample of Khlebnikov's verse:

> The smells of night – these stars
> In something something something,
> Where water somethings on something,
> Something something something,
> You come to something green
> From something something –
> My something teacher,
> Black, like something something.
> And another comes to meet,
> He is tired, like all the East,
> And in his hand something
> Red something flower. [1921]

Sorry, I couldn't find my dictionary.

overseer of the Kalmyks. Khlebnikov reported that his was the only house in the steppe: he grew up surrounded by yurts, the traditional tents of Mongolian nomads.

4   Roald Dahl wrote a story called *Skin* that featured a Kalmuck (*sic*) artist.

5   Waitz, in his *Introduction to Anthropology* (Eng. translation 1863, vol. 1, p. 135), quotes Bergmann and claims that the Kalmucks (*sic*) do not blush.

6   Darwin, however, in *The Expression of the Emotions in Man and Animals*, doubts this. Though he had never seen a Kalmuck, on page 316 he reports that a certain Mr Geach 'observed that the face, arms and breast of a Chinaman, aged 24 years, reddened from shame'. Thus might we not reasonably expect that a Kalmuck also will blush?

7   A news presenter on the Russian TV channel ORT is Kalmyk.

8   From a US Baptist Church 'Prayer Profile' of the Kalmyks:

The Kalmyks consider themselves to be strong Lama-Buddhist and [are] resistant to change. Buddhism is deeply rooted in the minds of the Kalmyks. With the fall of communism, as missionaries were allowed entry into the former Soviet Union, Kalmyks returned to Buddhism. The government financed a temple that was completed on 5 October 1996. Russians also brought Orthodox Christianity to Kalmykia, and Kalmyks consider Christianity a Russian religion. Both Russians and Kalmyks consider Evangelical Christianity to be a cult. As Kalmyks searched for their identity, they found it in Buddhism. Buddhism has become the Kalmyk culture and identity. They are drowned in Satan's deceptions. With the mixture of narrow-mindedness and in fear of persecution, they dare not come to Christ.

9   Kalmyk 'businessmen' were behind the Yeltsin-era Hungry Duck, at one time considered the most debauched bar in the entire world. One night a week alcohol was free for girls until 9 p.m., at which point they let the men in. It was like a rape camp in the centre of the city.

10   I once read a story in the *Moscow Times* about a police car chase. It ended when the criminals abandoned their car by the side of the road and ran for it. The cops found the corpse of a *Mr Kalmykov* inside the car. He had been shot in the head.

41

The bus from the temple took us into the heart of town, depositing us in front of the central concert hall, a large brick box. As there was nothing else to do, we decided to attend a performance by the State Orchestra. Joe went in to get the tickets, while Yosh and I sat on the steps of the concert hall, enjoying the spring sunshine.

Joe emerged a few minutes later, very excited. He hadn't managed to buy any tickets, but the woman at the ticket table had told him that he was the first foreigner ever to enter the building. Joe was overwhelmed, like he was the first European to enter Mecca.

I felt jealous. These days the world is infested with Europeans: you can't go anywhere without encountering German backpackers or twenty-strong mobs of Italian teenagers in bright yellow jackets. Go to Tamurlaine's tomb, and they're there . . . the Great Wall of China and they're there . . . Lake Titicaca . . . you'll never be alone. There will always be a European, guidebook in hand, expanding his or her mind.

And now we had spread the virus to Kalmykia. But at least we were the first. Or Joe was. Sort of. In the concert hall, at least. Yes.

Fucking Brian Kennedy.

42

Chess City: a mind-numbing voyage of extraordinary pointlessness

I

And so we come to the climax, the grand finale. Chess City.

Chess City never left my thoughts while I was in Elista, although I didn't have any interest in chess itself. But I was intrigued by Ilumzhinov's absurd vanity project. And yet, we almost didn't go.

The reasons were as follows: Joe and Yosh thought maybe a few hours extra spent lying in bed would be a better way to spend our time. We had seen a lot of nothing in the last couple of days and they weren't sure that Chess City would develop that nothing in any interesting way.

I, however, couldn't let go of the idea. From the start, I had intended the City of Chess to be the apex of my anti-holiday. I wanted a grand and bizarre pointlessness to conclude my stay in Elista. My fear was that it might be only a little strange and not disappointing enough.

Fat Cop, however, had pointed us in its direction and now I knew we could find the complex. In the end I persuaded the

Joe and Yoshi, exultant in front of the Palace of Chess, Chess City

others to go. I told them they could kick my arse if they didn't like it.

II

Ilf's and Petrov's *The Twelve Chairs* was the most popular comic novel of the Soviet Union. It sold millions and millions of copies that were, in the words of its English translator, literally 'read to shreds'. Before the curious among you nip out and buy it, let me advise you: don't bother. It's not funny.

There is a Kalmykia connection, however. The book centres on the adventures of its hero Ostap Bender, a charming conman who is travelling across Russia in pursuit of some precious gems hidden in the lining of an antique chair. Towards the end of the novel the quest brings him to a provincial dump called Vasyuki. Here he impersonates a chess champion and persuades the locals that he will put their nowhere town on the map if they give him cash. He proposes renaming the town New Vasyuki and transforming it into the chess centre of the universe, pledging that in future interplanetary contests will take place there. The gullible locals give Bender their money and he runs off with it, narrowly escaping a lynching.

Curiously, New Vasyuki is also the name of Elista's Chess City, and a statue of the fictional conman stands a few hundred metres from the entrance. Obviously the President of Kalmykia is not insensitive to the absurdities of some of his deeds.

III

In 1998 Ilumzhinov, recently elected head of the World Chess Federation, declared that Elista would host that year's Chess Olympiad. This, unsurprisingly, was not a very popular decision among the world's chess greats. They pointed out that

Elista was an obscure city lacking the infrastructure to cope with such a contest. Furthermore, it was almost impossible to get to. Why not host the contest in St Petersburg, which was (1) amply supplied with halls in which to hold the contest, (2) full of hotels for the players to stay in, (3) possessed an international airport, and (4) quite nice?

Ilumzhinov, however, insisted that the contest be held in Elista. He declared that all the objections regarding the city's unsuitability were easily overcome. He would build an 'Olympic village' containing luxury housing for the contestants and a 'palace of chess' devoted to the game where they would play. As for getting there, they could fly into Elista's 'international' airport via Moscow.

When asked how his tiny republic, with an annual budget less than half that of some Hollywood movies, was going to fund this development, he blithely explained that, of course, each country would stump up the cash for their representative's building. The Hungarian government would build a house for the Hungarian champion, the German government for the German champion and so on. It was simple!

It didn't happen that way. Instead, Ilumzhinov had to go to the federal government to ask for $150 million, so Russia wouldn't lose face in front of the world. Fortunately he had built good, solid relations with the corrupt alcoholic Yeltsin who obligingly coughed up the cash. The buildings were quickly erected, the tournament was played – and then everyone went home. Chess City, however, remained.

Ilumzhinov intended to lease the houses in Chess City as prestigious office space or luxurious living accommodation. The problem, of course, is that there is zero per cent foreign investment in Kalmykia, and thus nobody to hire prestigious office space or pay for luxurious living accommodation.

Interlude: the truth about advertising

All over Elista there were little posters that read, 'We buy hair.' They were stuck to every lamp-post, to every derelict building. The buyers were coming for two days and were interested only in hair of a certain length and quality.

I had never seen anything like that before. Soon there would be lots of shaved Kalmyk girls running around. I was impressed at human ingenuity. No matter how poor and derelict a people might be, no matter how far away, someone will always think of some way they can be used to benefit the rich. I envisioned the next generation of posters, once all the hair was taken: 'We buy fingers.'

Apart from the hair posters, there wasn't anything in the way of commercial advertising in Elista, not even one billboard for Coke. I noticed this on our last morning in the city, as we rode the taxi to Chess City. All the signs by the roadside were public announcements. They exhorted me to love Kalmykia, or to telephone my parents, or to play chess. Ilumzhinov was smiling at me, chesspiece in hand on that last one.

I had never been in an urban environment without advertising before. It was startling. It was eerie. Maybe, I thought, it was this absence that made Elista feel so much like the Twilight Zone. Without advertisements on the street there was nothing to remind its citizens of the rest of the world. There was only the President's face and, just beyond the city, the eternal, identity-erasing steppe.

Suddenly I understood that an advert for a Sony TV isn't just an advert for a Sony TV. It's a reminder that there's a country called Japan, and that there are links between your country and something outside itself. Advertising posters are portals to the beyond.

More than that, they assure us of the passage of time, that life changes, that old things die and are replaced with fresh ones. No billboard stays up longer than a couple of months. As sure as the seasons pass it will vanish, and be replaced by another, and another. And every time you look at a billboard, in the back of your mind, you are aware that it will soon vanish and be replaced with another one, more up to date.

Remove advertising posters and what you are left with are insincere public announcements that stay up for years, never changing, until they are all worn and peeling from the rain, wind and sun. Only exposure to the elements brings them down. The graphics, meanwhile, age even more badly and become depressing reminders of a time when you were younger and stronger.

I remembered one of my lecturers at Edinburgh University, a Marxist, bemoaning the appearance of adverts in recently democratic Romania. 'Ceauşescu's Romania may have been an evil dictatorship,' he said, a note of sadness in his voice, 'But at least the Communist state had the consolation of a landscape free of manipulative advertising.' I had thought he was an arsehole at the time. In Elista, however, I felt real anger at his smugness, his comfortable, well-fed complaisance.

Yes. I'm sure that when you couldn't buy meat in the shops, or when a policeman was beating you with a rubber hose, it always helped to remember the poor people in the West who had to look at all those ads for Coke. And I'm sure it's a great consolation for the people of Kalmykia in their poverty and obscurity today.

V

The taxi-driver, who had been silent for the whole journey, suddenly turned to Yoshi and spoke, asking a question that must have been burning in his soul. 'Are you Yugoslavian?' he asked.

'Er . . . no,' replied Yoshi.

VI

Chess City is a bright model village, one street long, lined with neat little houses, each of which has a colourful door and a tiny lawn. The Palace of Chess is located near the entrance to the development. It is a highly contemporary structure: a squat, conical pyramid of blue glass embedded in white concrete that stands four floors high. Perhaps in a more prosperous landscape the architecture would be nothing extraordinary, but transplanted to Kalmykia's post-industrial lunar landscape, this clean, clinical, contemporary suburb looks rather startling.

Aside from the houses and the palace, Chess City also contains an Orthodox chapel and a Buddhist stupa *demonstrating the republic's policy of tolerance towards different religious faiths. There is also a nice pond. This is the pond where Ilumzhinov's opponent Larissa Yudina was found with her head smashed in. Oh, Larissa! Why couldn't you just be quiet?*

Please note the silence. The silence of Chess City is something that should be commented on. It is something alien. It is the silence of ice forming in another galaxy.

VII

A young couple was necking on the steps of the palace of chess. They were fairly scraggy looking, as if they had spent the night asleep in the wasteland.

When she saw us, the girl tittered and whispered something to her man. He stared at us for a second, and then led her away, behind the palace. For a good stiff rogering, no doubt.

Apart from them, the streets were deserted. There were no cars. No people. The houses had plaques on them indicating that a government ministry had its offices inside. But those offices were empty.

VIII

There is an armed guard at the entrance to the Palace of Chess, so be careful as you enter. He does not see many people, and you may startle him. Answer his questions politely and honestly. Leave your bags with him. Only then will he grant you permission to study the palace and its treasures.

Passing within you will note that the Palace is cool and spacious. Light streams in through the glass walls of the pyramid. Look up and you will see the many flags and banners that hang suspended from the ceiling, stressing the international aspect of the compound. Grandmasters from all over the planet have played in these halls after all.

There is an interesting display of photographs on the ground floor, detailing the history of Chess City. There you can see the laying of the first brick, the blessing of the foundations by His Holiness Alexei II of the Russian Orthodox Church, the construction of the site. There are also lots of pictures of our young President Kirsan Ilumzhinov. Kirsan loves chess and has made it compulsory for children in Kalmykia to study the science of the game. He hopes that one day a world champion shall emerge from our small but proud nation.

IX

'Joe,' I said. 'Look at this. Who does that look like?' I was studying a photo of Ilumzhinov and another man, inspecting the foundations of the Palace of Chess.

'I'm not sure,' said Joe.

'I think it's Chuck Norris.'*

Joe stared long and hard at the solemn, bearded face. 'Fuck me! So it is! What's he doing here?'

For many years the charisma-free Mr Norris was mysteriously popular in Russia. At one time his mind-numbing TV show *Walker Texas Ranger* aired every night on Moscow's sixth channel. Chuck, meanwhile, capitalized on his popularity and had several investments in Russia, among them a hotel and a casino in Moscow. I wondered if his business concerns involved deals with Ilumzhinov. Perhaps he was involved in the construction of Chess City itself.

On the other hand, maybe Ilumzhinov just wanted another photo of himself beside a famous person to show off to his people with. The Patriarch and the Dalai Lama, OK. But Chuck Norris?

x

The second and third floors of Chess City are taken up mostly with chess tables. They stand neatly in file, row upon row upon row. There are no chairs, however, and there are no pieces on the boards. They gleam as though they have never been touched and, indeed, some of them have never been played upon. There are no scratches on the surfaces, no smudged fingerprints. These tables are things of beauty and must be preserved.

Thread your way carefully through the tables on the second floor until you come to the corner of chess champions. All the greats, such as Kasparov, Karpov and Bobby Fischer are there,

---

* Mr Norris is a third-rate action hero who has built an entire career on a tangential connection to Bruce Lee. I know who he is because my eldest brother was really into kung-fu movies when I was growing up and kept renting crap Chuck Norris efforts, instead of the movies with tits in them that I wanted to watch.

138

staring out at you from black-and-white photos. Continue walking until you come to the Chess Café. You may find it difficult to purchase any refreshments, however, as the café is usually shut. It would not do for the palace to become dirty, after all.

Pause to admire the beautiful mural depicting a Russian and a Kalmyk, sitting in a leafy glade, facing each other across a chessboard. It is a beautiful scene, a true picture of the inter-ethnic harmony that can be brought about by the love of this noblest and most high-minded of games.

And don't forget the Chess Museum, which contains numerous interesting exhibits! In its glass cases there are many old books, pendants from international competitions and chess sets. Pride of place, however, is taken by a huge wall rug that features an image of President Ilumzhinov's smiling face woven into its centre. He is very handsome, you know.

The museum has a full-time guide. She is particularly knowledgeable regarding the life and career of the Estonian master Mikhail Tal. Please, even if you are not interested, be polite. Our guide is sensitive, and easily hurt. She gets lonely sometimes. Put yourself in her place. Nod at appropriate intervals and echo the odd word here and there. Let her think you are listening.

XI

Chess legend Garry Kasparov is no fan of Ilumzhinov. Here is an excerpt from his testimony at the US Congressional Hearings on Corruption in Russia, 1998:

There is one transgressor who is extravagant even by Russian standards and I have watched his progress because it adversely affects my chess career. Kirsan Ilumzhinov is President of the tiny Republic of Kalmykia,

ruling over 360,000 impoverished people in the vast
empty steppes in the south of Russia on the Caspian Sea.
The President of this under-populated semi-autonomous
state has made an amazing career by attracting over four
thousand Russian corporations, including some household
names, to register in his self-proclaimed Off-Shore Zone.
The result is that these companies pay 5000 Euros per
quarter to a special presidential fund. This equates to a
multi-million dollar fortune for Kirsan Ilumzhinov, and a
significant loss to the central Russian tax base. This would
be like allowing Citibank-Travelers to register on an
Indian reservation somewhere in the US and pay no taxes
at all. At the end of 1995, Kirsan Ilumzhinov decided to
take over the ailing International Chess Federation known
as FIDE. His patronage and his subsidy give him full control over an International Federation based in Luanne.
The connection with Switzerland and the conduit this pro-
vides for his money is obvious.

On several occasions Kasparov has left FIDE in disgust at
Ilumzhinov's leadership. But wherever he gets it from,
Ilumzhinov has money, and that always brings the master
back into the fold.

XII

'Captain, we checked out the visitors to Chess City. They
were three foreigners – two Europeans and an Asian. We
found them in the little gallery on the top floor. I think they
were journalists or something. They were looking at the art.
Crappy wooden sculptures by a professor at the university.
Couldn't make head or tail of it myself. I followed one of the
Europeans around and watched what he was doing. I even
fiddled with my machine-gun a bit, to make him nervous. But

he was just a harmless fuckwit, it was totally clear. Wasn't even worth checking his documents. The woman on the entrance tried to charge us to come in. That was funny. Fuck that. We just walked right on in. Pay money to look at that shit? I mean, have you seen it? Fucking six-year-old kid could do better.'

XIII

'Where are you from?' asked the curator of an exhibition of wooden sculpture on the top floor. She was a young Kalmyk woman.

'Scotland,' I said.

'Really?'

'Yes.'

'I met a man from Scotland once before.'

'In Kalmykia?'

'Yes. He was an engineer.'

'Oh,' I said.

Brian Kennedy . . . Chuck Norris . . . and now some Scottish engineer. I wasn't even the first of my countrymen to set foot in the place. The longer I spent in Elista the more cheated I felt, the more I realized that, alas, there are no corners of the earth you can escape the footprints of predecessors. Not even in blank wastelands. The conversation, however, suddenly took an unexpected turn.

'What religion are you?' she asked.

'In Scotland?' I said, defensively.

'Yes.'

'Protestant,' I said.

'Did you see the Protestant church?'

'In Elista?'

'Yes. There's a Protestant church in the centre. It's on Lenin Street. You didn't see it?'

'No, I didn't.'

'Strange. It is in the centre.'

'Yes?'

'Yes. I go every Sunday.'

'Really?'

'Yes. I am Protestant. Perhaps you would like to come . . . with me . . .?'

'I'm sorry,' I said. 'We're leaving today.'

'Oh,' she said. 'It's a pity'

'Yes,' I said. 'It is.'

XIV

I said goodbye, and turned to leave. I was exiting the Palace of Chess, descending the steps to the ground floor, where I would reclaim my bag and step on to the street that led back to Elista.

But I didn't want to go. I felt a terrible, a ridiculous pang of separation. I missed this girl already. It was nonsense, of course, and I knew it. But it was there all the same. I wanted to continue our conversation. I wanted to find out more about her, to see where she lived, to hear her story, to find out how she wound up guarding the gallery of wooden architecture in the desert. Where did she learn English? What did she really think of Ilumzhinov?

It wasn't her, of course. I knew in an hour or so the feeling would pass. I'd felt it before, a couple of times, in places I'd connected with. It was always hard to leave. I had a sense of potential, of another destiny, another route hovering in front of me that I wasn't going to take. At moments like that I could feel another Daniel standing in the shadows, wanting to be born – a Daniel I would never know. I couldn't help my curiosity. Perhaps he'd be happier. More fulfilled. How could I just turn my back on him like that?

I imagined holing myself up in the hotel for a few months, with only the BBC and the strangers I met on the street for company. I'd be a stranger, a phantom. Weightless, like Brian Kennedy with his missing family: a man liberated from a past, from history. With the passage of time, though, I would begin to acquire substance. I would get to know the people. I would make friends, enemies. I would follow conversations to their end instead of finishing them as soon as they began.

Perhaps I'd spend my Sunday mornings at the Protestant church. And I could spend my weekdays helping out at the university, teaching English to young Kalmyks and Russians eager to engage with the world. I could write a column for the Elista *Evening News*, and ramble on about life in the UK for my readers. Messages from a distant star, and I the man who fell to earth, but an ET who had come voluntarily, enticed by the warmth and openness of Kalmykia and its denizens. I would embrace the void and become one with the void, and attain true communion of spirit.

I didn't want to be a tourist. I wanted to be something more. But how can you ever be anything more than a tourist when you know you can leave? When you know, not that your stay is temporary, but that it need never not be temporary?

You can't. You leave, and the people and the places recede into the distance. They become stories, a little splash of colour in your memories, but growing ever fainter with the passage of time. Just like the posters that read, 'We buy hair.'

MARI EL

1

A few months later I was sitting at home in Scotland trying to figure out what I should do with my life. My years of travel had been fine, but I needed to think of a different strategy. I was in the final phase of my twenties, and I couldn't keep on drifting around. I needed something new, some grand vision to shape the next phase of my destiny.

I thought about entering the diplomatic service, but couldn't be bothered with the exams. Then I thought about joining the British Council, but suddenly remembered it was crap. In Moscow, for example, the BC liked to spend UK taxpayers' money on importing DJs to the city's nightclubs. That was how it 'promoted contemporary British culture'. Nonsense. In desperation I looked into the possibility of working for some international mercenaries, perhaps in an organizational capacity. But the chances of breaking in were slim. I was in a quandary.

Then one day I decided to write a book.

2

I thought about it. A book would take a lot of time and energy. I'd have to go back to Russia. I'd probably never get it published. And even if I did I wouldn't make any money from it. Why, but of course! It made perfect sense! That's what I'd do!

I returned to Moscow and spent a couple of months writing about Kalmykia. One day while I was doing that I looked out the window and saw my neighbours in the opposite building having sex. A young blonde was sliding up and down on the cock of an unseen man.

That, surely, was a good omen.

3

I wanted to focus on Russia's European republics, and not just because I was too lazy to travel the extra distance to the Asian ones. No: I really thought I was on to something. Tatarstan and Kalmykia had radically altered my conception of Europe. I wanted to take it further and see if there were any other strange pseudo-countries lying in wait for me.

Ah, Europe! Glass buildings, Ikea . . . Neil Kinnock . . . Belgium. Not exactly inspiring, is it? Maybe that's why I was so fascinated by those 'hidden' Europeans – Mongols, Tatars, Adygey, Udmurt, Mari, Kypchak, Ingush, Bashkiri, who are completely ignored in 'Europe' as a cultural concept. They provided me with an antidote to the anaemic cappuccino culture that had smothered the western half of the continent.

Their names alone were exciting, so strange, so alien, so full of struggle, violence, survival. Every tiny reference to them in a history book I greedily devoured. Every mention in the *Moscow Times* I read. Even the ones about business and finance. If Tatneft, the Tatar state oil company, upped the output of its refinery, I took note. If an ice-cream factory in Ufa, the capital of Bashkortostan, started manufacturing a new flavour, I stroked my chin and said, 'Well, I never!'

After doing some research I decided to visit the Republic of Mari El, which borders Tatarstan to the north. I wanted to go because its indigenous people, the Mari, are the last true pagans in Europe. The Mari worship the same ancient nature gods their ancestors in the forests and villages did centuries ago. They kill animals to please their deities. I figured it had to be a strange place: ritual sacrifices in the shadow of nuclear-power plants, copious nudity, the ritual deflowering of virgins . . .

4

A few things would be different this time, however. First, I was going by myself. Joe had long since returned to the UK and Yoshi had gone back to Japan. After losing $10,000 in a hostel in Thailand he was bankrupt and his days as an Oriental Ahasuerus were over. I was alone in my obsession with bad places. This made me a little wary. Yoshi, for example, was far better than me at securing transport and accommodation and the general organization of travel. Joe, meanwhile, had a gift for attracting interesting and strange people. I was more of a conceptualist, a Brian Eno of the travel world. I had ideas, but I couldn't play any instruments. Not much use, really.

Secondly, I was worried I might get bored. What if I didn't find any pagans? What if I didn't find anything except locked buildings and derelict wastelands? Elista was fascinating because I'd never seen such emptiness before. But two surreal wastelands in a row would be too much. In Mari El I was hoping for . . . well . . . something to happen.

And lastly, of course, there was always the question of danger. As with Kalmykia and Tatarstan my plans to penetrate Mari El solo had disturbed my Russian friends. Russians are obsessed with the dangerousness of their country. They pride themselves on how it's too terrible for coddled Westerners with their baby-soft skin and quilted two-ply toilet paper. But I don't think Russia is dangerous at all. Not so long as you can avoid the police, the hospitals and the suicide bombers, that is.

5

After Elista we had gone to Astrakhan. And there we had a problem, because by the time we arrived, in the early evening, all the rooms in every hotel in town had been booked.

Or so they said. In the first hotel we entered the receptionist told us there were no rooms in the entire city. Not believing her, we decided to look for ourselves. But everywhere we went we were turned away. Astrakhan has a population of half a million and there are four or five large hotels in the city. It was early April – hardly peak season. I didn't believe that all the rooms in every hotel in town could be booked. I also watched in one hotel, as the receptionist who had turned us away gave out rooms to people who came after us. She caught my eye as she did so. But they were Russians, not foreigners.

I had no idea what was going on, and in Russia there's no point asking. In the end we found beds only because Yoshi abused the city in front of our taxi-driver. He took pity on us and rustled up a flat where we could stay. The next day I was attacked by a drunk and cursed by gypsies in the bus station. Astrakhan wasn't very good.

With this experience in mind, I decided to take no chances with accommodation or transport in Mari El and organize it all in advance.

6

It was easy enough to get train tickets. I found an agency on the net that could organize them for you and even deliver them to your door. It was only once they were in my hand and I compared the figure written on the ticket with the figure deducted from my bank account that I noticed I'd been charged 110 per cent commission. Nice.

The search for a place to stay uncovered a world of surprises. I had decided to rent a flat in the capital, Yoshkar Ola. When I typed 'Yoshkar Ola flats' in the Google search bar, however, I was led to a bunch of sites offering Russian brides to Western men. I tried the search again and once more was taken to aprettylady.com, russianbeauty.com, and the wonderfully named virginia.com. It turned out that Yoshkar Ola was a major centre of the mail-order-bride business in Russia.

The sites were fascinating. I was particularly impressed by virginia.com. There were over fourteen hundred women on offer and you could browse through them, looking at pictures and reading their letters. Most of the women professed a great interest in cooking and cleaning and generally being subservient, no doubt under the entirely correct impression that this would endear them to the men reading their letters in foreign lands. *Hello, dear friend!* they said. *Are you my soulmate?* With the click of a mouse you could have food parcels and cinema tickets sent to the house of your lady.

Browsing through all this, I found a link leading me to 'Natasha's flat'. Natasha rented out her apartment to the foreign men coming to the city to meet their wives for the first time. She had posted pictures on the net: it looked clean and comfortable. There were net curtains, a big sofa in the living room, and a double bed with a lilac cover. It cost $25 a night.

It was the bed that did it. I thought about all the trembling Russian beauties who had first been taken in the strong arms of a foreign man there. Men from Australia, America, Britain, Germany, who had flown around the world for love.

I could have found a cheaper place. But I had made up my mind. I wanted to stay in Natasha's flat.

7

What is a Mari anyway?

The most famous Finno-Ugric nations are the Hungarians, the Finns and the Estonians. They are descended from a tribe that, it is believed, emigrated west from the Ural mountains on the border of Europe and Asia thousands of years ago. Their languages and myths stem from the same roots and display many similarities.

But there are other, smaller offshoots of the original tribe living in Romania, northern Russia and as far away as the Ob river in Siberia. From the nearly extinct Livonians to the Nenets living on the shores of the Arctic Ocean, from the Udmurt to the Sami, to the Mordvins, to the Permyaks, to the Komi, to the Karelians, to the Mari. There are groups, sub-groups and sub-sub-groups. Each speaks its own language and has its own culture derived from the original mother culture. There are three types of Mari, for example: Hill Mari, Meadow Mari and Eastern Mari.

Add these three groups together and you have about half a million people, living mainly in the Republics of Mari El and Chuvashia and also in the Nizhni Novgorod region in Russia. Their history has been a hard and brutal one.

8

Some highlights from the history of the Mari

And what is that history? Let's take a quick look at some of the most important dates.

AD 551
The Mari living on the banks of the Volga first come under the subjection of a foreign power: the Ostrogoths. They remain that way until the . . .

SEVENTH CENTURY . . .
when the Bolgars move in and take over. A few centuries pass with the Mari living as their vassals and then in . . .

1236 ...
the Golden Horde arrives in the area. They crush the Bolgars but also crush the Mari.

1437–1552
The Mari live under the heel of the Kazan khanate. Like the Russians, the Mari pay tribute to Tatars. But they are also made to do menial work, repair town walls, build fortifications, and also have to serve in the army. The Mari live under their yoke until 1552, when the Russians sack Kazan and take over the Khan's territories.

1552–57
The Mari fight against Russian colonization. They lose.

1572–74
The Mari fight against Russian colonization again. They lose.

1581–84
The Mari fight against Russian colonization once more. And lose. A chronicler writes: 'The marshes, lakes and rivers were filled with the bones of the Mari and the earth saturated with their blood.' Many of them are resettled in the east. Russian colonization begins in earnest.

SEVENTEENTH AND EIGHTEENTH CENTURIES
Extensive pressure to convert to Russian Orthodoxy leads many Mari to emigrate. Their original national territory is divided between the provinces of Kazan, Vyatka and Nizhni Novgorod. The Mari, meanwhile, take an active part in two peasant revolts, one led by Stepan Razin and the other by Emelyan Pugatchev, which got as far as the Kazan Kremlin. The uprisings are cruelly suppressed; many peasants are beaten, tortured, sent to prison, or executed. Some lucky ones get all four.

1812

Napoleon invades Russia. The Mari consider the prospect of French domination worse than Russian domination and many join the army to fight the cheese-eaters. The Mari peasant Vassily Grigoryev becomes a national hero for taking part in the capture of Paris. In spite of this, however, for the rest of the . . .

NINETEENTH CENTURY . . .

the Mari territories are considered a backward region. People live in poverty. One out of every four babies dies in infancy. Frequent droughts destroy crops over large areas. There are only a few primitive factories producing glass, leather and wine. Eighty-four per cent of the Mari are illiterate. Scholars predict that they will soon die out.

1917

The October Revolution leads to the creation of the world's first socialist state. Toiling masses around the world rejoice.

1920

Like the Tatars and the Kalmyk, the Mari are given their own titular 'homeland'. The Mari Autonomous Oblast ('region') is formed. However, Russians and Uncle Toms are in charge and many Mari live outside its borders anyway. The Soviets begin the work of abolishing traditional holidays and repressing traditional beliefs.

1930S

Collectivization takes place. Mari villages are uprooted and transferred to work on enormous collective farms. A centuries-old way of life is destroyed. Stalin's purges begin and the majority of Mari intellectuals are exterminated.

1936

Time for a name change: the Mari Autonomous Oblast

becomes the Mari Autonomous Soviet Socialist Republic. Some paper mills open.

1950s
Russian industrialization and colonization intensifies.

1960s
Increased urbanization leads to a rapid decline in the use of the Mari language. Increasingly Mari becomes a mere 'language of the village'.

1992
Following the collapse of the Soviet Union the Mari Autonomous Soviet Socialist Republic is renamed the Republic of Mari El. It gets a nice new flag, too.

9

I left for Yoshkar Ola at the end of October. It was already snowing in Moscow.

In my carriage there were three young Russians, a guy and two girls. I immediately started thinking about how I could ingratiate myself into their company: after all, I had no contacts in the city and I was going to need help locating the pagans.

At first nobody spoke. We read our books. But after an hour or so the conversation began to flow. The guy, Andrei, was a cop in the Sokol neighbourhood of Moscow. He was going home to visit family. He and Masha, sitting next to him, had friends in common. Sveta, next to me, was also chatting away merrily.

Unfortunately my mind had seized up and I couldn't think of a gambit to enter the conversation. So I sat mute among them, reading *The Hitman's Handbook*, trying to follow the instructions on how to make a silencer.

After a while Andrei left to drink with the cops on duty in the carriage. They were totally hammered, staggering up and down outside the compartments, singing songs and toy-fighting each other. Then Masha also got up and walked out. That left me in there with Sveta. Finally my brain unfroze and I mustered up a few words of friendly introduction.

Sveta didn't live in Mari El. She was travelling en route to some shit-hole in Siberia to visit her parents. Obviously that connection wasn't going to get me far. Then Masha re-entered. Masha was very excited to discover I was British: she was a professor in the English faculty at the Pedagogical Institute of Mari El.

I thought my ship had come in. Not only was I liberated from the leaden chore of struggling to communicate in Russian, but she was an academic. Maybe she could help me find a pagan, through contacts at her institute.

Unfortunately I tried to rape her early on in our conversation. Or at least that's what she thought. When I asked how often she came to Moscow I think she heard, *Please may I cover you in kisses?* She waved her hand at me frantically, crying, 'I'm married! Look! Look! I've got a ring!'

That was annoying. Not to mention embarrassing. After that, it was difficult to maintain a tone of light banter. She kept looking at me nervously, like I was planning to jump her right then and there in the carriage. She was probably thanking God there was a policeman around to stop me. I nursed the conversation along, however, and eventually got round to asking her if she knew anything about the Mari pagans.

'No, I don't,' she said. 'I'm Orthodox.' She waved a cross at me.

I didn't see what that had to do with anything. I wasn't asking if she sacrificed babies to the sun god. But evidently Masha was rather sensitive. I told her I was a journalist and

I was researching an article on the topic of Mari beliefs.

'Ah . . .' she said. 'Well, you won't find any pagans in Yoshkar Ola.'

'No?'

'No. They live in the villages.'

Hm, I thought. *That could put a hole in my plans.*

'Well, do you know much about them?'

'Only that they pray to birch trees . . . and they have wizards, who put a *curse* on people who harm the trees.'

A curse on people who harm the trees? It sounded like pish to me. Superstitious hoo-ha. I was close to giving up, but then Masha offered to make enquiries in the Anthropology section of Yoshkar Ola's university for me. She also asked if I would talk to her students, to give them language practice. 'They are mostly young girls,' she said, eyes flashing, as if to say, *You'd like that, wouldn't you?* After all, I was the one who had so importunately attempted to storm her Chamber of Venus.

10

By the way, I'm not really a journalist. I just didn't want to tell her I was writing a book. I once lived in Prague and I met a lot of people there who claimed they were writing books. They were all fannies. From then on I always kept my own writing 'habit' secret, for fear that I would be identified with that legion of posturing Henry Miller wannabes.

11

The pagan fixation

Mari El consists mostly of trees and lakes. There are two hundred lakes. And lots of trees. If you look at a map of the republic, it's very green. There are trees, trees, trees and more trees. Tucked away among these trees are some villages and four medium-sized towns. And that's all.

The ancient Mari weren't literate. They didn't write books. Nor did they build temples or palaces or fortresses. They didn't leave any records of themselves. Russians and Europeans wrote their history, and they wrote it from the outside. They even invented their own name for the Mari, calling them the Cheremiss. And the Cheremiss appear only briefly as extras in the story of Russia's empire-building: as primitive squatters on land that was Russia's by right of destiny.

Trees, trees, trees. No books. No records. When oppressed, the Mari disappeared into the trees. Their history disappeared with them. Wise men, villains, lovers, dramas, sagas: a thousand years had vanished into the dark, devouring, sacred trees.

The Mari now lived in Russian cities, studied in Russian institutes. Many had been baptized into the Russian Orthodox Church. Some even spoke Russian as a first language. On the train to Yoshkar Ola I'd tried to spot Mari in the corridor. But you can't tell a Mari and a Russian apart. Physically, they're not that different. A lot of Mari even have Russian names.

So really, I didn't know what or who I was looking for. The 'Finno-Ugric identity' was too vague. All I had was one word: paganism. It was something to cling to.

12

Five hidden gems of the red city

I

Something you must not miss in Yoshkar Ola is the **Dead Ferris Wheel** in the Central Park of Culture and Rest. This

Dead Ferris Wheel, Yoshkar Ola

wheel, located next to a wooden fence behind the October Cinema *never moves*! It just grows older and older, slowly rotting before your very eyes!

II

The **Theatre Bridge** is a real treat for people who like paths that lead across water! Named for the Russian-language theatre that stands beside it, the bridge is long, broad, concrete, and lined with lamps! Intriguingly, many of the bulbs in the lamps have blown and never been replaced. This makes crossing the bridge at night a particularly hair-raising experience, especially if you hear the heavy footsteps of a stranger walking close behind you!

III

Enthusiasts for the punishment of felons should under no circumstances miss Yoshkar Ola's **prison**! This nineteenth-century edifice is situated in the centre of town, right opposite a *luxury block of flats*! Its walls are painted yellow and the bricked-up windows are painted red. The wardens actually live in apartments attached to the prison itself. Inside, prisoners not only run the risk of contracting new, drug-resistant strains of TB but also of getting impaled on the throbbing members of big, lusty cons!

IV

And don't forget to visit the **House of Culture for the All-Union Society of the Blind** for more blind people than you can shake a white stick at! This building is full of people who can't see! That's right, they're not pretending! Sometimes they perform blind concerts. Sometimes they have blind parties. I heard once they had a blind beauty contest too, though I've no idea how they judged that. I mean, really, how is that possible? I don't understand.

V

Lastly, somewhere you've really got to go is the **Newspaper Corner at the Central Park of Culture and Rest**! That's where they hang up the day's papers, so if you don't have enough money to buy a copy of *Moskovskii Komsomolyetz* you can read it there and find out what's going on in the world! Often they hang up pictures of tits and monsters that are supposed to live in the deep! The last time I went they had an amazing story about a brothel that operated next door to a boarding school in Odessa! All the young girls in the boarding school used the brothel's sauna to wash! They met lots of dirty old men in there! It was really amazing!

13

After a couple of hours' sleep the train pulled in to Yoshkar Ola. It was around 10 a.m. Winter had arrived there, too: the city was already covered in a thick blanket of snow. A crowd was standing on the platform to greet those returning from the big city. Masha stepped off the train and was immediately embraced by a big, burly guy: her husband, I assumed. She had told me he was an officer in the army. Just for good measure.

I meanwhile looked around for Natasha, my landlady. I didn't know what she looked like, but had told her to be on the look-out for a thin, transgendered individual with large breasts and a bushy beard. Since visiting Kalmykia I had spent some time in a Berlin clinic having a sex change, but had run out of money halfway through the op. I was a little worried I might get trouble on the streets of Yoshkar Ola. However, my predicament made it easy for Natasha to spot me. A tiny little woman with a flat face and bulging eyes ran up to me and grabbed my elbow: 'Daniel?'

I had also told Natasha I was a journalist researching paganism. On the bus back to her flat she said she knew absolutely nothing at all about them. 'Mari religion is of no significance to me.'

She did, however, know a lot about marriage agencies. There were over fifty of them in the city, serving a population of two hundred thousand.

'And I don't think there's anything wrong with them,' she said. 'The women here only want a better life, like everybody else. Our men are drunks. They are no good.'

I didn't know about whether the men were all that bad, but I couldn't criticize Russian women for wanting a better life. In fact, before coming I had resolved to put aside my prejudices about marriage agencies and mail-order brides and to respond to the people I met with sympathy and not condescension or glib comments.

Natasha told me that she often acted as a translator of the letters the women posted on the net. It was she who phrased those eloquent pleas for love, affection and a man with a steady income. She offered to introduce me to the head of the largest agency in Yoshkar Ola. He was an intelligent man who 'knew many things'. He might be able to help me find what I was after.

14

Natasha left me in the flat for a couple of hours, to rest and have a shower. I'm a bit of a dirty bastard, though, so I didn't bother with the shower part. Instead I mooched around, trying to get a feel for her flat.

Her last tenant had come about a month earlier. He was a guy from Germany, in town to pick up his bride, the second he had procured in Yoshkar Ola, after the first failed to meet his requirements. He stayed for a couple of days, and then departed, taking the woman to a new life.

I couldn't feel his presence in the flat, however. It was scrupulously clean, anonymous. Even the bedroom, which had looked like an Eastern boudoir on the net, seemed very utilitarian. I sat on it: the mattress was rather hard. The only traces I could find of the men who had passed through were a pre 9/11 American edition of *GQ* magazine and a year-old copy of the *Irish Daily Record*.

I expected an international love pad to have a special atmosphere. I expected it to have ghosts. It didn't. I couldn't feel anything.

I flicked through the *GQ* and a piece of paper fell out. It was a picture of Barbie, half coloured in, with a purple and an orange pencil. *Aha*, I thought. This guy had obviously found himself a woman with a little girl.

Suddenly, in my mind's eye, I could see them: the little girl, playing in the kitchen while her mother and this strange man made decisions that were going to alter her destiny for ever. And was he a good man, this man? And was she a good woman, this woman? And was she a happy little girl, this girl?

It felt awkward, like I was an intruder, but then my reverie was interrupted. The doorbell rang. Natasha had arrived to take me to Virginia. As we were leaving she looked me in the eye. 'I must warn you,' she said. 'The owner, Maxim. He is handicapped.'

And it's at this point, dear reader, that my narrative starts to get a little strange.

15

Lady of the week

OLGA 4421
Date of birth: 12 November 1983
Weight: 45 kg (99 lb)
Height: 168 cm (5'7")
Eyes: green
Hair: dark
Education: university

Occupation: student
Hobbies: art, reading, languages
Self-description: can be different
Ideal man: from twenty-five to forty-eight; 170 cm+ (5'7");
   family-oriented.
Marital status: never been married
Children: son Yaroslav, b. 5 March 2003

Hello! My name is Olya. And what is your name? I'm a girl from the nineteenth century, I just feel this way at my heart. I like poetry, wild nature and art. However, I'm very happy to live in the twenty-first century, otherwise, I would never have a chance to communicate with you. I think every girl is like a diamond. It can be either cut or not, either in a luxurious mounting or not. But it needs sunshine to shine with its beauty and glamour. Maybe you are my sunshine?

I'm going to become a clothes designer. This is a very creative profession and my greatest virtue is my vivid imagination. I draw and read a lot. The last book I read was *The Alchemist* by Paulo Koelyo. This book has taught me to take everything that happens in life, whether it's good or bad, as certain signs. I've realized that the path I'm walking along in life is leading me to you, that my happiness is in the other country. I have a good taste. I like nice clothes. I try to create harmony and beauty around myself, that's why it's always nice and cosy at my home. I like taking care of my home flowers and that's why I've chosen the profession of a clothes designer. Of course, the most beautiful flower of my life is my son Yaroslav. He is very little, he is only nine months old. Don't you agree that I being a young mother I look very good?

I have a good sense of humour, I'm communicative and easy-going. I won't have any problems with communication, because I know English very well. I value such qualities in men as care, intellect, attention, care and kindness. I like being courted, loved, valued and understood. Well, that's all for today. I hope we'll get to know each other better soon. Look forward to your letters,

Olya

16

The Virginia offices occupied the entire first floor of a multi-storey brick building and were very tasteful: a big, flashy digital clock and thermometer was attached to the corner and a stylized woman's face with full red lips hung over the main door. Natasha led me round the side to what looked like a service entrance. I followed her inside and found myself in the middle of a very pink office.

Natasha greeted the people she knew, but then stopped. In the corner there was a man, sitting in a wheelchair on a raised platform, watching everyone who went past. 'Maxim!' she said, startled. He was a little guy, about thirty, with a shaven head and piercing blue eyes, set in a soft white face. His head rocked back and forth slightly.

Natasha introduced herself. He couldn't remember her. But he knew who I was. Before I could say anything, he said, 'You are a journalist. You have come to find out about the pagans.'

I was startled. How did he know? What was going on?

'Er . . . yes, yes I have,' I said.

'In that case,' Maxim continued, 'you should speak to my brother Konstantin. He is acquainted with their high priest. Please enter our cafeteria and wait there. In a little while I will call my brother and then you can see if he is willing to help you.'

It was bizarre. Uncanny. Ridiculous. But before I could say anything a young girl was leading Natasha and me through to the café and Maxim had already turned his attention away from us. 'But how did he know?' Natasha whispered.

I had no idea. And I still have no idea. I never mustered up the courage to ask him. I decided instead to roll with the punches and let Maxim unfold what he wanted to unfold. I prefer mysteries to facts and Maxim's knowing was more unusual and remarkable to me than how he came to know.

However, I can speculate. The most likely explanation is that he guessed that, as Mari El was a dump devoid of interesting features, there was only one reason for a foreign journalist to have come . . . but then again, there was certainty in his voice. He wasn't guessing. He *knew*. How to explain that?

This leads me to my other, less convincing speculations: (1) he was telepathic; (2) he had a small diabolical imp in his service. The imp could see into the future and often shared its insights with Maxim. In return for its services, Maxim had forfeited his immortal soul to Satan.

See? Not very convincing.

17

Lady of the week

ZOYA 5422
Date of birth: 6 July 1974
Weight: 54 kg (119 lb)
Height: 174 cm (5'9")
Eyes: blue
Hair: blonde
Education: college
Occupation: modelling agency
Hobbies: travelling
Self-description: cheerful, optimist

Ideal man: from thirty to forty-five; 174 cm+ (5'9"); decent, open, bright
Marital status: never been married
Children: son, Vlad, b. 5 March 1994

There came a time when the need has arisen to treat a man as a partner for a future life. I understand that a dating service like this does not mean that your life can radically change at once. Changes require a lot of patience and time. I consider feeling comfortable with everything to be the most important ingredient in a relationship. I like cheerful people and I myself try to stay young, but boring people and dull situations make your desire to be beautiful disappear. Besides, time tells on your beauty, too. I prefer to lead an healthy style of life. I do not smoke. I have all the qualities a woman should have – fragility, tenderness, coquetry, an ability to forgive and to help. I know that I will make a good wife to my future husband.

I think that there should always be harmony in the life of any person. Everything that surrounds you like your house, clothes, food you eat should correspond to your state of mind. I love children mostly because they are curious to learn new things about the world just like I am.

I was not successful in my previous relationship. Now I have a nine-year-old son who I bring up on my own. My views on life and values have changed and now I am dreaming of having a strong and happy family. I can live independently, but I can say that I am old-fashioned because I can easily fall in dependence of a man. I want to meet a passionate, attentive person who should be responsible and full of energy. I will not make rush decisions, but let you express yourself.

Danger Zone

18

I didn't have much time to think about Maxim's paranormal abilities, however. In the kitchen, sitting across from me was a big guy, about fifty, with a droopy moustache and cowboy-style lace tie. His name was Dan and he was one of Maxim's clients. Remembering my discussion with Natasha on the bus I realized that this was my chance to get a story of mail-order love first hand, and to be sympathetic and non-judgemental about it. *No, he is not a creep*, I thought. He is not a lonely loser. Banish those thoughts now.

'So what brings yew to Mari El?' he asked. 'Lookin' for a wife?'

I told him I was a journalist (I was starting to feel more comfortable with the imposture) but before I could ask any questions Dan had already launched into his life story. He was, he told me, an engineer who made chemical weapons and built nuclear power plants. He earned 50K a month doing that. At one time he had customized Harley Davidsons for a hobby, but he was bored of that now. These days he worked as a freelance pilot, flying hunters into remote zones where they could kill the animals that usually escaped human attention. Dan was clearly an accomplished guy.

And yet he couldn't find love. He had been married twice: the first marriage produced two kids, both grown up now, but it didn't work out. The second marriage was fine, but his wife was much younger than him and she wanted children. Unfortunately Dan's jizzum-pipes had been clipped the first time round. 'I just couldn't bring her happiness, man. I had to let her go.' So he did. They were still on good terms. Now, however, he was looking for a Russian wife. American women were too materialistic, he said. All they thought about was your wallet. Russian women: they had heart, they had soul. They didn't care if you were rich or poor.

I myself had always suspected that the Russian women who went to marriage agencies cared very much whether a man was rich or poor, and that they usually preferred them to be rich. After all, it's no fun being hungry and poor in a wasteland.

And yet Dan hadn't had much success with Russian ladies either. The year before he'd corresponded with one woman for six months, then proposed. He flew to Russia, and met her parents. He went for walks in the local park with his beloved.

169

He showered her with gifts. He even got drunk with her father. Dan was ecstatic: he believed, in the immortal words of that great poet, Paul McCartney, that very soon there would indeed be 'no more lonely nights'.

Then, somehow, it all went wrong. His fiancée freaked out. She didn't want to leave her parents. She couldn't bear to leave Russia, her beloved motherland. And so Dan went home as alone as ever. But he wasn't bitter. He told me he had made lots of wonderful friends in Yoshkar Ola, and that was why he was back. To visit his friends.

At that moment, as the story of Dan's life and struggles lay open before me, a young girl entered the café. 'Maxim will see you now,' she said.

I thanked Dan for his story and went to talk to the mastermind of the operation.

19

Maxim stared at me, slowly, carefully, sizing me up. Apart from facial movements and some slight twitching in his fingers, he was completely paralysed. He didn't wait for me to ask questions but immediately called for one of his female assistants (there were several, all of them pretty girls, dashing back and forth between offices and the café) and had her dial his brother. She did so, and held the phone to Maxim's face.

'Konstantin!' barked Maxim. 'There is a journalist here from Scotland who wants to speak to you!' The assistant handed the phone to me. I pressed my ear close to the receiver: Konstantin was a small, distant voice. He sounded a little startled, as if he had just woken up even, but agreed to see me in a day's time, in the marriage agency. He didn't say what we would do, only that I ought to meet him. I handed the phone back to the assistant who disappeared into the kitchen.

Now I was left with Maxim. He was still staring at me, analysing me with what was obviously a ferocious intelligence. I remembered the tent on Coney Island, where I had met the world's smallest woman. I felt the same awkwardness. I smiled rather lamely at the paralysed man. It seemed like the right thing to do.

Suddenly Maxim asked me a question: 'Did you bring a coin for my numismatic collection?'

What? I thought. *What is he on about?*

'Er . . . no,' I said.

'It's a pity,' he replied.

'Yes,' I said. 'It is . . . if only I had known . . .'

What's this? I wondered. *Am I supposed to be telepathic? How was I to know?* And yet I felt guilty. I should have brought something, I thought. Some kind of gift for the strangers upon whose kindness I had always fully intended to call. It was thoughtless of me. I had an idea, a shit one.

'Er . . . I could send you some coins from Moscow, once I get back.'

'No, you can't,' snapped Maxim. 'It is illegal to send money through the post in Russia.'

'Oh,' I said. 'Oh.'

He had slapped me down there, alright. *Fuck it*, I thought.

Maxim continued to stare at me, his head rocking back and forth steadily. Every now and then his tongue would emerge and roll across his lips, like some parasitic alien that lived inside his mouth and wanted to see what its host was looking at. His tongue fascinated me: did he control it, or was it unintentional, the way it popped out?

Suddenly I remembered I was supposed to be a journalist. I ought to ask him some questions.

20

Lady of the week

ANASTASIYA 4517
Date of birth: 26 October 1970
Weight: 64 kg (141 lb)
Height: 173 cm (5'9")
Eyes: grey-green
Hair: light brown
Education: college
Occupation: nurse
Hobbies: reading, music, travelling
Self-description: merry, with sense of humour
Ideal man: from thirty to forty; 175 cm+ (5'9"); non-smoker
Marital status: never been married

If you are reading my letter, you are already a nice and interesting man. I am sorry that I cannot shake hands with you or look into your eyes. If we have something in common with you, you should write me. May be we are soulmates with you!

My name is Anastasiya, I am thirty-four y.o. and my height is 175 cm. I am energetic, cheerful, sociable and I have a good sense of humour. I am able to listen. I am responsible and serious. I do not bear the lie. I am romantic and I like to dream, I love life and I try to take only the best from it. Theatre, art, walks in the nature, travelling attract me. I like to read, to listen to the music, to dance, to meet new interesting people, to go in for sport.

I would like to meet a tall man till forty y.o. who has a permanent job, confident in himself, serious about meeting a Russian lady. Energetic, sensitive, tender, with a sense of humour, whom I could feel like behind a stone wall. In a man

I appreciate kindness, patience and persistence. I am tender and kind. And I would like to give the part of these feelings to a man who wants the same. I want to be just happy!!!

21

I decided to ask Maxim about Virginia.

'How long has your agency been open?' I asked.

'Six years.'

There was a long pause.

'How many people work here?' I asked.

'Eighty.'

Another long pause.

'Where do your customers come from?' I asked.

'Our largest client base is the US, followed by Britain. After Britain comes Germany.'

Long pause. Maxim looked down at the novel he had open and ignored me.

No doubt he suspected my motives for visiting Virginia. The marriage agency business never gets good press, after all. A few weeks before the *Moscow Times* had run a story about a guy in Washington who had murdered the wife he had brought over from Kyrgyzstan. This led to calls in the US Senate to make it more difficult for American men to import brides, as if all wife importers were murderers and abusers in waiting.

Nevertheless I persisted in extracting information. Painfully, question after question, I discovered that it cost about two pounds for women to register with Virginia and put their details on the web – unless they were older than thirty-five, in which case it cost three. He claimed his company had arranged sixteen hundred marriages. When I asked about the success rate, he told me they didn't keep records of divorces. It was too difficult to keep track of so many couples in so many different countries. He was too busy. In addition to the marriage agency he also ran a travel agency, a photo studio, an English school and a job centre.

Maxim, though, born with far fewer chances than most, had still become a kind of secret master of his city, a paralysed mini-mogul ruling over a small empire he had built out of nothing. In any country this would be impressive, but in Russia, a state that does not care for its weak, it was awe-inspiring. And Maxim knew this. His strength, his power shone in his eyes. And there was something in his employees' eyes also: a combination of respect, affection – and fear.

I too found him intimidating. Our long periods of silence were getting to be excruciating. I asked if he wanted me to go.

'No, no,' he said. 'Please, stay.'

Suddenly a woman rushed past. She was stunningly beautiful: a dark-eyed Egyptian, with refined features, full lips and, beneath her clothes, I could tell, a strong, lithe figure. Maxim was very eager for me to meet her and introduced us. 'Daniel,' he said, 'please meet my wife.'

'I'm terribly sorry,' she said in flawless English, 'but I can't stop. I must see my students now.'

Maxim beamed. She worked in his language school, teaching Arabic to Tatar Muslims eager to read the Koran in the original. A whole host of obvious questions formed in my head, precisely the same ones you are thinking right now, dear reader, but it was impossible for me to ask them.

Maxim was a remarkable man.

22

Lady of the week

Oxana 6669
Date of birth: 20 April 1954
Weight: 70 kg (154 lb)
Height: 165 cm (5'5")
Eyes: brown
Hair: dark
Education: university
Occupation: housewife
Hobbies: fitness, cookery, planting flowers
Self-description: tender, calm
Ideal man: from fifty-three to seventy; 165 cm+ (5'5"); kind,
  emotional, family-oriented
Marital status: never been married
Children: son, Anton, b. August 1977

Hello my Friend, I'm Oxana, I'm forty-nine years old. I may be described as a nice-looking dark-haired brown-eyed woman with a slight tendency to plumpness.

I was born and raised in Yoshkar Ola. However, I lived in Alma-Ata for a while. After having graduated in Economics, I worked as an accountant and economist. Now my primary job is a housewife and, quite frankly, I love it! I think it is as interesting and satisfying as it can get. Perhaps more ambitious and career-oriented people will disagree, but I'm certain that work and hobby should match, as they say. And this is the thing for me, being cosy and house-proud. I like cooking, sometimes experimenting and inventing new dishes, knitting and reading. As for fitness, I enjoy aerobics and especially swimming. Yet another hobby of mine is growing flowers and gardening.

I have a grown-up son who has been living in a different city for quite a while. We meet regularly, of course, but as long as he's started out on his own, the place reserved for him in my heart is free, in a certain sense. Now this flow of kind and tender feelings needs to be turned towards someone I could care about, could love and respect. So I hope to meet a reliable, loyal and kind man to love and be loved in return and to live happily ever after . . . I know he's out there somewhere, we just haven't met yet.

23

His wife gone, Maxim and I lapsed into silence once more. This silence lasted several minutes. I smiled awkwardly, while Maxim read his book. Then apropos of nothing, he spoke: 'The Mari people have very powerful magic,' he said.

'Really?'

'Yes. Their wizards are greatly feared. They place curses upon those who wrong them.'

'I see,' I said.

'Yes, their wizards are very powerful.'

I thought for a second about the 'neo-pagans' in the UK. They were always banging on about something called 'Wicca' – white magic. I thought I'd try that angle on Maxim.

'But what about white magic?' I said.

'White magic?'

'I mean good magic. Do the Mari wizards perform good magic too?'

'No. Never. Their magic is always evil.'

'Always?'

'Yes. You see, the Mari people are small, and resentful, and have a malicious character. Probably this is because they have always been conquered by greater nations. First they were conquered by the Tatars – a great, powerful culture. Then they were conquered by the Russians. Also a great, strong nation. So this has forged in the Mari a weak and fearful character. Their magic reflects this.'

'I see,' I said.

There was some more silence, while I thought about what he said. Then I came up with a question: 'And is belief in the power of Mari magic commonplace?'

'Oh yes,' he said.

'And what about Russians? Do they believe in it?'

'Russians also believe.'

'Really?'

'Yes. Let us conduct an experiment. Sasha!'

One of Maxim's assistants emerged from the café.

Maxim turned to me. 'Sasha is Russian,' he said. 'Sasha,' he asked, 'do you believe in the power of the Mari wizards?'

Sasha nodded. 'Oh yes,' she said. 'Definitely.'

Maxim spent the next twenty minutes stopping his employees and asking them a 'small sociological question'. All of them believed in the negative power of Mari magic. None of them could give any examples of it, however. The only person who scoffed at Mari magic as mere superstition was, in fact, the sole Mari in the office, a red-headed woman who worked as an English translator. She shrugged the question off with a laugh, as if it was ridiculous. She, evidently, was one of the urbanized Mari. More urbanized even than most of the Russians in the culture that had urbanized her.

As for Maxim, he was evasive. 'I would advise you to be cautious in your explorations. That is all.' He opened his eyes wide. His tongue rolled over his lips.

I, meanwhile, believed in Mari magic about as much as I believed in Santa Claus, the tooth fairy, and the pantheon of

Ancient Egypt, which is to say – not at all. But then, nobody asked me.

24

Reasons for resentment: some statistics

Fifty-two per cent of the Mari live outside their titular homeland, Mari El. Meanwhile, those who do live there are a minority in their own republic, outnumbered almost two to one by Russians. The President, too, is an ethnic Russian.

Over the last fifty years the Mari have become more urbanized. The percentage of ethnic Mari in the town population has slowly increased:

Year	%
1959	11.3
1970	15.6
1979	21.7
1989	26.1

This trend, however, inevitably entails Russification and the loss of a distinct Mari identity. Russian, after all, is the language of government, business and education.

Russian has also penetrated the home. In 1979 13.4 per cent of Mari families spoke Russian at home; by 1985 the figure had leapt to 33.4 per cent, and Russian had become the mother tongue of 23.3 per cent of urban Mari. Only 5 per cent of Mari children borrowed books in the Mari language from the libraries.

In the Soviet Union, Russians lived badly, but better than Mari. For example, in 1985, services in dwellings compared as follows:

	Russian %	Mari %
Plumbing	71.9	38.7
Sewers	64.7	31.7
Hot water	46.1	21.3
Gas	75.6	60.0
Telephone	21.3	16.4

These statistics probably reflect the fact that most Mari lived in villages with poor infrastructure rather than any active policy of repression by the state. Nevertheless it's highly unlikely, given the downward slide of everybody's living standards (outside Moscow) since the collapse of the Soviet Union, that this situation will have improved any.

Looking to the future, in 1994 a sociological survey found that 62.7 per cent of the Meadow Maris and 91.8 per cent of the Hill Maris used their native language to communicate with their parents, while only 23.3 per cent and 60.9 per cent, respectively, used it to communicate with their school-aged children.

The Mari have so far persisted as a separate group through fifteen hundred years of at times brutal subjugation. Their prospects have never looked good. At the start of the twenty-first century they still don't look good.

25

The silence dragged on. I couldn't decide whether it was entertaining or excruciating. Part of me was revelling in the bizarreness of the encounter, but another part was anxious. I kept expecting to be 'found out'. As if suddenly Maxim would look at me, and with those ice-cold blue eyes gaze into my soul and say: 'You are not what you claim to be. Your interview technique is risible. You are a fraud.'

That probably sounds paranoid. That's because it is. But remember: he knew who I was before meeting me. Wouldn't you be paranoid? I decided to ask Maxim about his book.

'What are you reading?'

'*It*,' he replied, 'by Stephen King. Have you read it?'

'No,' I said.

'Hm,' said Maxim.

I'd disappointed him again. Anyway, he started to read, ignoring me, sitting by his side. But quite quickly he reached the bottom of the page. And, of course, he couldn't turn it. He looked up. None of his assistants was around. So he sat there, staring at the page. I meanwhile watched his fingers. Occasionally one of them would twitch, impotently. This continued for a couple of minutes. It didn't occur to me to help him. And he never asked.

Finally one of his assistants walked past. He had her turn the page for him. Then he resumed reading. But very soon he reached the bottom of the page and it happened again. There was no one around to help, except me. I thought about turning it for him, but didn't know if I ought to. Would he be annoyed if I just reached out and turned the page for him? Would he think I was trying to ingratiate myself? I left him there. His head rolled back and forth in agony, looking for an assistant. None appeared.

Meanwhile, lots of women came and went before my eyes. Maxim's 'observation post' was set up directly across from the table where his female clients wrote their love letters. I saw young women, older women, beautiful women, plain women. Women for whom this was perhaps a game, others for whom it was a desperate last measure.

Maxim was thus able to oversee everything. He could watch the writing of the letters and then follow his employees with his eyes to a translation room and then to an IT room, where the messages of love were placed on the net. The doors to these rooms were open so he could see inside. Maxim, confined to his chair, was nevertheless everywhere.

The same went for his site. It was full of personal messages from Maxim to his international customers, reassuring them that he was a businessman, that they could trust him, that the women he offered were good, loyal women. Meanwhile, he worked intimately with the women who came to him looking for escape. He knew what his men wanted and what his women needed. While I was there one scary divorcee with purple cheeks came up and asked for advice on what to put in her letter. 'Remember,' said Maxim, 'he doesn't want a princess. He wants a wife. They all want women with the qualities of a wife.'

Just before I left, an older woman sat down with a young girl and began dictating to her.

'Look,' said Maxim, smiling. 'A mother has brought her daughter. She is telling her what to write.'

I had resolved not to judge anyone. And I didn't judge the woman or her daughter.

But it all seemed so damned sad.

26

I decided to go for a walk around town. But when I stepped outside it was already getting dark, and I didn't have a map. I also didn't know where the centre was, and there were no signs to indicate it. There were no visible landmarks. There was nothing except concrete and tarmac and the odd tree poking up out of the dirt. I wound up walking along a motorway lined with dilapidated blocks of flats.

I walked along this motorway for half an hour until the city stopped. It just crumbled away. Beyond lay emptiness.

Wasteland. I decided to go back.

Along the way, I noticed that people were staring at me. This made me nervous: what did they see? What was so strange about me? Could they tell I was a foreigner? After years in Russia I was pretty adept at passing myself off for a local. It was easy: I shuffled along with a miserable expression on my face and betrayed no interest in my surroundings whatsoever.

I wondered if it was my walk. I was walking quickly, with a sense of purpose. I saw that everyone else was just drifting around aimlessly, like the snowflakes floating down from the murky grey sky. I slowed down. People stopped staring.

Soviet mosaic, downtown Yoshkar Ola

I address the youth of Yoshkar Ola

Maxim had asked if I would attend his English school's 'conversation club' that night. It was an opportunity for some of his 'ladies' to practise their speech with native speakers. I was intrigued by the opportunity to meet some of his female clients, whose letters I had read on the net. Not that I planned to marry any of them, you understand. Honest. No, I just wanted to see if I could put faces and voices to some of the lonely people. In particular I hoped to meet a young woman who, on the net, had almost flashed her tit at her prospective suitors. Not that I wanted to get closer to her tit, you understand. No. Actually, my motives were darker. For underneath the tit was a small piece of text explaining that she was looking for a husband because her last one had just died in the war in Chechnya; she was alone in the world, save for her infant child.

Life is brutal. And yet in her picture she had a warm, almost naive smile. Her text was naive too. She exercised a dark fascination on me. Why did I want to see her? Was it sympathy? Voyeurism? A strange commingling of both? Anyway, it doesn't matter because she never turned up. Instead, much to my surprise, I was confronted by two of my countrymen.

I didn't expect to meet Glaswegians in Mari El. One of them was in his twenties but had a 1970s bowl haircut with neat ear-flaps, like Joanie's boyfriend Chachi in *Happy Days*. The other was old and shrivelled and looked like a monkey. So far, so comprehensible: they were ugly, so I could easily imagine they found it difficult to attract women back home. However, they denied they were looking for wives.

'I'm a web designer,' said Bowlcut Boy,' . . . er . . . on a business trip, and my "friend" here is keeping me company.'

This was a nonsensical cover story. Russia has many expert software specialists and web designers who work for a fraction of the cost of a Glaswegian with a daft haircut to maintain. He was ashamed of himself, and lying.

If they'd come to the conversation club sharking for brides, however, they didn't stand much chance. Most of the 'ladies' in the class weren't looking for foreign husbands. A lot of them weren't even Maxim's clients, but friends of his English teacher and students at the local university. I told some stories about life in Moscow which they found much more interesting than the ones about the UK. They were open and curious and optimistic. They dreamt of making it big in the capital of their own country.

Dan also was there. He talked about the American dream. He encapsulated it thus: *You can have anything you want, so long as you work hard*. I could see that the girls found him extremely boring, as, no doubt, most women do. I felt sorry for Dan. After all, he flew planes and built chemical weapons. That should have made him very interesting. But it didn't. He was still very dull. And very lonely. And he couldn't understand why.

The Scots annoyed me. I found it difficult to maintain my non-judgemental position regarding them. They were trivial and insensitive. Bowlcut Boy complained about the litter on the street and talked about the lap-dancers in Faraon, Yoshkar Ola's main nightclub. Monkey Man grunted every now and again. Nevertheless, I did my best to like them as I was getting hungry and hoped to leech a good meal on their coin. They were rich 'web designers' travelling on 'business', after all. They'd mentioned they were going to a restaurant after the conversation club. So I laughed at their jokes. I pretended I was interested in what they had to say. Then, once the chat was over, I hung around shamelessly, hoping they'd invite me to join them. They didn't. I ask you: is that any way to treat a fellow countryman? Wankers.

So instead I staggered out on to the street alone and hungry and keen to be alone for a while. I walked up and down looking for a place I could buy food, but all the shops were shut, except those that sold alcohol. In the end I found two cold cabbage pies in a dismal off-licence located in a dirty basement. Then I went home and watched Russian TV for several hours. It was an uplifting evening.

28

The Planetarium

There are twenty-five planetariums in the Russian Federation. Many of them are now closed. For example, the Central Planetarium in Moscow is closed, and has been for ten years. It is a crumbling shell located next to the Zoo, next to the monkey enclosures. It smells of monkey piss.

The Planetarium in Yoshkar Ola, however, has been open continuously since 1958, although it has not received any government funding since 1992. Avdokia Krylovna, its current curator, cares for it herself. She cleans it, paints it, maintains the lamp, replaces bulbs. Avdokia Krylovna is a bitter woman. She despises the government. But she loves the Planetarium. She loves space, the stars, the cosmos. She loves the hard certainties of science.

The day I visited I arrived late and the Planetarium was closing. But Avdokia Krylovna was kind and let me come in for a private showing.

There were rows of little wooden chairs inside and a Yuri Gagarin head sitting on a shelf at the back. In the middle of the room stood a strange mechanical device, several metal globes with multiple coloured glass eyes. It looked vaguely sinister. I sat down and gazed up at the curved ceiling. I didn't actually know what a planetarium was, as I'm not interested in astronomy at all. I only wanted to go because I thought the word was beautiful. Say it to yourself: *planetarium, planetarium.* It is, isn't it? I expected some kind of observatory. But the domed ceiling, round like a church cupola, was closed. There was nothing to observe save peeling paint, and my breath drifting upwards in fluffy white clouds. It was below zero in there.

Avdokia Krylovna took her position at a control panel at the back. She switched off the lights and I was abruptly plunged into darkness. But the mechanical device in the centre hummed and came to life; it lit up and from its multiple eyes shone forth our galaxy, stars upon stars beamed on to the darkness of cupola.

The planets and the stars revolved above me while Avdokia Krylovna, in her beautiful voice, told me stories about the cosmos. For the first time since I was nine I felt an interest in our cold, empty universe. Yes, Venera, Yupiter, Saturn, Merkur . . . the planets were amazing things, they were poetry, pure poetry. I understood the mystery and awe the ancients had felt before the illuminated night sky. It all made sense. I perceived it unthinkingly, with the perfect logic of a dream, the logic that goes deeper than reason.

Avdokia Krylovna showed me the surface of Mars, all dry and pitted with craters, then the surface of Pluto, eerie caves full of ice. Then she showed me our planet, and Yoshkar Ola itself, where we were sitting, not still, but moving, spinning through space. The revelations continued. I was entranced: more, more! Don't let it stop! The universe *is* amazing, it is!

But then Avdokia Krylovna lost me. She showed me a picture of Sagittarius and traced the shape of the hunter in the stars. I couldn't see it. She showed me pictures of the Great Bear, and the Little Bear, the Plough, the Virgin . . . I couldn't see them either, I couldn't see any of them. I even started to smirk. *Ha! Bullshit!* I thought. *It looks nothing like a bear.* My moment of vision was over as soon as it had begun. I was blind again.

Avdokia Krylovna switched on the lights. My journey through the cosmos was over.

29

Anti-tourism

I

I had a day to kill before meeting Maxim's brother.

I spent the first part of it wandering around the city. I found the usual Soviet stuff pretty quickly – the eternal flame, the Central Park of Culture and Rest, some big, concrete 'palaces of culture'. It was a Sunday, however, and all the museums were closed. So were all the theatres. Unlike in Elista, however, I wasn't very excited by this emptiness. In fact, I found it dull and a little depressing. That was probably because I was alone, without my friends Joe and Yosh. I missed them.

II

After a while I found myself counting Lenins. As far as I could see, Yoshkar Ola had three: one in the central square, one in the park of culture, and another, lurking behind some bushes on Communist Street, like a furtive cottager. That last one had surprised me in the dark as I made my way home the night before. He even had his hands in his pockets, fumbling with his gonads.

I thought three was excessive, not to mention anachronistic and drearily unimaginative. It was high time the authorities in Yoshkar Ola flexed their imaginative muscles and started

The Towers of Yoshkar Ola

erecting new, modern statues with a contemporary relevance that might draw the world's attention to their sleepy republic. I myself had a few ideas: (1) replace the Lenin in the central square with a monument to Andrei Chikitilo, Russia's most prodigious serial killer; (2) recast the Lenin in the park of culture so that it has an H. R. Giger 'chestburster' alien erupting from his ribcage – Lenin could look really shocked and frightened; (3) the 'cottaging' Lenin could be replaced by a ribald sculpture of a skeleton masturbating.

The possibilities were endless.

III

Once I'd run out of Lenins I decided to cross the bridge in the centre of town. There was nothing else to do. As soon as I stepped on to the bridge, however, the sky grew dark. A storm blew up out of nowhere and by the time I was halfway across wet snow was whipping me across the face and ears.

Reaching the end I saw a little girl, hand in hand with her mother, coming towards me. She was wearing a woolly cap and was tapping a stick on the ground. As she passed I saw her eyes were shut. 'How strange,' I thought, 'to play a game like that with her mother – pretending to be blind.'

As they passed, her mother caught my eye. There was anxiety and dread in her face.

The little girl wasn't playing at all, of course. She was really blind. I laughed, but it wasn't a laugh of amusement. It was a laugh at how strange my thought had been. Why had I thought she was playing a game?

IV

On the other side I found a housing scheme in the snow. I was too tired and hungry to walk any further, however, so I turned back and crossed the bridge into the centre again. Once I was there, however, I experienced a minor existential crisis.

What am I doing here? I wondered.

I'm researching a book, I replied.

But why? I retorted. *What's the point?*

I thought about it. *It's something to do, I suppose.*

But then I started to get worried. *What if I don't meet the chief pagan? What then? What am I going to write about? I think I covered absolute emptiness in the last section.*

It was true. I needed some new shit. Suddenly any further exploration seemed pointless. An infinitely empty Sunday was simply a rehash of what had gone before, no development of my theme, whatever the fuck that was.

I decided not to walk any more. It was futile, as all action is futile. I went back to my flat.

v

Once back in the flat, however, existential crisis or not, I got bored. So I tried calling Masha, in the hope that she could give some shape to my life, for an evening at least. Even though our chat on the train had been awkward, she had suggested something about meeting me in town at the weekend, maybe showing me some local landmarks and going to a restaurant. That last part sounded especially appealing. I was finding it difficult to feed myself. There were no decent food shops around, just alcohol kiosks and an open-air market selling potatoes and lard. The 'restaurants' I had found, meanwhile, were scabby canteens only slightly better than Elista's Sputnik Café.

So I called Masha and got her mother. She gave me Masha's mobile number. Masha was at the market, buying potatoes and lard. I called her and she sounded shocked, panicked. 'Let me call you back,' she said.

About an hour later, she called. 'Well,' she said, 'there's an

American-style pizza place in town, it's on Sovietskaya. Maybe you can go there *yourself*. And there's a big cinema in town . . . Maybe you could go there . . . *yourself*. Oh, wait, my *husband*'s calling me. I have to go. Will you still talk to my students, by the way?'

I felt rather irritated. Masha was under no obligation to help me, but then *why the fuck had she given me her number and said she would?* My irritation was exacerbated by hunger. It wasn't a growling, painful hunger, but rather a sly and subtle undertone. I felt light-headed and a little numb. My body was a heavy object I had to drag around with me. I was really pining for a decent, preferably free meal, but there were none to be had. I thought back to the Glaswegians. They were probably drinking coffee and smoking big cigars. And getting lap-dances from cold, malnourished village girls in Faraon, Yoshkar Ola's only nightclub.

VI

Some hours passed. It grew dark. I reflected on the day's discoveries. There hadn't been many. Aside from some bilingual street signs, there was little to mark Yoshkar Ola out as the capital of an ethnic republic. If I didn't succeed in my meeting with Konstantin the next day I'd be in trouble. I felt as though Kazan and Elista had deceived me. They were so radically strange, so different. I had expected to find something similar in all Russia's republics. Now, however, I suspected they were exceptions, not the norm. Yoshkar Ola was barely aware of itself as an ethnic republic. It was barely aware of itself full stop. This was a problem, if I was going to write a book.

I did like its name, however, which is Mari, not Russian. I liked rolling it off my tongue, the two words joined together, the way locals said it: *Yoshkarola*. It sounded magical, strange, mysterious. Even translated it was still beautiful: 'Red City'.

Can you imagine living in Red City? It sounds magnificent. My hometown in Scotland is called Dunfermline, which sounds prosaic, mundane. And it is. Dunfermline is one of the dullest towns in the country, a dead dump with a few historical ruins and a lot of charity shops, in which the frail forms of the soon to be deceased can be seen passing their twilight hours rooting around for cheap clothes. I don't like it very much.

Yoshkar Ola is also a prosaic and mundane city. I certainly wouldn't want to live there. But it has a beautiful name.

30

At this point I would like to segue smoothly into a section detailing the true origins and beliefs of the Mari pagans, maybe give a little information about their myths and rituals, that sort of thing. It would lead in nicely to my first meeting with the High Priest.

But there's a problem, best expressed by an exchange I had with Diana Yefremova, an archaeologist at the Mari State University. 'I'm researching an article on the Mari pagans,' I said. 'Unfortunately there's not much information available in English.'

'You're telling me,' she said. 'There's hardly any information available in Russian, either.'

The serious study of Mari culture began only about fifteen years ago, in the late *perestroika* period. Prior to that, the state's goal was to eradicate Mari culture and assimilate the Mari into the Soviet mass, not to encourage a separate identity and culture. Consequently, most information about the Mari had been written from a Marxist–Leninist perspective and sounded something like this:

Many years ago the Mari lived in poverty and ignorance. They suffered from double oppression – from the Tsar's officials and from the local authorities. They had to work hard and to pay all kinds of taxes. They lived a hard hopeless life. As the Mari couldn't see any way out of the misery and poverty they set their hopes on the other world ... [Continue with infantile tone, enumeration of quaint local customs, then miraculous arrival of Great October Revolution setting them free from oppression, superstition and ignorance blah blah blah ...]

Even though serious research had begun, there wasn't much money to conduct it with, and there was very little evidence to go on anyway. The Mari had left no monuments to study. Their beliefs were passed on orally from generation to generation. As a result of the Revolution, however, a great fissure had come into being, a seventy-year gap between the present and the past. It was a blank, a void. How could you be sure the beliefs of the current Mari pagans were the same as the beliefs of their ancestors?

Diana, the archaeologist, told me that very little could be known exactly. The oldest monument connected to the Mari dates back to the ninth century, although the neighbouring Udmurt people, who, as we will see are even more lacking in symbols of an identity, claim it is theirs. No other monuments appear until the sixteenth century. The study of these sites has turned up only animal bones – that is to say, there is no evidence the Mari ever ritually murdered humans, in spite of what most Russians in the area seem to think.

The first written record of the Mari and their customs didn't appear until the eighteenth century, when an Austrian journalist voyaged into the woods to make a study of them. He provided a list of their gods, a description of some of their rites and holy groves and the information that there was a fixed priestly class. From his list we know that the Mari today worship the same gods as they did three hundred years ago: but whether those gods are the same as the ones they worshipped before that is impossible to prove.

As to the content of their beliefs, Diana was reluctant to give me much information. 'I'm an archaeologist, not an ethnologist,' she explained. She told me that there was a chief god called Yuma, and an evil god called Keremet.

She did, however, tell me about sacrifices. 'In times of catastrophe,' she said, 'such as epidemics, people gather in the groves to make sacrifices to the gods. They torture the animals more, so that they die slowly, to show God how much the people are suffering.'

Apparently the distinction between pagans and shamans is that, for pagans, animals act as intermediaries between humans and gods. Shamans, on the other hand, enter the spirit world themselves and commune with the deities directly.

I found that very interesting. I was even a little envious. I'd like to be able to commune with deities directly.

31

Mari culture

Meanwhile I asked myself: what books, what music exist in this lost zone? What unknown geniuses do they have? We have seen that the Tatars have many, and that though the Kalmyks have few, they are very proud of them. And the Mari? Well, I spent a lot of time looking and . . .

I

On Leninsky Prospekt in Yoshkar Ola I found a Mari-language dramatic theatre. It is a large Stalinist job with pillars and porticoes, very grand and impressive. Most of the plays in its repertoire were translations from Russian. When I visited, however, the season had not yet begun, although it was already late October. I therefore have no idea whether the performances were any good or not.

II

Propped up outside the Palace of Culture 'Thirty Years of Victory of the Great Patriotic War', I saw a poster for a traditional dance ensemble called 'Mari El'. As noted earlier, Kalmykia, Tatarstan, Buryatia, perhaps all Russian republics have traditional dance ensembles, bequeathed to them by the Great Stalin. Kitsch costumes and happy songs about spring would still seem to be the main consolation offered by the Russian state for the loss of one's ethnic identity.

III

As Russian cities all have the same street names, when you find an unfamiliar one, it is probably derived from a local worthy. Looking at the map of Yoshkar Ola I found only one: Chavain. He was a Soviet writer, allegedly the 'father of Mari literature'. I couldn't find any of his books on sale.

Subsequent research turned up other names, all of them Soviet. Aside from Chavain, 'Y. Shketan', and 'Sh. Ossip' had also written books which, apparently, had been translated into other languages. They weren't available in their homeland, however. In fact, the bookshops contained nothing whatsoever on the subject of local peoples, local authors or anything of that ilk. The most I managed to find was a set of postcards celebrating the four-hundredth anniversary of Yoshkar Ola, a city founded and built by Russians.

IV

I did find a house museum for a local composer, but I have forgotten his name. He was the 'father of professional Mari music'. He taught in a local high school in the 1920s. When I went to the museum I found a little wooden shed sitting in the shadows of some concrete apartment blocks. The shed was closed.

That was all I managed to uncover of Mari cultural production. I did, however, attend a concert of Tatar pop music and watch *Bad Boys 2,* starring Will Smith and Martin Lawrence in Yoshkar Ola's nice new Rossiya cinema with Dolby stereo surround sound. *Bad Boys 2* was particularly interesting because it taught me how to say, 'Kiss my black ass' in Russian: *Potselui moi chorny zad.*

32

Meanwhile I was told: if you want to encounter real Mari culture, then go into the villages! The people can't even speak Russian there!

Oh, the authenticity!

I thought about it for one second: maybe I would find something. Like shabby houses and land allotments. Poor people. Pies I'd never eaten before.

I was told about the villages by one of Maxim's marriage clients, a burly American called Steve from Philadelphia. Maxim arranged trips to these Mari 'reservations' as part of the standard bride-collecting holiday package. The thought was bizarre: here were these remote villages and they were full of American men prodding things. If I was a peasant, the last thing I'd want would be a wealthy Westerner swishing into town all wrapped up in Gore Tex and taking a picture of me as I milked a cow.

Collapsed house, near the museum of some composer or other

In fact, I hate it when wealthy Westerners harass peasants in villages in search of some bogus authenticity. To me that kind of tourism is based on nostalgia and a belief that there is some kind of essential truth and beauty in the poverty of foreign lands. Shit, I say. There's as much truth in the graffiti on a Manchester housing estate, or in a dirty shopping centre in Dundee. Visiting noble peasants isn't about discovery, it's about escapism.

I prefer to leave them alone.

33

Peledysh Pairem

Finally, after more digging around I managed to uncover some information regarding a Mari festival. Unfortunately it wasn't one invented by the Mari.

The sacred calendar of the ancient Mari included a great number of holidays and holy days, which the Soviets of course tried to eradicate. In their place they instituted secular alternatives. The most successful of these was Peledysh Pairem – 'The Holiday of Flowers'. First celebrated in the Mari village of Sernur in 1920, it replaced the religious holiday of Semik which had taken place in late May/early June.

The first Peledysh Pairem began with a poem. The locals congregated in the village square and were addressed with the following piece of horse-shit:

If you're worried about the future of your people,
If you are fond of your national clothing as white as snow,
Your mind as quick as lightning,
Your eyes as sparkling as stars,
Onar's power in your bodies,
Your tongue as mild as wax,
Your songs as beautiful as the bird's singing,
Your soul as gentle as the butterflies' wings,
If you want the Mari people to rise high up to the Moon and
To shine as bright as the Sun
Celebrate Peledysh Pairem in your settlement.

'If you are fond of your national clothing as white as snow . . .' Hm . . . verse? Or literary cumstain?

According to contemporary accounts, however, Peledysh Pairem was a rip-roaring success. The village was bedecked with political posters and red flags. Tables in the street groaned under the weight of Mari national dishes. There were concerts, dances and sporting competitions with embroidered napkins and towels for prizes.

But it wasn't all fun and games. There was an exhibition of the first books to be published in the Mari language. Then a Party-approved Mari intellectual, O. Shabdar, recited some poems, eulogizing the beauty of his homeland and also, of course, praising Lenin and the great Soviet government. 'When the celebration was over nobody wanted to leave. The people brought some bagpipes and trumpets and spent the night in joyous revelry . . .'

And there you go. Centuries of fear and trembling before the gods replaced by vapid shite. As is often the case, however, vapidity was no obstacle to success. Peledysh Pairem soon spread to other villages in the region. It was first celebrated in Yoshkar Ola in 1923. There was a performance of *Yamblat Kuvar* ('Yamblat's Bride') by Chavain, the aforementioned state-appointed father of Mari literature, to mark the occasion. It is still celebrated today.

34

My meeting with Konstantin was arranged for 9.30 in the morning, a most inhumane hour for talking with humans. But I had no choice. Cursing, I crawled out of bed about an hour beforehand, ate a piece of hard Swiss roll to stave off the hunger and then set to thinking, *What exactly am I going to ask him?*

I wasn't sure. I was still hoping to get to a sacred grove. It was the goal I had set myself, to give shape to my stay in Yoshkar Ola. That said, I hadn't spent much time thinking about what a sacred grove actually was. Perhaps if I had I wouldn't have been so keen to go. After all, what's so exciting about a bunch of trees? Nevertheless I needed something to aim for and it seemed like a viable option. Like Chess City, there was a whiff of strange and unorthodox discovery, of seeing something few others had. Maybe Konstantin could tell me how to find some holy trees or, better yet, take me to some himself.

Then, I thought, maybe he could introduce me to some Mari, too. I was writing a book about them, after all. It might be useful. Yeah! Thus armed with a plan of action, the existential doubt of the previous day melted away, like a snowman in July. I felt quite excited.

35

One of Maxim's assistants, a guy called Feodor, was standing at the entrance to Virginia sniffing coke. He had chopped a few lines on a mirror and was snorting them through a rolled-up thousand-rouble note.

'Gotta get my morning buzz . . .' he said, wiping his nose. 'Gets me through the day . . . All these needy bitches and desperate Americans . . .'

Just then, a small boy with no arms ran out of the building and started pleading, 'Daddy, Daddy! Give me *koka*!'

Feodor smacked him across the nose. 'Fuck off!' he roared.

The little boy ran away crying, his nose bleeding profusely. Feodor looked up and saw me, standing rather awkwardly in front of him. He knew who I was, and what I wanted. 'Konstantin is waiting for you inside. Please come with me.'

I followed him. Although it was early, the agency was already humming with action: people were coming and going,

Standing, left to right: The author and Alexei Izergovich Yakimov, High Priest of the Chi Mari; *seated, left to right:* Konstantin Sitnikov, Maxim Sitnikov

I could see a woman sitting at the writing desk, composing a love letter. The assistant showed me a door. 'Konstantin is waiting in this office.'

I stepped inside. A little guy was sitting at a computer. He wore glasses and had pale blotchy skin. He was pudgy, slightly squishy even, as if, were I to handle him, I might leave my fingerprints in his flesh. I noticed also that he was sitting in a special chair, the kind with wheels, and his arms hung loosely from their sockets, resting on a board across his knees.

'Please, come in,' he said, smiling. 'Take a seat.'

The world is full of surprises. Konstantin wasn't taking me to any sacred groves.

Konstantin was slightly less paralysed than his brother. Whereas Maxim's body was entirely useless, Konstantin appeared to have marginally more movement in his fingers. *Whoop-de-doo*, I thought. *Lucky him.*

I introduced myself and explained I was on a mission to locate pagans.

'And what about you?' he asked, smiling. 'Are you a pagan?'

It had never occurred to me that someone might think I had a serious, *religious* interest in paganism. It worried me. Did I look like a dirty hippy? A New Age crystal-healing type?

'No, no,' I said. 'I'm just interested from a . . . scientific point of view. I think it's amazing that these ancient beliefs have survived into the modern age.'

'Yes . . . it is. Because you know, this isn't some nonsense cooked up by Western hippies in the 1960s. This is the real thing. These people really believe in these gods. They are quite sincere in their beliefs . . .'

'Oh yes,' I said. 'I know.'

There was a small photo album sitting on his board. He indicated it with a jerk of his chin.

'I'd like to show you some pictures.'

I opened the album. Two grave men in white robes with long beards stared out at me.

'The man on the right is the High Priest,' said Konstantin. 'The man next to him is a . . . how do you say . . . clairvoyant? He travels through the spirit world.'

'Really?'

'Yes. In fact, he says he has been to . . . what do you call it? Hell.'

'Really?' That sounded interesting. 'What was it like?' I asked.

'I'm sorry?'

'What's hell like? I'd like to know.'

Konstantin didn't answer.

I turned the page and there was a photo of him sitting, grinning in his wheelchair by an enormous oak tree, surrounded by people carrying meat, pancakes and loaves of bread. It was a rather bizarre image.

'I took part in their prayers this summer. I am Orthodox, but the Mari permit outsiders to attend, so long as they participate in the rite. I brought some meat for the gods.'

'Was it a special type of meat?' I asked.

'No, no. It was perfectly ordinary meat. I bought it in the local supermarket.'

Konstantin's eyes twinkled. He had a keen sense of the absurd, and none of his brother's ferocity. I felt very relaxed around him.

Just then there was noise from the corridor outside. Konstantin craned his neck to look behind me. 'Ah!' he said. 'The High Priest has arrived.'

37

The grand entrance

Alexei Izergovich Yakimov, the *Shnui On,* the *Verkhovnii Zhretz,* the High Priest, the Chief Druid, the leader of the Oshmari-Chimari All-Mari Religious-Spiritual Pagan Centre and Spiritual Head of the Chimari entered the room. A tall, imposing man in flowing white robes, he paused to utter a blessing in his deep sonorous voice before sitting down. A shiver ran down my spine. Never before had I encountered a man who radiated so much authority, so much spiritual force. I was overwhelmed. Without thinking, I dropped to the floor and bowed before him. 'I am honoured, honoured!' I cried.

Alexei Izergovich extended a long bony finger. 'You may lick the sacred dirt from underneath my fingernail,' he said.

38

The grand entrance (2)

Alexei Izergovich Yakimov, the *Shnui On*, the *Verkhovnii Zhretz*, the High Priest, the Chief Druid, the leader of the Oshmari-Chimari All-Mari Religious-Spiritual Pagan Centre and Spiritual Head of the Chimari burst into the room, arms and legs flailing, wearing an old fur hat and carrying a beaten-up plastic bag. He was a tall, spindly, nervous old man with a long nose and alert, beady black eyes that darted around under thick, bushy black eyebrows. He also had a very long beard.

The beard was magnificent, a real holy man's beard. Around his mouth it was a deep black, but as it travelled south it gradually became whiter and whiter, contrasting sharply with the shabby black coat he wore.

He looked around, shook my hand and then scratched his head and ran his fingers through the beard. There was nowhere for him to sit. Konstantin called for one of Maxim's assistants to bring a chair. Alexei took off his hat and coat and sat down, smoothing his wild mane of steel-grey hair. Under the coat he was wearing a tweed jacket; under the tweed jacket was a white shirt embroidered with ethnic designs. I noticed a white badge stuck to his jacket lapel.

'Oh!' he said, 'Oh my goodness! I forgot! I completely forgot to take off this badge from this really important religious congress I was at! I was a special guest there, you know!'

Speaking of badges, and names, in Russia everybody is given three names at birth: first name, patronymic and family name. While the first name (freely chosen) and last name (your father's) follow the same rules as names in Western societies, the patronymic is a little different. It is derived from your father's first name.

For example, if we look at Josef Vissarionovich Dzugashvili (Stalin), we can deduce that the murderous tyrant was the son of a man called Vissarion Dzugashvili, also probably not very nice. Alexei, meanwhile, was the son of a man called Izerg Yakimov, a name as startling to Russian ears as it is to British ones.

It is customary to refer to older men and women by first name and patronymic, as a sign of respect. For example, I always called my seventy-year-old landlord in Moscow 'Yevgeny Mikhailovich'. Plain 'Yevgeny' would have been shockingly familiar and something of an insult to a man of his years.

I noticed immediately, however, that Konstantin referred to Alexei Izergovich simply as 'Alexei'. Considering he was the venerable High Priest of the Mari religion, this was startling. Rapidly, however, I found myself doing the same. I tried correcting myself but there was something about him that made 'Alexei Izergovich' sound ridiculous. Perhaps it was his own informality, perhaps his eager, curious childlike quality. Whatever, I refer to him here as 'Alexei', not from a lack of respect, but simply because that's who he was.

40

Alexei claimed that he didn't like to show outsiders his holy garments, but he had brought them with him none the less. If he felt comfortable, he'd show me.

I was suspicious. I had been in his company for only about one minute, but already I couldn't believe that Alexei was a shrinking violet. That badge he had 'accidentally' forgotten to remove . . .

Sure enough, about two minutes later he pulled his conical priest's hat from the bag and put it on. There were three circles on the white felt hat which, he explained, represented air, earth and water, 'the three elements without which we cannot live'. Then he pulled a big address book out of his bag. He asked me to write my name and country in it. I wrote it in English and in Russian. The old man peered at the writing. He passed over the roman lines and looked at the next set of characters. It took a few seconds before he realized he was reading his own alphabet.

'What?' he said suddenly, startled. 'Hey! He did it in Russian!' He beamed at me, and then tried sounding out my name: '*Dan-ee-yell Koll-derr . . . Shotlandiya*. Hey, where is Scotland? I tried to find it on the map last night but couldn't.'

'It's next to England,' said Konstantin.

'Is it north?' he asked me.

'Yes,' I replied.

'It's part of England?' asked Alexei.

'No, it's next to England,' said Konstantin.

'What's the difference?' asked Alexei.

'It's a different country,' I said.

'Scottish men wear skirts,' said Konstantin.

'Skirts?' asked Alexei.

'Yes. And they play the bagpipes.'

'Ah . . .' said Alexei. It seemed to ring a bell.

'We eat porridge too,' I said.

'I thought that was the English,' said Konstantin.

'No, that's us,' I said.

'Ah . . .' said Alexei, stroking his beard. 'Scotland, Scotland. I see . . .'

41

Alexei was well practised at discussing his beliefs to outsiders. He explained that the Mari were not animists: they did not believe that the trees themselves were divine, though some of them were sacred. Instead they had a hierarchy of gods whose blessing they invoked through prayer and sacrifice. Alexei mentioned the following nine deities as the main ones:

Tunia Yuma	The Father God, Creator of the World
Tun Yuma	Chief God
Serlagish	The Saviour God
Osh Kech Yuma	The God of light
Pursho	The God of Fate
Shochinava Yuma	The Holy Mother
Kava Yuma	God of the Sky
Mlande Yuma	God of Wealth
Chumblat	God of the Holy Mountain

There were, however, numerous others. Each god was responsible for his part of the world or human life, and under him were many 'spirits', assistants with more specific duties. Each had to be invoked according to what the supplicant desired, whether it was a rich harvest, luck in hunting, or conception. Sometimes a prayer sufficed, but the gods preferred sacrifices. Can't say I blame them. So would I, if I was a god.

The sacrifices depended on the rank of the god. To the chief gods, such as Osh Kech Yuma, Tun Yuma, or Tunia Yuma it was necessary to offer a horse or a goose. To the other, smaller gods, a duck, or a calf, or a hare might suffice. A red cock protected against fires. Pigs and goats were not deemed suitable offerings.

Alexei waxed lyrical over the last time he had presided over the sacrifice of a horse. 'Ah . . . it was in 1996. During our "prayers for the world". We had a thousand people in the grove then. They came in on buses from lots of different villages. And the horse, it was a beautiful red one. Expensive, too. You can't sacrifice a beauty like that too often. I didn't sacrifice it, mind; my assistants did. Four of them. It's not my job to kill animals. No, no; I'm High Priest. I don't kill. I bless the offerings.'

He continued, 'After they killed it, they cut the body into parts and put the separate parts on different plates, decorated with folk motifs. We got a local artist to paint them for us. We then put the innards on the fire to Yuma. Then I lit a candle and we boiled the parts of the horse in a great cauldron while all the people prayed with me, for half an hour. Cloth belts stained with the blood of the sacrificed horse hung from the trees. Nobody was allowed to taste the soup, not until after the prayers.'

'Are women and children allowed to participate?' I asked.

'Yes, yes. All the people eat the sacred soup – the women, the children, the men.'

'What about dogs?' asked Konstantin, with a mischievous smile.

'No, no dogs.'

'Cats?'

'No. No cats either. They're not allowed.'

This was all very benign. I got the impression that Alexei was trying to impress upon me the *normalcy* of his belief, that it wasn't about witches, magic and curses, as (for example) Maxim and most Russians thought. It was about living in harmony with the universe.

But I was curious about Keremet, the evil god, the Satan. I started to formulate a question, but as soon as I mentioned his name, Alexei went crazy and began waving his arms in the air. 'Keremet? Keremet? We don't pray to Keremet! Who told you about Keremet?'

Konstantin tried to calm him down. There was an English lesson taking place in the next room and he was disturbing the students.

Suddenly Alexei relaxed, and he told me a little about the god.

'He is a little devil, who causes evil to test us.'

In fact, it turned out that there were two groups of Mari, those who prayed to Keremet and those who did not. The Chi Mari ('Clean Mari' – thus named because they had never accepted Christian baptism), of whom Alexei was the spiritual leader, did not.

'Well, not very often,' he said.

42

Maxim wanted to meet the High Priest, so we moved to his 'viewing platform' in the centre of the agency. I greeted him cheerfully and casually, but in fact I felt uneasy. His stare made me feel as though he was looking around in my soul, rummaging through all the drawers where I keep my secrets. And I was still perplexed by his eerie prescience of two days before, his knowing in advance who I was and what I had come for.

Alexei plopped himself down next to Maxim and pulled out a copy of *Who's Who in Mari El* and pointed at his photo. 'That's me,' he said. 'The High Priest of the Chi Mari.'

I noticed that the delegate's badge from the conference had mystically returned to his lapel.

Maxim studied the entry. Then he turned to me. '*Who's Who in Mari El* – a list of the three thousand most significant individuals in our republic. I also am in this book.'

Alexei wanted Maxim to put his name in his address book.

Maxim pointed out that he couldn't move his hands. 'Ah!' said Alexei, 'Well, you can dictate it to me.'

Maxim sounded out his name and Alexei copied it into the book, echoing Maxim as he wrote. 'Sit-ni-kov . . . Sitnikov . . . sounds familiar . . . Hey! That's Konstantin's name!'

He looked up, but Maxim was distracted, calling to his wife. Alexei peered at Maxim, and saw the wheelchair for the first time. Then he looked at me. His beady black eyes sparkled.

'Aha!' he said, tapping his nose, as if we were both in on a great secret.

43

Maxim's wife joined us at the table. He introduced her as a journalist from an Egyptian newspaper. Maxim shot me a wry glance, but she looked unhappy at the deception. Alexei, however, was really excited. He had never met a journalist from so far away before. He asked her to write her name in his book too. It was about fifty words long. As I can't remember it I'm going to call her 'Sahra'.

Alexei began his spiel, the same one he had given me, about sacred groves, Tunia Yuma, all that.

Sahra wasn't very interested, however. She interrupted him: 'Yes, yes, but how do you know that this is true?'

Alexei laughed. It was such a silly question.

'My father told me.'

'Yes, but how do you know that what he said was true?'

'Well, his father told him.'

'So? How did he know?'

'My grandfather was a very wise man. He was a priest. He cut the forest to grow corn, but he knew to leave a grove, as a temple. He knew many things . . . he was descended from a line of *karts*.'

'But what was his source?'

'Ah,' said Alexei, 'you must understand that paganism is the oldest religion in the world. The Egyptians were pagans, the Ancient Greeks were pagans. In Japan they had shinto-ism–paganism. And in India Hinduism . . .'

'Hinduism isn't paganism,' said Maxim.

'Well, it's like paganism,' said Alexei. 'And in Tibet . . .'

'They're Buddhists,' said Maxim.

'Are they?' said Alexei, 'Oh yes, that's right. So they are. Anyway, paganism is older than Christianity, older than Judaism, much older than Islam.'

'OK, so it's old,' said Sahra. 'But how do you know it's true? Who told you this?'

I chipped in: 'Do you have a book?'

'A book?'

'In your religion. Do you have a holy book?'

'Yes, we have a book. In our stories, there is a great book.'

'He's talking about a mythical book,' said Maxim.

'No,' I said. 'I mean, do you have a book like the Bible, or the Koran – a source book for your beliefs?'

'Oh, that kind of book,' said Alexei. 'No, no we don't.'

'Then how do you know?' asked Sahra. 'How do you know it's true?'

Sahra was clearly disturbed by Alexei's existence, disturbed by the thought that he might be right and she could be wrong, and that Allah could be a myth. Her entire people then would be destined for whichever sector of hell it is that is reserved for heretics. I asked Alexei about the afterlife.

'What about when you die?' I asked. 'What happens?'

'Ah,' said Alexei. 'When you die . . .'

'I mean, is there a judgment?'

'Yes, all the people will be gathered . . . but God won't have to ask questions. He will already know who has done good and who has done bad . . .'

'And what happens to those who have done bad?' I asked.

'If you're good, you go to the right. If you're evil, you go to the left.'

'And then what?'

'Er . . . it's not clear. But the bad are punished. Some people return to earth as spirits. I have met people from other side, you know . . .'

'Who is your prophet?' demanded Sahra, suddenly.

'Prophet?' echoed Alexei.

'Yes, who told you all this?'

'For example,' I said, 'Christians have Jesus, Muslims have Muhammad. Who is your prophet?'

'We don't have one,' he replied.

'You have the tradition of your ancestors and that's all,' said Maxim.

'Yes,' said Alexei.

'I've had enough of this,' said Sahra. She pushed the stool aside and walked away.

Alexei laughed. 'She's a feisty one,' he said.

44

Suddenly, from out of nowhere, a tall, bony woman appeared at the table. 'I'm a journalist too,' she said. 'And I've studied the Mari. I was at their sacrifices earlier this year.'

She began distributing photos around the table. I was about to pick one up when Alexei roared and leapt to his feet.

'What's this?' he cried. 'What's this? It's an outrage! Heresy! Sacrilege!' He was waving a picture around in his hand. The journalist was trying to snatch it back from him. 'This is outrageous! Outrageous!'

Across from us a teenager was writing a love letter. She looked frightened.

The offices of the Virginia Travel Agency, one of Maxim Sitnikov's five enterprises.

'Alexei Izergovich,' said Maxim, 'please calm down.'

Alexei, however, continued to wave the picture in the air and fulminate.

'What's the matter?' I asked Konstantin.

'Ah,' said Konstantin. 'In the picture a woman is preparing the sacrifice. For Alexei, this is sacrilege. These Mari belong to a different sect.'

'A woman!' cried Alexei. 'A woman! And she's doing it all wrong!'

After ranting for about a minute, however, Alexei suddenly sat down again, calm and relaxed. The journalist gathered up her photos and beat a hasty retreat. Alexei pursed his lips and looked around.

'Is that all? Any more questions? Questions?'

Nobody had any more questions. I asked if he would show me a sacred grove.

'Ah, you don't want to go,' he said. 'It'll be covered in snow. There's nothing there. It's rubbish this time of year.'

I was persistent, however. This strange and wily old man had piqued my curiosity. Now much more than before I wanted to see a holy grove. I wanted to spend more time with him. Eventually he agreed to take me the next day. In fact, it took hardly any persuading. Then he gathered up his stuff and scurried out the door, explaining that he was late for a meeting with an artist who was painting a ceremonial plate for him.

I thanked Maxim and Konstantin and left Virginia once more. From having arrived in Yoshkar Ola with no contacts and no strategy, my quest for pagans was picking up. Via the telepathic paralysed owner of a marriage agency I had met the Chief Druid. The omens were good. It looked as though I was going to be successful.

45

The trouble with pagans

The existence of different, opposed pagan sects took me by surprise. I had expected the Mari to all believe the same things, mainly because there weren't very many of them. Of course, that was rather naive. Divisions emerge in human society whenever a group contains more than one person.

It wasn't only the rift between existing groups of pagans that concerned me, however. There was also an unbridgeable gap between the modern pagans and their ancestors. I asked Alexei how he knew that his prayers were the same prayers as his forefathers, that his rituals were the same. He answered that he didn't. His prayers and rites were part invention, part recollection.

This ambiguity was intensified by what I discovered in a

214

book I bought in the Mari State Museum. It was, I might add, the only book I found in all of Yoshkar Ola on the topic of Mari folk culture. It was a collection of short interviews with old Mari peasants, mostly recorded in the late 1980s and early 1990s, as the last generation to grow up with their native beliefs was dying out. There I found a list of the main Mari deities. They were:

Ketse Yuma	God of the Sun
Mardezh Yuma	God of the Wind
Yur Yuma	God of Rain
Ur Yuma	God of Animals
Tergya Yuma	God of Birds
Oshketse Yuma	God of Midday Sun
Vud Yuma	God of Water

If you look back a few pages you will see that this list is almost entirely different from the one Alexei gave me. The descriptions of Mari prayers in the book were also different.

Also, as far as I could tell, the Mari gods themselves seemed to be little more than names: these old people didn't give any information about their characteristics to the anthropologists who interviewed them. I remembered a passage I had read in a book about early Roman religion years ago. The Romans had a god of dung, called Sterculus. Naturally, I thought this was pretty funny and wanted to know what he looked like, what kind of character he had, and whether he featured in any myths. The book, however, said that the original Roman gods were little more than names attached to functions. You invoked Sterculus when you spread dung on the fields. That was all.

I wondered if the Mari gods were like this. There were no pictures of them. There weren't many stories about them. The peasants spoke mostly about the sacred groves. Groves had to be kept clean and tidy. You couldn't eat the fruit or the berries in the grove. If you blasphemed in the grove, you fell ill and died. In the book there were plenty of stories of women and men and Russians who picked fruit or killed animals in a grove and mysteriously died. There was only one story about the evil spirits who roamed the fields at night, however, and all it said was that there were evil spirits.

The more I looked, the more the Mari and their beliefs slipped away from me. It was possible that there was information they didn't like to share with curious scientists and journalists. Their ancient beliefs had survived partly because of their reclusiveness, their difficulty to reach.

There is no way I can write with any authority on Mari paganism. That's the work of an anthropologist willing to spend years among the different groups collecting, collating and comparing information. As yet that work hasn't been done.

46

The Secret Master of Yoshkar Ola

Meanwhile I had had another brilliant idea for a movie, perhaps my best yet.

It occurred to me as I was crossing Krasnoarmeiskaya Street at the point where it meets Volnova Street. It was about three in the afternoon and I'd spent the first part of the day wandering round the centre, looking unsuccessfully for books on Mari history and culture.

The title came to me first: *The Secret Master of Yoshkar Ola*. I liked it. By the time I was halfway across the road I knew what it was about: an entirely paralysed crime boss who ran the city, with a crew of able-bodied and fiercely loyal henchmen. He was unspeakably cruel and consumed by a demonic lust. His headquarters were full of naked and nearly naked girls who acted as his assistants: making cups of tea, dialling numbers on the phone, dancing for him, moving his limbs for him so he could pretend he wasn't paralysed . . . and, of course, performing 'other' services too.

By the time I'd reached the other side I was toying with the idea of making him a certifiable loon as well: like maybe he gave his commands through a glove puppet which the girls stuck on his arm for him. Yes – he wasn't the boss, the puppet was. Or at least it was the highest authority, which he consulted for really big decisions. He was a remarkable ventriloquist and could project his voice on to the puppet, which was utterly psychotic.

As for who would oppose him, I thought maybe he had a paralysed brother, a journalist, who set out to bring him down. This was a difficult task as the police were on the evil brother's side and, of course, the good brother couldn't move or do anything without help. But perhaps he'd gather together a small band of loyal friends who'd help him blow the whistle on a big white-slaving deal his brother was setting up, selling young girls to Israeli brothels as slaves or something like that, while promising them work. Once in Israel their captors would get them hooked on drugs, steal their passports and lock the girls in basements where repulsive men with facial deformities and missing limbs would have their way with them. Yes! They were sex slaves for evil amputees!

The good brother would uncover the plot and reveal it to the world at large, thus saving the citizens of Yoshkar Ola from the tyranny of the evil white-slaving overlord. There would also be a scene where the good brother made love to a really beautiful sex-slave girl, an escapee who had fallen in love with him. It would be a graphic and yet tender scene, a plea for recognizing the essential humanness of the disabled. Naturally this would rule out the possibility of American financing, but I figured Germans might go for it.

I arrived home and prepared some lunch. The plot needed working on, but the premise, essentially, was complete. I was satisfied with my work. But, for now, let us forget about film scripts, pagan priests and marriage agencies. Instead, please follow me on a diversion, an existential tour of a lost zone . . .

47

The night voyage: an interlude

I

I first had this feeling in St Petersburg, when I rented a flat on the outskirts of the city. The walk to the metro led me past vast roads and massive towers. The roads were so huge and long that they tapered off, disappearing at the horizon, where the earth met the sky. The towers, meanwhile, were positioned at odd angles, so that they hid each other – you couldn't see what lay beyond them. I felt I was lost in a vast, numinous labyrinth.

I wondered if there were not mysteries and miracles taking place in that maze. Were there perhaps strange monuments that nobody knew about? Hidden, secret relics, that few people had ever seen? After all, nobody walked those streets – they climbed into cars, or buses, or underground trains and sped past them, never pausing to contemplate the secret beauty they contained.

It occurred to me that it might be more interesting to forget the centre with all its pompous historical baggage and study the concrete suburbs instead. They were more alluring. Nobody had ever seriously considered them as a garden of hidden delights before. I resolved to go back a year later and spend a few days wandering around the concrete suburbs, looking at open windows and graffiti, picking up discarded toys and junk, listening to conversations . . .

I never did, however. I had other things to do. I had to make money. I had to survive. In Yoshkar Ola, however, I thought I could at least make a sketch towards that idea: the suburbs there were smaller, and easier to negotiate on foot. As a consequence, they were less awe-inspiring, but nonetheless fascinating. In these buildings Mari, Russians, Tatars struggled to stay alive, experienced ecstasy, despair, disillusionment. In these apartments they wept, shat and came. Surely I would find something there?

I didn't tell anyone I was going to do this, however. They would have said I was mad and laughed at me. Or told me that it was a dangerous plan and scolded me . . .

II

I made my first attempt during daylight, crossing the Theatre Bridge to the valley of apartment buildings that lay beyond it. It was extremely cold and an icy wind cut through my jacket. The bridge developed into a broad, broad street lined with concrete tower blocks, each eleven storeys high. They led off in a straight line that appeared to terminate in a wasteland.

I noticed that the concrete blocks were different from any I'd seen before. They had different designs on the balconies. And I was intrigued, but also repelled by the long stretch ahead of me. It wasn't easy to commit myself to it. I knew I'd get tired and hungry and then I'd have to walk back. Besides, the twin tyrannies of history and beauty were calling me. There was the State Museum to visit, the Planetarium.

Shouldn't I try one of those instead?

I caved in to pressure. I only made it about a hundred metres into the suburb, as far as a mysterious statue of an unknown great man. He looked oriental. He had his arms folded and one finger under his chin as if he was musing on something. But on what I had no idea. Who he was I had no idea. I took some pictures. People stared at me. Then I went back.

III

I was more cunning the next time. I went at night. I was alone in the city, I had no friends, and there were no places to visit. It was boring to sit in the flat and watch Russian TV. What else was there to do except walk around a housing scheme? I knew that this time I wouldn't be tempted back by museums and cafés and such shite.

On the other hand it was also (theoretically) more danger-ous. Maybe I'd get attacked by a gang and have to run for it. At the very least a drunk might give me some hassle. Or maybe the cops would stop me. That, however, only made it more enticing, as I figured once the bruises had healed I'd have a good story to tell. So at around ten I set off for the suburb.

IV

Once more I followed the bridge to the statue of the unknown genius. After the statue, however, all identifiable landmarks fell away. The buildings ran ahead of me to the wasteland. On the right and on the left, meanwhile, they were identical. There was nothing to choose between them.

I decided to turn right simply because it led to another bridge across the river, a bridge that terminated in front of my home. Looking back, however, I think that perhaps this was a mistake. I was showing an unwillingness to surrender myself to the concrete, to the long paths, to the nothingness, to the central act of getting lost.

Nevertheless, that was the choice I made. So I walked on and for a while, nothing happened and I saw no one. Then, however, I turned a corner and found myself on an alley where I found (*choose one of the following*): (a) a human ear; (b) a mysterious, triangular blue key; (c) the black book, *Necronomicon*; (d) Lord Lucan; or (e) none of the above.

I found another alley, long and exactly the same as the one that had preceded it. After that I found another alley, long and exactly the same as the one that preceded it. Then I found another, long and . . . you get the idea. Growing frustrated, I followed this last one to its end until the street-lights vanished and I almost stumbled into a bog. Discouraged, I turned back and retraced my steps towards the bridge. Along the way I saw some drunks and a few lone women scurrying home in fear.

Something almost happened as I was crossing the bridge. A police car stopped and waited as I walked towards them. I thought the cops inside were going to pick me up, and maybe steal my money. But then they drove away.

I arrived home, cold and hungry, and ate some *pelmeni*, Russian mud-food I had found in an all-night liquor store. They didn't go down well and I felt rough. Then I watched Russian TV for a few hours. Then I went to sleep.

And that was it. No mysteries. No secrets. Nothing at all.

48

The sacred grove

I

The old bus drove us out of town past flat snow-covered fields and crumbling houses. I was sitting next to Alexei, holding his

Alexei at prayer

holy staff for him, listening to him talk about killing and gutting animals for God. It was as if he were the master of some evil cult, and I the acolyte. The other passengers stared at us. I wondered if they recognized him. After all, according to *Who's Who*, he was one of the three thousand most significant people in Mari El. However, I don't think they did. The looks we got were not those of recognition, but of confusion, even fear. I liked that.

II

Alexei referred to me using *ti*, the familiar form of you, and immediately I felt included. I wasn't standing on the outside. I was participating. I remembered Konstantin had brought meat to the summer sacrifices and thought, *Perhaps I ought to have brought something.* But I didn't know yet what was

222

going to happen. Nevertheless, I sensed that I was going to be doing more than just watching.

I tried to get Alexei to talk about his past. Who had he been for the first sixty years of his existence? He told me he was an *udarnik*, a Soviet 'shock worker', building cities in Siberia and railways in Kazakhstan. But he wasn't very interested in the past. No; he preferred to talk about his sudden self-reinvention ten years earlier, when he had become High Priest. The Soviet Union had collapsed and there was a flowering of Mari self-consciousness. Alexei returned to Yoshkar Ola from Siberia to be a part of it. People were openly practising their old religion and somehow he got himself elected High Priest. He was vague on the details.

He was, however, very detailed on the things he got for free because of his status as High Priest. He enumerated train tickets to conferences, hot meals and hotel rooms and how much they usually cost. This only made me like him more, as I also enjoy scabbing things for free. We were players of the same game, but he was better at it than me. He was the master, I the acolyte.

III

Our stop was in the middle of a wasteland. I followed Alexei off, but as I stepped down from the bus the ground collapsed beneath me. My foot went straight into an icy puddle of water, up to the ankle. It flooded my shoe and I felt the cold grip each and every toe simultaneously.

'Bollocks,' I said.

'You should have worn boots, you should have worn boots!' said Alexei.

'I left them in Moscow,' I said. 'I didn't think . . .'

'See that?' said Alexei, interrupting. He was pointing at a half-built block of flats. 'That used to be a meadow. It was beautiful. But now they're building flats, ugly flats. And look at them! Cheap! Shoddy! Ugly! Pah!'

'Yes, they're not very nice,' I concurred.

'Over there! Over there!' cried Alexei, pointing at a snow-covered field, ringed with trees. 'The grove is over there!'

He set off. I followed.

IV

The path led us down a slope and across a field. Sometimes we had to trudge through deep snow, other times we struggled to keep our balance as the path turned to sheet ice beneath us. Alexei found it particularly difficult as he had cunningly chosen to wear plastic boots that gave him no grip whatsoever.

I asked him about his family. He had numerous brothers and sisters, spread all over Russia. The eldest brother was dead. Alexei had been married twice ('I know it's not right,' he said, 'but I've been alive a long time') and had a daughter who lived in Moscow. However, he wasn't interested in talking about his personal life. He had other things on his mind.

'I'm seventy-three,' he said, 'but look at me! Strong as an ox! Strong as an ox! I never get sick! Yes! And I'll tell you why! I never drink. I never smoke. And, of course,' he paused, 'the most important thing.'

'What's that?' I asked.

'God,' he said, pointing upwards.

'Yes . . . God,' I said.

He was silent for a moment. Then he continued. 'See that over there?'

I looked. I saw nothing. The land and the sky were both blank.

'Yes,' I lied.

'That's the main road. That's the road the cars follow for dachas.'

'Ah.'

'Yes! There are dachas here! Dachas!'

Dachas are little wooden country cottages, summer homes, where people grow vegetables and fruit.

'I've got a dacha, you know. It's not far from here, not far at all. I'm going there tomorrow to get some preserves!'

'I see.'

'Yes, we made preserves in the summer, now we're going to . . . Wait! Look over there!'

'Yes?'

'That used to be a pioneer camp! A pioneer camp! But some New Russian bought the land and built a house on it!'

'Really?'

'Yes! He just bought the land, and now . . .' He paused. 'Now the kids have nowhere to go! Progress!' He tapped his nose.

'Um,' I said.

Alexei paused.

'Hey – you do understand Russian, don't you?'

'Yes . . .' I said. 'I understand almost everything . . . but my grammar is bad. It's difficult to speak.'

'Ah! As long as you understand!'

Satisfied, he continued merrily chatting away about roads and dachas. But I had stopped listening. It was extremely icy underfoot and I didn't want to be distracted from the difficult task of staying on my feet.

v

We plunged deeper and deeper into the forest, and Alexei grew more and more animated as we went. He pointed out which trees were holy and which not.

'This one's a fir,' he said. 'It represents eternity . . . and this one, it's a birch, that represents a woman's tenderness. An oak

225

– that's for strength, and a lime, ah, a lime . . .'

Suddenly he stopped. 'Hold this,' he said, handing me his bag. He then stalked off, disappearing into the trees.

What's this? I thought. *Have we reached a particularly sacred spot? Is he going to offer up a prayer?*

I looked for him in the woods, and caught a glimpse of his white beard. Then I saw him do a kind of squat and shortly after that I heard a trickling sound, which quickly became a drumming sound, like a thin jet of liquid being sprayed against a solid object.

VI

We walked on and on, and on. I lagged behind, looking around for something that could pass for a sacred grove. I expected a circle of ancient oaks, mighty trees with thick, thick trunks and sprawling branches, exuding an aura of mystery, of fear. The kind of things I'd seen on *Robin of Sherwood* as a boy: the oaks of the gods, the oaks that would kill you, or strike you blind if you didn't treat them with sufficient respect.

But I couldn't see any. I was surrounded by birch trees, scrawny sticks poking out of the snow. They grew in no particular order, and were no more than forty or fifty years old. I couldn't imagine I was near one of the nine main groves Alexei's ancestors had planted three hundred years ago.

That isn't to say, however, that the birch trees were not sinister. They were very sinister, as all Russian forests are. One of the most famous atrocities in Russian history took place in the Katyn forest, near Smolensk. There, thousands of Polish officers were shot by the NKVD and hastily buried. The Soviet government blamed their deaths on the Nazis, and it wasn't until the late 1980s that the truth was revealed.

But the Katyn forest is not the only one where victims of the regime lie. The soil in Russia is full of skeletons. Its trees grew strong and multiplied, feasting on the juices of the murdered. To Alexei, they were holy. To me, they were towering symbols of a mute, omnipresent evil.

VII

Alexei pointed out footsteps in the snow. 'Do you see? Someone has already been here today! Yes, the faith is strong.'

I had expected a green Stonehenge. But actually, the grove was rather humble. It consisted of an open semi-circle of oaks and a small cluster of birch trees. Now it was easy to understand why a full 360 groves had survived seventy years of Soviet oppression. If you weren't told you were looking at a holy grove, you wouldn't know. It was possible to see the hand of man in the arrangement of the oaks, but it was equally possible to imagine the apparent order was natural, a happy accident.

The central oak, however, was a real beauty. It stood apart from the other trees in a clearing, its broad trunk erupting from the white ground and spreading into thick, sinewy black branches that clawed at the sky. As we walked closer I noticed colourful rags hanging from the branches.

I had seen this before: scraps of cloth tied to the branches of a fir tree in a forest in provincial Russia, or on a bush growing by some dachas in the suburbs of Moscow. Even on the thorns of a dry shrub sprouting from the dusty steppe near a canyon in southern Kazakhstan. It's a remnant of Slav pagan beliefs. You tie a rag to a branch and make a wish. Evidently the Mari pagans also did this. But here I felt something different.

Imagine, for a second, that you meet a modern man, dressed just like you, sane and reasonable, with a technological education even, but who happens to come from a people

227

who have been hiding in a forest for the best part of a thousand years.

Now everybody knows that Hallowe'en was originally a pagan festival, but that through Christianity and secularism it withered away to a children's holiday associated with scary masks and the consumption of sweets.

But imagine that the beliefs of his ancestors are still alive in this man's mind, and that when you talk to him you realize that the night of 31 October is a time when the darkness *is* alive with powerful demons that mean to do him harm. And he believes in those demons in the same way that he believes a picture will appear when he turns on his TV. And that he is scared senseless of those demons.

That's what it was like standing next to Alexei in front of the tree.

VIII

Alexei saw that some of the rags were in fact shreds of plastic bags. He didn't like this at all. 'It's not right' he said, shaking his head. 'Our people, there's so much they don't know. They need me to teach them.' He hesitated, deliberating whether to remove the plastic. Then he shook his head. 'Let it be,' he said.

The back of the tree revealed a sorry sight. Alexei showed me the wound where it had been attacked with fire. A man could have climbed inside that charred hole. And at the very base of the trunk there was a scar from a chainsaw. Alexei sighed sadly, tutted, shook his head.

Probably, I thought, the tree was attacked by Russian Orthodox believers opposed to the Mari and their 'Satanic' magical rites. But Alexei didn't think this likely at all. He was convinced it was another, enemy Mari sect. Furthermore he claimed that some members of Yoshkar Ola's police belonged to this sect, so there was no way the culprits would ever be caught and punished, or that the tree could be effectively protected.

'We need to put up signs. To say that it's sacred. But we don't have any money.' He ran his fingers through his beard. 'Three hundred years this oak has stood here,' he said. 'And it comes to this.'

He shrugged, and led me into the cluster of birch trees.

IX

The preparations for prayer were meticulous and elaborate.

First, it was necessary to clean the grove. Alexei walked around, chattering to himself, picking up bits of litter. The ground was thick with bushes and dead branches and it was difficult for him to walk across it. Meanwhile I was standing gazing blankly on the edge of the grove, holding his holy staff. Once it was sufficiently clean, Alexei broke off a branch from a small tree and, using a knife, whittled it into a more regular shape. He then brought it over to me and thrust it into the ground in front of a large birch.

Alexei took the staff from me. 'Watch this,' he said. 'The Patriarch of the Orthodox Church may have a fancy bishop's mitre, but I bet his doesn't double as a table!'

He unscrewed the bolt on the top, and thrust the staff into the ground, next to the branch. Then he pulled a square piece of plywood out of his bag. The plywood had a hole in the centre: he placed it over the screw sticking out of the staff and reattached the bolt. *Et voilà!* We had a table.

Alexei then took some embroidered cloths from his bag and placed one over the makeshift table; the other two I helped him tie around the tree.

After checking that the cloths were straight, Alexei took a small wooden board from out of his bag. In the centre of the

229

board there were three circles enclosed within a larger circle, from which rays of (presumably) light radiated outwards. The circles represented the earth, the sky and the water: 'The three fundamental elements without which there is no life,' said Alexei. Glued to the bottom of the board was a piece of paper with the words OSH KECHE YUMA – Great White Yuma – written on it in bold black letters. The paper had been scrappily coloured in with a felt-tip pen.

I helped Alexei tie the board to the tree. It took a few minutes for him to get it the way he wanted. The first time we did it he thought it was hanging squint, so we had to do it again. The second time, however, he was satisfied. He stepped back. 'Nice,' he said, admiring his efforts. 'Pretty. That's very pretty.'

Then Alexei took a circular brown loaf and an old Fanta bottle from the bag and put them on the table. The Fanta bottle contained home-made berry juice. He also pulled out two empty yoghurt cartons, to serve as cups. I wondered if he was going to make a libation, or if we were going to participate in some kind of communion. I wondered if I was supposed to have an offering for the god too, but Alexei didn't ask me for anything.

He took out a little porcelain candlestick, and placed it on top of the bread. Then he put a thin beeswax candle, exactly like the ones they burn in Orthodox churches, in the holder. He also had a wind-shield, constructed from another Fanta bottle he had cut up. 'Clever, eh?' he said, as he placed it around the candle. It still took several attempts to light the candle, however, as the breeze kept extinguishing it.

Once all this was done Alexei stepped back to admire the ensemble. 'Yes,' he said. 'That's nice. That's really nice. Very pretty.'

Finally he took off his jacket. Underneath he was wearing a white shirt, embroidered with ethnic designs. He pulled his conical High Priest's hat from the bag, smoothed down his thick black hair and placed it on his head. On the front it had the same three circles as the board. He turned to me.

'How do I look?'

'Fine,' I said.

'No, I mean, is the hat on straight? Is it on straight?'

'Yes, it's on straight,' I said. In fact, it was actually slightly squint: the three circles were not perfectly aligned with the bridge of his nose.

'Then we can begin.'

X

'We are going to pray to Holy Mother Earth. I'm going to ask for a blessing for you, and also for a fruitful harvest in the year to come. Do you have a coin?'

'Hm?'

'A coin, like this.'

Alexei showed me a silver one-rouble piece. I took a similar coin from my wallet.

'We need to wash the money, to make it clean for the goddess.'

He knelt down and scrubbed his rouble with snow. I copied him. Then Alexei stood up and pushed the coin into the bread, so that it was half embedded. I did the same. The loaf looked like one of those blind fish that trawls the sea-bed eating crap, the coins its unseeing eyes.

Alexei began to pray. He bowed his head and suddenly streams of words were pouring from his lips, one after the other, incessant and unending. It was the first time I had heard Mari spoken. The sounds were short, clipped, they rushed to follow each other, rather like Japanese, only even more frenetic. Periodically he would pause, take a deep breath and then continue. I heard 'Yuma' rise to the surface once, only to be swept away in the torrent, lost in the rush of the sacred.

I was struck by the resemblance in style to the Orthodox rite, whereby priests also intone long, semi-musical prayers. Perhaps Alexei had copied his style from the Russian Church: he had admitted, after all, that the exact details of the Mari rite were lost during the Soviet period. The main difference was that, after intoning one section of the prayer Alexei would pause, run his hands through his beard two or three times, and then resume praying. And, of course, he was praying in front of a tree to the Earth Goddess, instead of an iconostasis.

I stood there listening and watching. After a few minutes I heard my name. Alexei switched to Russian. 'I'm praying for you now,' he said.

'O Yuma, please grant Daniel success in all he does. Give him health and prosperity and joy in his work . . .'

But he spoke so fast I lost track of the blessing. Once it was over, he paused, took the bread, and bit a chunk out of the side. He passed it to me, and I bit a chunk from the other side. We drank the holy berry juice.

Alexei knelt before the tree and reached the climax of his prayer with another stream of Mari and more stroking of the beard. Then he stood up. It was finished.

'Yes,' he said. 'That was nice. That was good. I'm glad we did this.'

I was blessed.

49

Postscript (1)

And it would be nice if I could leave Alexei like that: just him and me standing in the forest, shivering, bonded by the ritual of blessing. That would be a good ending. A tidy ending. Nice and 'authentic'. The story, however, has a postscript.

I asked him about the patterns embroidered on the cloths tied to the tree. 'Those two birds, kissing – what kind are they? What do they represent?'

'Dunno,' said Alexei. 'They're just birds.'

Then I took some photos. Alexei was a willing subject, coming up with a wide range of suitably priestly expressions as he posed beside the tree and the holy bread:

ALEXEI: Hey! Take one of me praying! Like this! And how about like this? Is that good? What about like this?

DANIEL: (*shutter snapping*) Yeah baby, yeah!

He also took a few pictures of me, but I was freezing my nuts off; consequently, in the photos, I have a look of anguish on my face. We packed up, and set off back along the path to the bus stop, Alexei carrying the bag, me carrying the staff.

Alexei started talking about Stalin and how he had collectivized the Mari villages. It was all rather interesting and I was concentrating hard so I could understand. The path, however, was very icy, and Alexei kept slipping in his plastic boots. He had just invited me back to his flat for a cup of tea when he went flying.

Oh no, I thought. *He's a really old guy and maybe he'll break something*. I rushed to grab him before he hit the ground. I broke his fall, but when he looked up I saw there was a huge flap of skin hanging loose from his nose and that blood was pouring from it. With horror, I realized that yea verily, I had whacked the High Priest in the face with his own holy staff.

He sat there, startled, dazed, staring at me. Here was an old man who had gone out of his way to do something nice for me. An old man who had invited me to his house for tea. And he had been so excited – 'So you'll come? You'll come to me? For tea! Excellent!' In return, I had ripped a chunk of flesh out of his nose. I felt very, very guilty.

'Maybe you should have let me fall,' said Alexei.

50

Postscript (2)

And while it would not exactly be *good* if I could leave Alexei in the forest, it might be better than what happened next. For the story is not over yet. The postscript too has a postscript.

I rode the bus with Alexei back to his flat. His nose was streaming with blood the whole time and I was acutely conscious of the silence that now divided us. He had not, however, revoked his invitation to tea. We went into a shop to buy bread, and I watched closely to see if the sullen girl working behind the counter recognized him, if she realized she was serving the High Priest of the Mari. But she remained sullen and it was clear that she had no idea at all who he was. Alexei was just an eccentric old man.

Alexei's apartment, meanwhile, was a single room and kitchen in a crumbling concrete low rise from the Brezhnev era. There were no carpets on the floor and the walls were unpapered. Instead of a clock in the kitchen there was an old watch nailed up by the door. The furniture was spartan and uncomfortable. '*Kak skromno miy zhivyem!*' he said, as I stepped into the hall. 'How modestly we live!'

Alexei's wife, a chatty round *babushka* prepared food for us. She was kind and gentle. As we ate she asked me about my family, my country. Like her husband she wasn't sure where or what Scotland was. I talked about Loch Ness: I thought it might help.

'We have a monster,' I said. 'It lives in a lake.' But that only confused her further.

'A monster? He has a monster? What's he talking about?' she asked her husband.

Alexei however, was intrigued. 'Yes, I've heard of that,' he said. 'It's probably not a monster. It's probably the guardian spirit of the lake.'

After lunch Alexei and I went through to the living room. There was an ancient TV, two beds and an old sepia portrait of Alexei's father, the head of a collective farm, on the wall. By the door stood his desk, covered in papers. Behind the desk there was a notice board covered in articles about paganism. In the left corner of the room, by the window, was the 'red corner'.

In devout Orthodox households it's common to have a 'red corner' given over to an icon. The Communists made it a place for portraits of Lenin. Alexei evidently liked the tradition too, although his corner, of course, was pagan.

There was something strange about Alexei's red corner, however. Aside from one small plaque with the three circles and OSH KECHE YUMA inscribed on it, it was full of stuff about him. There was a photo of him, smiling. There was a big article about him, mounted on card. There was even a wooden doll – with his features painted on it. Alexei showed me each of these things, glowing with pride.

Then he opened a big fat file full of copies of articles – about him. He showed me every single one, pointing out photos and his name, which was always underlined. This took about half an hour, and he grew more and more excited, prodding at his favourite lines and quoting himself.

'Have you shown him the *Who's Who*?' called his wife from the other room.

'Yes, yes!' he replied. 'Long ago!'

I had been speaking Russian for six hours and my head was beginning to swim. It was time to leave. But Alexei wanted me to stay a little longer. 'There's time! There's time! You haven't seen it all yet!' he cried. He stood up and walked over to the ancient TV and pulled out a file sitting under it. 'I've kept this since my days in the Red Army,' he said. 'It's fifty years old!'

The file had a title. *Alexei Izergovich Yakimov: Collected Works, vol. 1.* He laughed a little at that. Then he threw it open. It was full of brittle yellowing newspaper clippings.

'I wrote these,' he said. 'I wrote them all. I am an educated man, you see.'

He went through the clippings, forty years' worth, from Siberian newspapers, from Kazakh newspapers, from the local Mari newspapers. There were thousands and thousands of words, on the glories of Soviet construction, reports from building sites, tales of heroic labour – with the odd lyrical interlude on the joys of love or spring tossed in – stretching from the mid-1950s to the early 1990s.

'I wrote that, I wrote that,' he said. 'Look, that's me! Me!'

'All my life,' said Alexei, 'I've wanted to write a book. I never succeeded. But I'm writing one now . . . and, with God's help, I'll succeed.'

Suddenly Alexei's transformation from Soviet shock worker to High Priest made perfect sense. His remarkable story was in fact rather banal. His life was not so contradictory after all. There was a unifying theme: the drive for fame. He wanted to see his name in print. He wanted to be somebody. He had become High Priest and see: a journalist from Scotland had come to see him! They knew about him even in faraway lands!

Alexei had made a mistake: he shouldn't have shown me the clippings. It made him seem smaller to me.

I didn't want that.

51

By *smaller*, however, understand that I mean human and

flawed, that he was less of a miracle, that I could understand him. There had been mystery; now there was not. I do not mean that I considered him a fraud, adopting the mantle of High Priest solely to get the attention he craved. He believed in his gods with a simple, unanguished faith. That was obvious to me. But he also used them for his own, unspiritual ends. He had taken his faith and manipulated it to satisfy a deeply felt need for attention and recognition. But that it was a genuine belief I did not doubt.

However, when I got back to Moscow and told people about him the response was always the same: 'Ah! So he just wanted to be famous.'

This irritated me. It was so lacking in nuance, so lacking in sympathy. As if people wanted to negate him, to brush him aside. *Ah! So that's what it's all about. He's not really a pagan. He doesn't really believe in all this strange stuff.* Thus the unknown is banished and you are left with just a little lost man, a failure. The world becomes reasonable, comprehensible. The world becomes safe.

I found myself becoming defensive, protective of Alexei. But for some reason it was difficult to explain what I thought: that a man can believe but exploit his belief; that he can love, but abuse his love. Surely that's obvious?

People are complex and contradictory. People are messy. Alexei is both an egomaniac and a sincere worshipper of his gods. And furthermore, even though he is an egomaniac, I don't blame him. He wants to be great, to be famous. And why not? Why not demand big things? Why settle for the life of an electrician in Kazakhstan? I can't condemn him for it.

And I hope you, dear reader, will also resist the facile urge to dismiss him and allow him room to be both an egoist and a man inspired by ancient gods.

52

Dreams

I kept a notebook of my dreams in Yoshkar Ola. It was the bed that did it. Sleeping there, in the nuptial chamber, on the sheets of so many lovers, I wanted to see if the ghosts of coitus past came to haunt me in my sleep. Did those awkward first embraces leave any psychic traces on the room? So many lonely cocks entering so many desperate vaginas, all of them utterly alien to each other. Shuddering orgasms, shame, disappointment, the clinching of a deal. Surely, surely the atmosphere had to carry some hint, some reminder of the sad dramas that had reached the climax of their first act there?

The first night I dreamt nothing in particular. I think I replayed some of the conversations from the train and dreamt a little about my life in Moscow. I don't know. I couldn't remember properly when I woke up.

The second night, however, I had an interesting night vision. I was sitting, huddled into myself at the top of an escalator. People were riding up, and striding past, barely taking any notice of me. And I kept asking myself, *Don't they recognize my evil? Don't they see that I am evil?* But none of them did.

Then Alexei arrived. He showed me a chart listing all the people I had noticed and addressed in my mind. Then he began to explain which ones he had cursed, how and why.

On the third night I dreamt of Konstantin. He was going to America and it was my job to accompany him. But as the day of our departure approached I began to wonder if I was really up to the job. Could I care full time for a paraplegic? I'd not only have to wheel him around but also dress him, wash him, feed him, take him to the toilet. Wipe his arse. Pull up his pants. I grew more and more panicked and I was about to back out – then I realized we were already in New York and it was too late.

On my fourth night I dreamt I was standing in the middle of Yoshkar Ola, staring at an old notice stuck to a lamp-post. It was an advertisement for the circus. I gazed in wonder at the pictures of monkeys, elephants, clowns, balloons. Then I saw that the circus had already been and had long since moved on to another town. At exactly that moment a flock of pigeons began to flutter around me – at my shoulder, my eye-line, my waist, at my feet. I backed away from the announcement, trying to escape their embrace. Meanwhile a fierce old woman was glaring at me, as if I had upset the pigeons, or shouldn't be standing there thinking about the circus.

Actually, that last one wasn't a dream. It happened my first morning in the town. After the first three nights I didn't keep a dream diary. You need to write that stuff down as soon as you wake up. I couldn't be bothered. I preferred to sleep.

53

After Alexei had revealed his soul to me, I wandered back to my flat. I was confused and tired and I wanted solitude. Once I got there, however, I felt restless. I didn't want to stay in. So I called Masha and offered to speak to her students. She asked me to come around six. That gave me a couple of hours to sit in a chair staring into space, processing everything I had seen and done in the last couple of days.

It was a cold and icy walk to the pedagogical institute, and by the time I got there I was hungry. Her students were pleasant but shy and I couldn't be bothered talking. One of them asked me about haunted castles and I said, 'Yes, we have castles . . . and some of them are haunted.' Another asked me about traditional Scottish food and I talked about fried Mars bars for a while. I don't think they believed me.

Afterwards Masha walked me home. She reminded me she had a husband and also waffled on about Soviet film. I told her I thought Moscow was an evil city that devoured human souls. She didn't invite me back to her house for food.

54

Five easy faeces

One day, as I was leaving the flat, I was momentarily distracted by five fresh dog turds, resting on the mezzanine between the first and the ground floor.

It wasn't exactly a long journey to the patch of grass round the back of the building. The owner of this dog (or dogs – the turds looked like they belonged to a couple of yippy terriers) was evidently a very lazy person and a shockingly inconsiderate neighbour.

The turds sat there for three days. I watched them grow shrivelled and hard. Then, on the fourth day, they were gone.

I myself disappeared soon afterwards.

UDMURTIA

1

Shortly after my trip to Mari El I heard from both Joe and Yoshi. It was now almost three years since our first trip to Kazan. Yosh, the great voyager, had set fire to his car on top of a hill in Spain, and had flown back to Japan for good, planning to get a job and get married. Joe, meanwhile, was in England, where he had secured thrilling employment working for Prontaprint, designing bus-stop signs and doing the lay-out for Little Chef menus. I suppose that's life. You can't keep floating through the cosmos for ever. Sooner or later mission command orders you to return to earth.

But do you have to obey? Around this time, I had a dream where I saw a cosmonaut. He'd been orbiting the earth for years and had just received the order to return to human society. His days in space were over. But the cosmonaut, alone for so long, had grown estranged from people, and preferred solitude and the contemplation of the stars. And though not going home meant he was to drift in space for ever, floating amid dead rocks and dust clouds, that was what he loved, that was he wanted to do. So, ignoring his commander, he switched off the intercom, and set forth to drift eternally among the stars and planets.

The dream fascinated me. I thought the cosmonaut's action was noble, beautiful and even rational. He would live and die alone but, on the other hand, he would have the knowledge that he'd been true to himself, and what life he had left would be spent among the stars, in the deep dark infinity of space which he loved. Nobody would know what he discovered. Nobody would care. But it was interesting to him, and that was enough.

I admired this lost cosmonaut. I drew a picture of him and

hung it on my wall, above the maps of the republics in this book. I slept under those maps, that face. Each night I drifted through dreams. I never saw him again, though I often wondered how he was doing.

Like Joe and Yoshi I felt the pull of home. But I decided to ignore it.

2

I had decided to visit the Republic of Udmurtia, on the basis that it had a strange name that echoed the words 'ugly' and 'mud'. Apart from that I knew nothing. So I did some research and discovered that the capital, Izhevsk, was home to Mikhail Kalashnikov, inventor of the world famous AK-47 assault rifle. Infinitely more people have died from that gun than the victims of Hiroshima and Nagasaki combined. Kalashnikov was a genius of death. I found this encouraging. I had also read in a few Moscow tabloids that Udmurtia was crawling with serial killers, slaughtering their victims in the shadows of the factory smokestacks. That too was enticing.

But what about the Udmurt? I wondered. They, after all, were what I was really interested in – another tribe lost in the shadow of the Russian behemoth, dwelling in this forgotten Europe. After the proud Tatars, the frankly bizarre Kalmyks and the druids of Mari El I was eager to know what this particular lost nation was about.

3

The Udmurt, like the Mari, are a Finno-Ugric people, and their destinies have followed a similar path: colonized first by the Tatars, and then by the Russians, and forced to work as vassals for both. Only, where the Mari had fought against their dominators and maintained their beliefs, the Udmurt . . . hadn't.

No; not for the Udmurt were the pleasures of conquest and expansion, of raping and looting and pillaging. They'd never made war against anyone. They didn't want to force other tribes to bend the knee, to adopt their gods. When pressurized by the Russians they converted from nature worship to Christianity. Most of the time, however, they just ran away, retreating deeper into the forest.

The Udmurt had spent their existence farming and hunting and getting married and reproducing. Certainly they'd cooked up a religion and some folktales, and they had a separate language, but that doesn't take much effort. Every culture that has ever existed has done it. Humans do it by default. You can hardly praise them for it. The Udmurt had built no cities and written few books.

The Udmurt today constitute a small minority even in their own nominal homeland. They number only six hundred thousand, about 30 per cent of the republic. And they are in the process of assimilating to Russian culture completely. In villages the Udmurt language is still spoken, but it is rarely written. More and more Udmurt, however, are moving to the cities.

In fact, for many Udmurt, the process of assimilation is already complete. They have lost their language, their beliefs, everything. These people, I thought, were their own ghosts. They were a name, a memory, and that's all.

4

This, however, only made me keener to go. I was excited by the challenge. Most people choose to visit areas where the culture is exotic, where the inhabitants maintain their beliefs. I think they believe this is authentic in some way. Why not, however, visit one where the culture is already lost? Where assimilation is well under way? That, surely, is just as authentic, just as truthful. It's the trend the world is following, after all. It's why the French write language laws. Why so many Brits resist the EU, why Scotland kicks against England, why the individual kicks against death. We dread the loss of our identity. We want to be distinct, to leave a mark on the cosmos.

Yes, it was time to encounter a people who weren't clinging on for existence, who weren't asserting their importance. In Tatarstan, in Kalmykia, in Mari El I had encountered a ferocious straining, an attempt at self-assertion in the face of global indifference . . . The Udmurt, however, were doing something very different. They were . . . surrendering. Of course, that probably wasn't how they thought of it. But they were. It was a simple trade-off. In exchange for a better life – the jobs and educational possibilities of the city – they were letting go of themselves. That was the price – and it was a price more and more were willing to pay.

And why not? I thought. Why cling to identities that are just an accident of birth, after all? Why not shift to a new one? Ah, I thought. That's what I'll do. I'll stand up for the assimilators, the invisible ones. The meek shall inherit my book. I'll write a poem of praise to the peaceful.

5

Izhevsk, my Izhevsk

Ancient cities were built on rivers, next to seas, in deserts, along trade routes. Even after millennia these cities often preserve their original shape. Moscow is like this: circular ripples

246

Hammer and sickle, Izhmash plant, Izhevsk

of streets spreading outwards from the historic splash of the Kremlin on a hill. London, too, spreads along the bank of the Thames, like some nasty rash given the land by the river.

Izhevsk, on the other hand, is built around an ironworks, founded in 1760 by some Russian aristocrat or other. For a long time it was merely a collection of huts, a big village designed to house the serfs who worked the furnace.

Infractions in work discipline meant chains, the collar, beatings. Life was brutal. Russians, Tatars and Udmurt frequently ran away, disappearing into the surrounding forests. The masters of Russia, however, were pleased with the factory. They built a huge church to thank God for the many fine weapons it had produced for the country.

In the 1930s, however, the country had new masters. The church was destroyed and Izhevsk was declared the capital of the Udmurt homeland, even though few Udmurt lived in the city or worked in the foundry. Only the ironworks grew, spreading into a huge complex of factories named Izhmash that produced weapons, cars, motorbikes and heavy machinery. Udmurtia, home of a people who had never waged war against anybody, became the centre of the Russian arms industry. Fate sometimes favours a heavy-handed irony.

The main factory of Izhmash sits on the edge of a pond and has ten huge chimneys, which drool smoke into the sky above. It is surrounded by a labyrinth of streets without names, where nobody lives: there are only more factories and offices to service them. Those streets are not designed for walking. You take a bus or a car to the building you want, enter, and then exit. Inside the factories there are blast furnaces, melting iron, reducing the hard, dark substance to a bright seething liquid. Men work there, in masks, to shield their faces from the heat. Stick your arm into that hot light and it will disappear. Outside, meanwhile, the factory hums, it thrums. Its thrumming is carried on the wind throughout the streets of Izhevsk. It is the soundtrack, the backdrop to life.

And what lies beyond Izhmash? Well, there are . . . more factories. And of course, flats to contain the people – Russian, Tatar, Udmurt, Chuvash, Mari – who work in the factories. And there are cinemas and alcohol shops and also a circus, for when people grow bored of life at the furnace and crave a little distraction.

6

My railway carriage contained four humans. Aside from me, there was an old guy in a cheap shiny Russian suit and two women. The old guy liked to touch me. He touched my knee whenever he got up to go to the toilet. 'Excuse me,' he'd say, and then touch my knee. 'Excuse me,' he'd say when he sat down, and touch it again.

Maybe he was just being friendly. As for the women, they were divorcees in their early thirties. One was fat and blond, the other thin and a redhead. The redhead was very bitter. She bitched and whined a lot. In particular she bitched and whined about the old guy.

'Are you going all the way to Izhevsk?' she asked.

'I hope so,' he replied. 'How boring!' she exclaimed.

The old guy didn't reply. He was too startled. I said nothing at all for about an hour and then climbed on to my bunk where I was silent for the rest of the journey. That was about twenty hours of silence. It disturbed my travelling companions enormously, and gave me great pleasure.

7

The train stopped at several towns during the night. At around midnight the train wheezed to a halt and I heard a clamouring from outside. I looked up and saw a bizarre procession of crystal, vases, chandeliers, soft toys, even furniture, parading past the carriage windows.

Voices yelled at us to buy the goods. The hungry, desperate citizens of this town worked in factories that paid them in the items they produced, so the only way they could make cash was to flog things to the night trains that would stop for twenty minutes in their town.

The fat blonde got up to look. She smiled, and shook her head at the people on the platform.

'I don't want your stuff,' she said to one man, laughing. He was holding a giant teddy bear in his hand.

She was greatly enjoying herself, enjoying the separation, enjoying the sense that she had wealth and they had none. She was returning home to Izhevsk from Moscow after all, where she had no doubt been reminded continually that she was a poor hick from the provinces. Now it was her turn to feel big.

And thus the weak get their jollies lording it over those even weaker than they are.

8

Russian iron road

Russia, are you not speeding along like a fiery and matchless troika? Russia, where are you flying? Answer me. There is no answer. The bells are tinkling and filling the air with their wonderful pealing; the air is torn and thundering as it turns to wind; everything on earth comes flying past, and looking askance at her, other peoples and states move aside and make way.

As the train moved through the night I thought of this passage from Gogol's book *Dead Souls*. I often did when I travelled through Russia. It is a favourite quote of writers on the country; usually they are expressing how the Russians are a wild and crazy bunch and all that. I think it appeals to Westerners with withered souls sitting in armchairs, dreaming of a life of daring, of a land where there are still risks.

Well, I decided to answer Gogol's question once and for all by taking notes of everything I saw out the window from Moscow to Izhevsk. And I saw . . .

Fine, fine towns of concrete high rises and broad streets. The stations inform me they are called Arzamas, Zeleny Dol, Mozhg, and, my favourite, 92 km.

Enormous and filthy vats of oil.

Very strange machines with long arms and odd bodies. They sit on tracks, rusting. I cannot fathom their function. They look as though they have been designed expressly to rot and look ugly.

Trains rush by, and yet there are no passengers on them. The empty carriages are lined with wooden benches. The eye feels uncomfortable just looking upon them.

Huge factories lit up at night. I look inside, however, and see they are abandoned. Nothing moves. It is easy to imagine that this is their permanent state, that they must always be empty.

Small towns, seemingly without names, stranded by the side of the tracks. Indeed, names would be wasted on them. Why grant them an identity they do not have? They are holes, pits, for humans to live in.

A moment of poetic beauty: light reflected from the train on the edge of the neighbouring track. It gleams, dazzling, alongside us, and races from darkness into darkness.

Wooden homes, buried in the night. Mostly they are abandoned. Every now and then, however, a solitary light illuminates a single window in a vast plain of darkness.

Two men, squatting by a smoky fire about a hundred kilometres from Moscow. One of them has a thick beard and shaggy hair. *Are they fugitives?* I ask myself.

A prison: barracks, barbed wire. Watchtowers, where fat guards sleep, their guns propped up on their knees. Very grim in the March mud and slush. Painted on its walls, the legend: PEACE TO PLANET EARTH.

Under a glowering sky, a tin Pushkin stands next to some shacks.

So we can see: the troika is racing through a wasteland full of junk and poor people.

9

Journey to the centre of the room

I

The weather was extremely drab when I got off the train at about two in the afternoon. But that was OK, obviously there was no point seeing Udmurtia when it was nice. I wanted to see it in the conditions of the other forty-nine weeks of the year, the way its citizens saw it. I'd been worried that spring might break through before I got there, as it was mid-March. Fortunately that hadn't happened. It was cold and dismal in Izhevsk, with filthy, six-foot-high snowdrifts lining the roads and trees thrusting like dead black sticks out of frostbitten concrete. I took a cab to the Hotel Centralnaya, passing the Izhmash plant on the way. Driving up a hill, I saw its huge chimneys looming over the city. It was quite exciting, beautiful even – albeit in a bleak, dispiriting way.

Settling in my hotel, however, I was immediately struck by a feeling that I had no idea what I was doing. I had come in search of ghosts. How was I to explain it to people? How was I to explain it to myself? What the fuck did it mean?

Fortunately I had a plan. It was this: don't leave the hotel room. No, *stay there and fast!* Isn't that genius? Isn't that brilliant? I figured that no travel writer had ever done it before. Well, maybe it had happened, but no one had been honest enough to write about it, that was for sure. It would solve lots of problems too. I wouldn't have to find any food. I wouldn't have to find any entertainment. I wouldn't have to learn anything about the Udmurt. No, I'd just sit on my bed and meditate, and maybe have a few visions. It would be nice. Maybe I'd even draw some pictures or write a few short stories. I'd get hungry, of course, but it would be nothing compared to the hunger religious visionaries of earlier ages had suffered. No, it would be good. I could write in great detail about the architecture of my room and my relationship to it. It would be a first: an in-depth literary study of a hotel room in Izhevsk.

II

So, let us begin: the room was a narrow cubicle with a hard bed, a TV, a table, a chair and a small dresser with a phone book of the city in it. There was no phone, however. The wallpaper was a faded orange-yellow. No bathroom, no shower: just a sink with a single sorry tap that dribbled cold water. There was also a small radio above the bedstead that I couldn't switch off. I could only turn the volume down. There was only one station. People were talking about art and politics on it. And even with the volume down you could still hear them whispering.

My view was of the courtyard: a large concrete square, enclosed by the wings of the hotel. I could see, *Rear Window*-style, the rooms of other guests, but nobody was having sex or killing anybody, so that was disappointing. Written in the brickwork on the top floor was the legend: LET IT ALWAYS BE SUNNY.

My room was 'third class'. There were no second-class rooms. I could have paid for 'luxury', but I didn't want to. It

253

was three times as expensive and I wanted a certain amount of privation. It seemed indecent to travel to Udmurtia and be comfortable.

III

I unfolded the map on the table, studied it for a few minutes and then lay back on the bed, where I did a little work on constructing Izhevsk in my head, mainly focusing on a street in the west of the city where numerous serial killers lived. Near by there was a set of train tracks where, I decided, they liked to dispose of their victims' remains. The cops often found sacks of dismembered limbs there, left in skips, as the killers were comparatively tidy. Then I shifted my attention to another region, on Metallurgist Street, where there was a flat containing a man who liked to draw maps of the cosmos. It wasn't exactly our cosmos as he had added some extra planets to the solar system and invented other features: for example, Laika, the first dog in space had been transubstantiated and was now a divine sun located at the heart of all things. Nevertheless, he insisted that this was a true picture of creation. His walls were covered in intricate drawings and calculations. During the daylight hours he drove trams.

Maybe if I'd set my mind to it, I could have stayed in the room. Maybe I'd really have got into it, and started to enjoy myself. Alas, after about two hours my attention wandered and I began to feel self-conscious. What if the cleaning ladies came in and found me, half naked and in a trance? That would have been a tricky one to explain.

'Hi,' I'd say. 'I'm exploring your hotel room.'

Worst of all, curiosity had got the better of me. Reluctantly I got up and left to explore the city.

10

I wound up wandering up and down a grid of long streets for hours, amid Stalin-era apartments, cinemas and shops. Here, in the residential and commercial district, there was no sense of a centre, so I decided to create my own. I placed the circus, which I had glimpsed from the taxi en route to the station, at the heart of Izhevsk.

I like the circus. I like acrobats and illusionists and clowns. I like midgets. I like monkeys. I like bears on roller-skates. And I especially like it when the circus is cruel – like the time I saw some dwarfs and pinheads crucify a monkey in Kazakhstan. That was really good.

So I retraced the route of the taxi, going downhill, taking great care not to trip on the ice, which had a nice surface layer of water on it. And as I went my excitement mounted. When I arrived I saw that the circus was brand new, made of red bricks, with weird, futuristic neon lights attached to the walls. I became very happy indeed. The poster outside described a fantastic sounding show: *Snow White and the Seven Dwarves on Ice*. I let out a squeal of anticipation.

Then I walked up to the ticket office, and saw a notice taped to the window: 'Due to sickness among the artistes this weekend's shows have been cancelled.'

I staggered back on to the street, reeling from the disappointment. Nearby on the steps an old woman was clutching her ticket in rage, literally spitting in disgust. Her disappointed grandchildren hovered sad-eyed at her waist as great globules of flob rained down on the pavement around them.

'Now what are we to do?' barked the grandma.

It was a good question. I drifted back up the street towards the hotel, passed a strip joint and stopped outside a large, yellow neo-classical building with white columns that looked like a museum or a mansion but was actually a cinema.

I stepped inside. It was nice. They'd done it up. There was even a computerized floor plan, so you could choose your seat with great exactitude. Alas, then I studied the films advertised. *Blueberry,* a psychedelic French western starring Vincent Cassel and Juliette Lewis. Shit. *Brother Bear,* a Disney effort based on a theme-park ride, I think. Cumstain. *The House of Sand and Fog.* Some Oscar-nominated melodramatic tripe of great worthiness. Cancer lump. The only film that halfway tempted me was *The Last Samurai,* starring the mighty Tom Cruise. I figured it might have some fifteen or twenty minutes' worth of killing in it. Suddenly, however, I became aware of a braying and guffawing and cackling all around me. Teenagers. That was the last straw. The wise words of Thomas à Kempis in *The Imitation of Christ* came to me: 'Be seldom among young people and strangers.' I walked out.

Following this, I drifted around the city growing hungry and cold in the dark. I felt like a ghost, a wraith, some kind of insubstantial fleck. I was scared of being noticed, of being spoken to. I was worried that someone might realize I was a foreigner and ask me what I was doing in Udmurtia. I still hadn't found a decent answer. My journey to Izhevsk seemed pointless. I didn't understand what I was up to, though it had seemed to make sense in Moscow.

In the end my feet led me to a place called 'Mig Mag' an ersatz McDonald's located in the International University of Eastern Europe, an institution, surprisingly, I had never heard of. I located a quiet corner behind the door and sat myself down there, where I quickly polished off my *Big Mag* and fries. Mig Mag was obviously quite a big deal in Izhevsk as lots of young people kept coming in, dressed to the nines. Sitting there I felt safe and secure and, after eating, pulled out a notebook in which I wrote down lots of ideas. Among them were:

'The girls in Izhevsk are skinnier than the ones in Moscow.'
'Izhevsk is better than Yoshkar Ola.'
And –
'Izhevsk is about 30 per cent cheaper than Moscow.'

I was deeply moved. After a while, I began to see parallels between Mig Mag's interior design and the radical suprematist paintings of the great Russian avant-gardist painter Kazimir* Malevich. Indeed, I thought that whoever was responsible for the interior decor was a visionary.

I felt sad I would only have a few days to experience Mig Mag. I felt comfortable here. Nobody stared at me, and the food reminded me of food I had eaten at home. I even thought that Mig Mag was actually better than McDonald's. Then it occurred to me that I might be losing it, and it would probably be for the best if I returned to the hotel for the night. I did so, and vegged in front of Udmurt TV for a few hours before falling into a deep and dreamless sleep.

11

A note on the Udmurt language

There are many reasons not to learn Udmurt, and most of them are obvious. Nevertheless, the language adds a few extra arguments against itself through its extraordinary complexity. Those who studied German in school will recall getting annoyed at the language's four grammatical cases. Udmurt has many more: eight cases for animate objects and a full fifteen for inanimate ones. *But that's not all*: nouns and pro-

---

* Did you know that Charles Bronson's real name was Kazimir? Thought not.

nouns also change their endings for their first, second and third person forms, *and* for their singular and plural forms. Thus inanimate nouns have about two hundred possible endings for the speaker to juggle with.

As for verbs, Udmurt has six *past* tenses alone. Three of these have the curious function of indicating that something might have happened, but the speaker can't say for sure, as he didn't see it himself. Good getting that cleared up, then. Also intriguing are the special 'fictitious' suffixes that mean pretending to do something or, on the other hand, pretending not to. I've always thought English could do with some of those. Meanwhile, the word 'not' conjugates rather like a verb, and the verbs used with it have special forms. The only concession to simplicity is that there is no concept of gender. There aren't even separate words for 'he', 'she' or 'it'. But that isn't simple: it's just confusing.

Do people really speak this language?

12

Some other fine cities of the Udmurt Republic

VOTKINSK

Ah, Votkinsk! Founded in 1759 as an industrial community for an ironworks, today it is a bustling city with a population in excess of a hundred thousand. The city's main employer is the Votkinsk Engineering Plant (*Votkinsky mashinostroitelny zavod*).

GLAZOV

The city of Glazov is in the north of the Udmurt Republic, on the left bank of the river Cheptsa. Formerly the village of Glazovo, this fine town was granted urban status in 1780. It too has a population that exceeds a hundred thousand. The biggest industrial concern in the city is Cheptsa Mechanical Plant (*Chepetsky mekhanichesky zavod*).

SARAPUL

The city of Sarapul was founded in 1780 on the site of the village of Voznesenskoe and grew into a trade centre and port on the Kama river. Today the population stands at about a hundred and ten thousand. The light and food industries are of great significance in Sarapul.

KAMBARKA

In 1761 the village of Kambarka was established to house the workforce for G. Demidova's ironworks and is located on the left bank of the Kama river. Seventeen thousand people live in Kambarka, not far from a stockpile of the chemical weapon lewisite, which, fortunately, is scheduled for destruction before 2010.

MOZHGA

Mozhga began life in 1835 as a village for the employees of the Syuginsky Glass Factory (*Syuginsky stekolny zavod*). Fifty thousand souls live in Mozhga, the only industrial centre in the south-west part of Udmurtia.

13

Election Day

My second day in Udmurtia, 14 March 2004, was Election Day in Russia. Not only was President Vladimir Putin standing for re-election against an assortment of cranks and nobodies but the people of Udmurtia were electing a new president for their republic also. I thought it might be interest-

Izhmash. The black blobs in the picture are men fishing through holes they've drilled in the ice. There's not much to do in Izhevsk.

ing to observe both elections. It was something to do, after all. So after dragging myself out of bed I went out to find a polling booth and see what was going on.

While searching for a booth, I observed many interesting things. I saw old men sitting on the frozen Izhevsk pond, fishing through holes they had cut in the ice. I watched as my form was twisted into curious shapes in a hall of mirrors in the Summer Park. And then in the city bazaar my heart stopped as a beautiful, buxom, red-lipped girl beckoned me over to her stall to buy a slab of raw, bleeding liver. The one thing I didn't observe, however, was voting. I could see posters instructing people to vote (they didn't say who for, as it was covertly acknowledged Putin had no serious contenders) but no people.

Then at last, after about three hours of searching, I stumbled on a polling station. It was located inside a concert hall, and was identifiable by a set of flags at the entrance and loud, Russian pop music blasting out of speakers mounted over the doors. A steady trickle of people shambled in and out, not all of them pensioners.

In the lobby I found a bookshop and a stall selling cabbage pies. Following the stairs I came to the first floor of the concert hall. Up there I found a bored cop, two tables with a few cheerful ladies sitting at them, and on their right some cubicles with curtains where the people of Izhevsk were casting their votes. I was mildly paranoid that the cop might sense I was an alien and ask me what I was doing, but no such thing happened. In fact, the atmosphere was extremely mellow, almost like a holiday.

I started to observe. First, I observed the list of candidates for the Federal Election. Putin had recently tossed Russia's richest man in gaol for tax evasion and this seemed to have successfully scared off all his serious opponents. The leader of the Communists had declined to stand, nominating a deputy instead. Taking this logic further but going for laughs, Vladimir Zhirinovsky, leader of the ultra-nationalist LDPR, had nominated his bodyguard. I recognized only one candidate – the half-Japanese Irina Khakamada, a descendant of a samurai family, who represented the 'liberal' forces in Russian politics.

'Liberal' meant Yeltsin-era free-market radical. She was

running a vociferously anti-Putin campaign, claiming he was an enemy of freedom and an oppressor, etc., etc. There had indeed been a lot of hoo-ha in the world media about Putin crushing democracy, but I was rather sceptical. I had lived in Russia under Yeltsin and didn't believe the democracy he had achieved was worth preserving. It benefited only a tiny proportion of extremely rich thieves. The rest of the country was abandoned to starve and die, prematurely if at all possible.

After observing the Federal candidates I moved on to join a wizened old lady studying the Xeroxed mugshots of candidates for the Udmurt presidency. They were a grim-looking bunch. Underneath each picture, however, you could read lots of information about how many cars and homes each candidate had, what jobs he'd done, and how much money he had in the bank.

I found this fascinating. For example, the incumbent Alexander Volkov owned a hut that covered 32.4 square metres of land. I imagined the hut: was it a nice, new one, freshly painted? Or was it an old shabby shack, containing only a set of ancient rusty gardening tools?

I had read in the *Moscow Times* that Volkov faced a serious challenge from Yevgeni Ovdyannikov, a heart surgeon (who owned four cars). I was perplexed then to see Ovdyannikov's younger brother Yuri running a separate campaign. Aside from having the same name, they also had the same qualifications and job, about the same amount of money, and they looked pretty similar too. I wondered how one was supposed to choose between them.

Aside from the two Ovdyannikovs there were numerous other candidates, none of whom seemed to stand for anything. They were all independents running on little or no platform. My favourite was a man called Sergei Kletenkov. He had no job and no bank account. He was an ethnic Tatar, from Tatarstan, who lived in a flat that covered 63 square metres. He was thirty-eight years old, didn't live in Udmurtia and had no apparent reason for standing for election. Nor could he expect to get many votes. Nevertheless, judging by the smile on his face in the photograph, he was an extremely happy man.

This was all very perplexing, and I raised the question of Kletenkov and the two Ovdyannikovs a few days later with a local news reporter.

'Why would people vote for an unemployed Tatar who lives outside the republic?' I asked. 'And why would two brothers run against each other?'

'I don't know,' she said. She hadn't paid any attention to the Election. She, a professional journalist, hadn't even heard of the Tatar.

In fact, nobody had heard of Kletenkov. The Election was regarded with a mixture of despair and apathy. Volkov was not hated with the fervour Ilumzhinov's opponents feel. Nevertheless, he too was accused of wasting money on vanity projects (in his case a presidential palace, the new circus and a zoo) while ignoring the plight of the republic's poor. Nobody, however, doubted he would remain in power. One person I spoke to speculated that all the candidates were in Volkov's pocket: that the Tatar had been put up to attract the votes of Udmurtia's Tatar population, and that the two brothers were intentionally splitting each other's vote to ensure that neither challenge was too successful.

It seemed like a reasonable explanation to me. The next day it was announced that Volkov had won with 54.3 per cent of the vote. His nearest challenger, the elder Ovdyannikov had polled 19 per cent. Meanwhile, in the federal election, Putin won with over 70 per cent of the vote. All in all, it was a good day for the status quo.

14

'Udmurtia is Proud of You'

Taken from the public notice board on the central square:

Larissa Nikolaevna Pavlova – senior examining
    magistrate, Industrial Region, Izhevsk
Nikolai Alexandrovich Bezborodov – chief weapons
    constructor, Izhmash Factory, Izhevsk
Valery Fedorovich Vasev – head of collective farm,
    Sharkanski Region
Leonid Petrovich Chuvashov – combine-harvester driver,
    'Motherland' Collective Farm, Mozhginski Region
    Vladimir Vasilievich Semakin – Minister of Finance,
    Republic of Udmurtia
Ludmilla Ivanovna Vakhrusheva – therapist, Central
    Polyclinic, Sarapul
The employees of the Izhevsk Plastics Factory
The children and teachers of Kindergarten No. 30,
    Sarapul
The workers of the Svetlanskoy Bakery, Botkinsky Region
Viktor Vasilievich Grebenshikov – serial rapist and
    murderer, Kambarka

15

Two weeks before leaving Moscow I had contacted the international affairs section of the city of Izhevsk, asking for assistance in setting up interviews and meetings and that sort of
thing. I didn't think saying I was composing *an existential
voyage to the heart of non-being* would be very persuasive so
instead I explained I was writing a book that would reveal the
fascinating world of Russia's European republics to readers in
the West who knew nothing of it.

A man named Andrei Chulkin replied, excited by the project. He offered to set up interviews with significant personages in the republic. I decided to surrender myself to his ideas, and to the official representatives of Udmurtia. That way, I thought, I would see how the republic represented itself to me, and thus how it saw itself. It seemed to fit my plan of pursuing assimilation and integration.

The day after the Election I was sitting in Andrei's office. He was a thin young man in a cheap suit with melancholy eyes. He was busy on the phone trying to contact historians, artists and politicians. Unfortunately it was 9 a.m. on a Monday and none was around. He kept getting cleaners and security guards instead, and after he had introduced himself they would hang up. I sat in the corner, watching Andrei become more and more flustered and embarrassed.

It was my first visit to a provincial bureaucrat's office and it was depressing. The furniture was bulky and uncomfortable, the wallpaper was striped like prison pyjamas, and the computers were old and clunky. Everything was dark and grimy. Andrei himself seemed dwarfed by his surroundings. I imagined myself in his position. That made me more depressed, desperate even. I had experienced life as a civil servant briefly in Scotland and it had made me physically ill from boredom. What if I was trapped, like Andrei, in Izhevsk, struggling to climb the greasy pole of promotion for a couple of hundred dollars a month? An accident of birth was all that separated me from him. Promoting Udmurtia to the outside world might be a strange task, but it's no stranger than most of the other pointless tasks we occupy ourselves with.

Andrei hung up the phone. 'The problem is', he said, 'that nothing opens until ten.'

'I see,' I said.

Silence hung in the air.

'You know,' he said, 'if you really want to see Udmurt culture, you should go to the villages. We have a reconstructed village, a museum reserve you could visit.'

'Ah,' I said, and let the suggestion die in the silence.

'Hm,' he said.

We were silent again.

'What about the Tchaikovsky Museum? Tchaikovsky was born in Udmurtia, you know.'

'Yes,' I said.

Silence.

'Are you Russian or Udmurt?' I asked. I was sure he was Russian, but I wanted to see how he reacted.

'Russian, of course,' he replied, looking at me curiously.

Silence.

'What about the Election? Who won?' I asked.

'Volkov . . .' He paused and now gave me a long, wary look, as if I was a spy.

I decided to keep quiet and let him get on with organizing some meetings. Eventually he managed to get through to some people. Then he drew some maps and marched me into the corridor, clearly anxious to get me out of his office as quickly as possible.

'*Goodbye!*' he said, pushing me into the lift. The doors closed. And that was that.

16

Udmurtspotting 1

'Do you see that boy there?'

   'The one with red hair?'

   'Yes. He is almost definitely an Udmurt.'

   'How do you know?'

The building of the Izhevsk City Administration. Some people spend their entire working lives here.

'The colour of the hair . . . the freckles . . . the high cheek-bones . . . the slitty eyes . . . these are usually the signs of an Udmurt.'

'I see.'

17

I took the bus back to the central square and followed Andrei's map to the Municipal Gallery. It led me directly to a shopping centre. I stood there confused for a bit, until round the side I found a small door. After rechecking the map a few times I stepped inside. A woman was sitting at a desk next to a pile of tickets. I introduced myself. She looked puzzled.

'Who sent you?'

'Andrei Chulkin, from the City Administration.'

'Who?'

I showed her a piece of paper Andrei had given me. It had a name on it: Natalia Gennadievna.

'Natalia Gennadievna is unavailable right now. Maybe you can wait?'

'No, it's all right,' I said cheerfully. 'I'll go in and have a look around.'

I paid five times the Russian ticket price to enter. Evidently my connection to the City Administration and status as a 'journalist' didn't count for much, nor indeed my holy task as a chronicler of the Udmurt. I was just another foreigner to be milked.

The exhibition was called *The Light from Icons* and it was very boring. There were lots of pictures of Jesus and angels on the walls. I had no idea why Andrei had sent me. I was about to cut loose when suddenly a small, round woman with glasses appeared at my shoulder.

'I am Natalia Gennadievna. How can I help you?'

'Er . . .' I said.

I had no idea if she could help me or not. Andrei had been so quick to get me out the door he hadn't actually told me anything about who I was going to see or what he'd arranged. As for me, I wasn't sure either. The doubt I had been experiencing since I'd got on the train had not gone away. What was I looking for? I kept forgetting.

'Er . . .' I said. 'I'm writing a book about Udmurtia . . .' Apart from that I couldn't think of anything else to say. I stared at her blankly. She stared back.

'Well,' she said. 'I have a tour group to show round right now. Maybe you can look around yourself and come to the office later. Then I'll be happy to answer any questions you may have thought of . . .' And with that, she vanished.

There was a partition in the gallery, and behind it I could see some pictures of Mikhail Kalashnikov. That seemed more interesting. There was no way into the exhibit from the icon room, however, so I went back into the corridor to find an entrance. The door was locked. A passing cleaner explained: 'You have to pay for that one separately.' I returned to the ticket woman and paid five times the Russian price. An aged woman came and escorted me to the hall. Once we were in, the aged woman sat in the corner keeping an eye on me in case I tried to steal things.

18

A short history of the Kalashnikov

Mikhail Timofeevich Kalashnikov was born to a peasant family in the Altai region on 10 November 1919. Thirty years later he received the Stalin Prize for inventing one of the greatest killing machines in human history. By the mid-1990s the AK-47, or one of its later modifications, was in use in fifty-five countries around the world and had killed more people than the Hiroshima bomb.

Kalashnikov was a tank sergeant in World War II but after being wounded was evacuated to Kazan, where his recovery took longer than anticipated. And so, stuck in Tatarstan, miles from the front, he began thinking of other ways to help the war effort. His early efforts at rifle design were rejected, but deemed promising enough for the Soviet authorities to send the young Kalashnikov to work with some of the great gun designers of the era.

In Kazakhstan he produced the first prototype of what was to become the legendary AK-47. After successful testing it actually entered mass service in 1949, the same year he won the Stalin Prize and became chief weapons designer at the Izhmash plant, a position he held until his son Viktor took over (although Kalashnikov senior remains an adviser at the plant).

Kalashnikov's rifle, however, was patented only in 1997, by which time something like 70 million were already in use all over the world, in some fine countries in Africa, and also Afghanistan and Vietnam. The Izhmash plant hired a foreign legal firm to track down its royalties and prosecute countries producing pirated versions of the weapon. A licence to manufacture Kalashnikovs costs between six and ten million dollars. It is already produced in nineteen countries, among them not only the usual suspects such as Egypt, Israel, India and China, but also peace-loving Holland and Sweden.

By contrast only 7 million models of the American assault rifle, the M-16 are in circulation. Perhaps it is a question of price, but the Kalashnikov is also lightweight and easy to dismantle. The average blindfolded schoolboy in the Soviet Union could take one apart in thirty seconds.

The Kalashnikov, however, is more than just an instrument of death. It's a cultural icon. You can listen to the song, you can buy the T-shirt. Perhaps the most beautiful use of the AK-47 image, however, is on the national flag of Mozambique. It was adopted in 1973 after a war with Portugal as a symbol of freedom. A few years down the line, however, it was felt that the symbol was too militaristic, and efforts were made to find a new national emblem. The people of Mozambique, however, liked the rifle and it stayed.

19

Among the exhibits on display were a rack of AK-47s,

Kalashnikov's drawing board from the 1950s and some certificates and awards he had received, including the one from Joey Stalin himself. Then there was a reconstruction of the Kalashnikov living room in the 1970s, his exercise bike and, on the walls, photos of the great man – though it seemed nobody had owned a camera in the K. family between 1950 and 1990. Thus Kalashnikov appeared solely as a benign, smiling old codger with slightly Asiatic features and a pot belly. Always laughing, always joking, salt of the earth. There he was, laughing with his son, his grandkids, his wife and President Volkov. Oh, and Colonel Qaddafi.

Before leaving Moscow I had managed to find Kalashnikov's fax number and contacted him for an interview. Kalashnikov wasn't Udmurt and had nothing at all to do with the theme of my journeys. But it was hard to resist. I wanted to shake him by the hand and look into his eyes.

My letter to Kalashnikov was very flattering. I referred to him as 'by far the most significant figure in the Udmurt Republic' and said nice things about his achievements. A few days passed without any reply, and then at last a thin piece of tissue paper rattled through my fax machine. It said:

Gospodin Kolderr!

Unfortunately I am not giving any interviews to anybody at all right now because I am too busy writing my own book about my life and experiences. Indeed, this book may one day see print in English and many other languages.

If you are interested in my life and work may I suggest that you visit the bookshops in Izhevsk while you are in Udmurtia. There you will find copies of several books about me and by me.

If you need still more information about me, perhaps it

will be possible for you to talk with one of my representatives.

Regards

M. Kalashnikov

P.S. Word on the street is that you're a cunt.

He had signed the letter himself, in the shaky scrawl of a very old man marked for death. I hastily composed a reply and fired it back to him. It said: 'Fuck you, old man.'

20

Kalashnikov, of course, is a legend, but nowhere more so than in Udmurtia, where he is a small god, the only world-famous citizen in the entire republic. Kalashnikov was mentioned on every website and Udmurtia's tourist brochures featured him prominently. 'You might even have a chance to meet him,' they promised. In a local bookshop I found a book signed by Kalashnikov going for $50, and also a weird painting of the city with his face hovering over it, like some ancient wizened deity. In the Izhmash Museum, meanwhile, along with every edition of his rifle, there were yet more pictures of the grinning weapons designer, this time posing alongside world leaders, African mayors and the Patriarch of the Orthodox Church. It reminded me a little of Ilumzhinov's personality cult in Elista, only these people had come to see Kalashnikov and not vice versa. They got kudos from him.

Myself, I had some doubts as to whether K. ought to be thus fêted. Robert Oppenheimer at least had some regrets about the bomb he created. Kalashnikov's glee at designing the world's top gun could hardly be contained. He walked with a laugh, bursting with pleasure. Of course, world peace is a fantasy and John Lennon's trite 'Imagine' makes me puke.

War is inevitable. Nevertheless Kalashnikov could at least have feigned a little thoughtfulness.

A modicum of decorum, please.

21

But wait, what's Kalashnikov got to do with anything? I was in search of the Udmurt, not some wily old fuck gun design-er . . .

I knocked on the door of Natalia Gennadievna's office and stepped inside.

'Come in, come in!' she said, indicating a seat. 'Now how can I help you?'

I was better prepared this time. 'I'm writing a book about Udmurtia and the Udmurt,' I said. 'And we must assume that the reader knows nothing. I want the basics about the Udmurt people, their history, their relations with the Russians.'

'Well, I can't help you,' she said. 'I'm Russian. We're all Russians here.' The two other women in the office laughed. 'All I can tell you about is Izhevsk.'

It turned out that Andrei had sent me to see a tour guide who worked in this gallery, which featured exhibits by local artists. Even so I figured she had to know something, so I switched on my tape-recorder and started asking questions. And indeed, she could hold forth on many subjects at great length. She knew a lot about the Izhmash plant, for example. She told me that Russia's first motorcycles had been manufac-tured in the city and knew when the first one had rolled off the production line, giving me the serial number of the specif-ic model. Then she told me some stuff about Kalashnikov, Izhmash and the founding of the city. But when it came to the Udmurt . . . well, frankly she knew fuck all, as my mother would say.

'What can you tell me about Udmurt cosmogony?' I asked.

'Eh?'

'About their gods, their creation myths, that sort of thing?'

'Er . . . they had many gods and they sacrificed animals to them.'

'OK, but what about the creation of the universe? How did it happen?'

'No idea. Why don't I tell you about our Year of Culture? Did you know that Izhevsk is City of Culture for the Lower Volga Region in 2004?'

'Oh, really? What does that mean?'

'Well we're having some film retrospectives . . . that sort of thing.'

'For example?'

'Er . . . I think there's going to be a festival of French cinema. But I don't have the programme in front of me right now.'

I tried to steer her back to the Udmurt.

'What about the Udmurt character? In what way are they different from Russians?'

I was sure she'd have an answer for this. Russians are very good at talking about their souls and what distinguishes them from the other nations on earth. Sure enough, Natalia Gennadievna thought a bit and then she spoke.

'Well, you see, we Russians are a very open people, very friendly, with strong emotions. But the Udmurt – they're very shy. Very closed. They prefer to stay in their communities. Now, however, more and more are coming to the cities for work. And it's very sad, but when they come, they assimilate completely – they lose their language, their history, everything.'

After that she talked a lot about Izhevsk's new circus. She was a great admirer of the circus art and told me that one of Russia's great bear-tamers, Ivan Kudriantsev, came from the

Monument to the friendship of the Russian and Udmurt peoples

republic. As she described him I developed a strong feeling that I had actually seen him perform in Volgograd, where a man in a top hat had made a bear roll downhill on a skateboard on its front paws. That was pretty cool. When I asked if he was Udmurt or Russian, however, she couldn't tell me.

'Udmurt . . . I think.'

I thanked her, and left.

22

How Udmurts turn into pigs: a true story

When I was in America I met an Udmurt girl. She was washing dishes in the same camp as me. Anyway, she told me a story about her village. A witch had cast a spell on her to bind her to a man she did not love. The thing is, the spell really worked. She couldn't leave this guy, and was full of fear. She became depressed all the time. In the end she had to go to another village to have the spell lifted. And then, of course, she could never go home. She moved to the city and hasn't been back to her village since.

But that's not all. She told me that in her village there was an old woman who could turn into a pig. Or at least that's what people believed. This is what happened: a pig got loose and rampaged around the village. The people chased it, but they couldn't catch it. Eventually it broke into somebody's house and started destroying everything. The man who owned the house jumped on the pig and tried to stop it, in the process tearing its ear. Then the pig charged out the door, through the gate and was never seen again. It disappeared into the forest, where, one might expect, some wolves made a meal of it.

But living in the village there was an old woman. And the

next day she appeared with a bent ear. The residents of the village looked at each other and nodded wisely. The old woman and the pig, it was clear, were one and the same. The old woman was a witch, and one with powerful magic besides.

23

Udmurtspotting 2

A couple of times on the street I stopped and tried to spot some Udmurt. I'd been told that they constituted 20 per cent of the populace. On the one hand, it didn't sound like much. On the other hand, it meant that for every fifth person that passed, one of them was an Udmurt – and that did sound like a lot. So I'd stand there looking – but I could never tell. It was pointless.

24

It wasn't Natalia Gennadievna's fault that she couldn't tell me much about the Udmurt, of course. That wasn't her job. She'd been trained to memorize facts about Soviet factories and great Communists of the region.

However, about twenty-four hours later, I found myself in the State Museum, awaiting an audience with some real experts on Udmurt culture. That, at least, was what Andrei had told me.

'I've come to explore the interconnectedness of Udmurt and Russian culture,' I explained to the museum director.

'Ah,' she said. 'Then I'd better find someone from our Ethnology department.'

A few minutes later a slim, middle-aged lady with cropped, bleach-blonde hair arrived.

'I am the ethnographer,' she said. 'How can I help you?'

'I've come to find out about the Udmurt,' I said. 'Their history, their culture. I want to explore their soul.'

'Hm,' she said. Her brow furrowed. 'Well, we've got nothing about that here. We do have an exhibition on the life of Udmurt women and national holidays, however. What if I tell you about that instead?'

25

She showed me a dead tree stump that had multi-coloured rags tied to it. It made me think of the sacred oak Alexei had led me to in Yoshkar Ola.

'Udmurt women liked to tie ribbons to trees on holidays,' she said.

Yes, I thought, quite excited. *This sounds good. Nice and juicy.* I knew the ancient Udmurt had an ancestor cult, and that they believed their forefathers lived on beneath the earth. I also knew that the ribbons on the trees were connected to this belief somehow. However, the guide was already moving on to the next exhibit.

'Wait,' I said.

'Yes?'

'Why did they tie the ribbons to the trees?'

'Er . . . different reasons,' she said, getting ready to move again.

'But what do the different colours represent?'

She hesitated. 'Er . . . different things.'

'What about the blue one, for example?

'Well, I can tell you that the white one represents purity.'

I could tell I was making her uncomfortable, so I allowed her to move on. Next she showed me what I can only describe as some wooden . . . things. I knew they were used for making clothes, but that was only because I had seen them in a museum of wooden architecture in Novgorod where the information was also provided in English. She banged on about them for a very long time. Andrei had kindly furnished me with an interpreter, a student from a local institute called Feodor. But Feodor wasn't able to help much as the vocabulary of flax preparation had somehow never been included in his course of study. He kept saying things like: 'And then they'd do . . . something . . . with this . . . thing . . . before taking the . . . stuff . . . to another . . . thing.'

It didn't bother me, though. I didn't give a fuck about the 'things'– they were evidence that peasant life was rather hard and rather dull. No revelations there. I just kept on nodding politely, hoping she'd hurry up and finish.

After spending about fifteen minutes at the 'things' she showed us some dummies in national dress. As she rambled on I noticed she was using the word 'Russian', 'Udmurt' and even 'Chuvash' interchangeably. More than anything else, however, she used the word 'Russian'.

'Wait a minute,' I said. 'Are you talking about the Russians or the Udmurt?'

'Oh, er . . .' she said, 'There's no difference. The two cultures have been intertwined for so long that it's really impossible to distinguish which traditions belong to which people.'

Yeah, right, I thought. *If you asked a Chuvash or an Udmurt, I'm sure they'd be able to tell the difference.*

The Russian/Udmurt obfuscation didn't shock me, however. On the contrary, it was exactly what I'd expected. The Soviet Union had spent the best part of its existence systematically eradicating national differences. The people running the museum had grown up under that system. Furthermore, regardless of whatever lip service it paid to multiculturalism, the Russian state probably still thought assimilation and integration were good ideas. Pretty clothes, pretty festivals, but we're all the same really. No mention of the fact that the Udmurt were still sacrificing horses to the sun god long after the Russians had been Christianized. No mention of Udmurt attitudes to their colonial masters. No mention of resistance, resentment, dissent. No, there were no differences. Just: this wooden thing is a different colour from that wooden thing. This necklace was a little more elaborate than that necklace. What lay under these cultures, what gave fire to them, what gods they worshipped – that was left well alone.

On reflection, though, there's nothing particularly Russian about that. It's the norm in all 'multicultural' societies, liberal or not. Minorities may be allowed their traditional clothes, picturesque festivals and tasty food – but the secular law of the state always triumphs over whatever religious customs the immigrants have brought. The goal is and always will be the marginalization and neutralization of the minority culture, regardless of what official voices say.

Anyway, I listened to the woman for about an hour. But I can't recall anything more about what she said. It was mind-rape and I just clenched my teeth and waited for it to finish. We were at the last tableau in the exhibit when I woke up again. It was a dummy of an Udmurt girl getting dressed for her wedding – and the guide was droning on about the wedding customs of Russians and Udmurts. They were pretty much the same of course: both societies married their girls off young; both societies demanded dowries.

'But', said my guide, 'I think perhaps the Udmurt festival was more elaborate and . . . prettier.'

I was quite startled by this sudden expression of . . . opinion . . . of judgement. She didn't say why she thought the Udmurt ceremony was better. There was no evidence, no argument. Only: 'But maybe that's because I am an Udmurtka.'

26

Up until that point I had assumed she was Russian. She looked like a Russian; she dressed like a Russian. And she spoke about the Udmurt as if they were Russians.

Ah well, Natalia Gennadievna had told me that the Udmurt assimilated, that they lost their language and culture. With that would go most of their sense of themselves also. That's the ultimate colonization: when you see yourself through the eyes of your colonizer. That's what had happened to this woman.

It's inevitable. The Udmurt number only six hundred thousand. The Russians number well over 100 million. Perhaps the only reason these nations survive is because the Russian empire has always been sloppy. If the Udmurt had been based in the US, for example, they'd have been absorbed long ago. There used to be over sixteen hundred Indian languages: now there are almost none. There are still a hundred and thirty languages in Russia, however, which has been trying to stamp them out for longer.

In the modern world, however, it's forbidden to crush and absorb minorities entirely. Unless you're a psychotic Third World dictator, and even then it's not really approved of. The Udmurt, then, I thought, are condemned to a long twilight. They will continue to assimilate, but they'll never be allowed to assimilate fully. There will always be the word 'Udmurt' hanging over them, preventing them from identifying fully with the only culture they have: Russian. That is their destiny: even when they are no longer Udmurt, they will still be 'Udmurt'.

Suddenly I felt very sympathetic towards this woman. I thanked her and smiled. She smiled back. I looked in her features for something I could recognize, something I could take away with me as Udmurt, as a sign of who she was. High cheekbones? Ginger hair?

There was nothing. Nothing at all.

27

Udmurtspotting 3

There was a huge billboard across the street from the Central Hotel. On it there was an enormous photograph of a smiling woman in traditional Udmurt dress. The costume was pretty fantastical: a long pointed hat, long dangly earrings, lots of jewellery, and a red-and-white dress. It looked like a costume from *Star Trek*. The legend read: IZHEVSK, CAPITAL OF UDMURTIA. I couldn't focus on it for very long, however, because it was one of those billboards that changes, and it had two other images on it. The picture kept vanishing to be replaced by an advert for cars and then by another, for vodka.

28

The Udmurt State Theatre

I

My meetings weren't going quite as I'd expected. I was hoping that Andrei would provide me with a golden key to the offices of the movers and shakers in the republic: the top historians, writers and politicians. He had hinted I might get to meet the Prime Minister. But I had been in Izhevsk for days and the people felt far away, as unreal as ever. Perhaps it was inevitable. Indeed, I hadn't come expecting to find some essential quality, but nevertheless I felt I had . . . missed somehow. I was still outside, lost, unconnected.

I was optimistic for my next encounter, however, in the

Udmurt State Theatre. For a start, it was not Andrei's idea, but mine. I'd been dismissive of 'national theatres' in my journeys to the other republics because I thought they were artificial creations of the Soviet state without any origins in the authentic culture of the people they were supposed to represent. Indeed, if you look back at my section on Tatarstan you'll see that I referred to the Tatar National Theatre fleetingly and noted that pigeons were crapping on it. Now, however, I thought this was presumptuous on my part. Perhaps travel had done what it was supposed to do: broadened my mind. Now, I asked myself, who was I to decide what was 'authentic' and what was not? And, furthermore, did it really matter? Might not the Udmurt people find value in it, even though it was not their creation? All cultures borrow, steal and mutate forms they take from other sources.

On a simpler note, I also thought it would be interesting to have a look around one anyway, as I like theatres. I wanted to meet the director, and get a backstage tour.

II

The Udmurt State Theatre was located on the ground floor of what looked like a university dormitory, across the street from the Central House of Metallurgists and Izhevsk's main Cathedral. The Cathedral, one of the only pre-Revolutionary structures in the city, had a beautiful golden spire. It sparkled against the drear greyness of the sky and the dissolving mounds of slush in the street.

I entered the theatre vestibule and spoke to the woman behind the ticket window, introducing myself and explaining that Andrei Chulkin of the City Administration had sent me. She hadn't heard of me and knew nothing about my visit. I heard some discussion and then the door to the lobby opened.

All Mice Love Cheese

A man with glittering eyes and a black goatee resembling the Master in *Dr Who* asked me who I wanted. Andrei had given me a piece of paper with a name on it. I showed it to him.

As soon as the Master saw that he smiled. 'Ah! You are very lucky! Anna Yakovlevna has been with the theatre for many years and knows all about our actors and our history. Please, follow me.'

III

Originally I had planned to attend a performance at the Udmurt Theatre. I wanted to hear the language, to see the stars of this most obscure of troupes, to be exposed to a world of stories I knew nothing about. Andrei hadn't been too keen on me attending, however. Nor had the managers of the theatre. There was going to be only one performance that week, and it was for children between the ages of three and five. It was called *All Mice Love Cheese*. Furthermore, it was in Russian.

Nevertheless, I planned to attend. But Andrei had set up my meeting with Natalia Gennadievna for when it was on, and thus thwarted me.

IV

The Master walked quickly, leading me up stairs, along corridors, past a display of photographs. Along the way we passed something shaped like an enormous head covered in tarpaulin, crowned with a large conical red cap.

'That's Lenin,' he said. 'Used to stand in the foyer. Our young actors . . . transformed him.'

Anna Yakovlevna, at least, was expecting me. When the Master opened the door to her office she leapt to her feet. 'Ah, the journalist! Please come in!'

Anna Yakovlevna had a very simple office: an old table, a

285

wardrobe and a bookshelf. I knew the tale of this theatre already, familiar from a thousand feature articles on Russia. It was the same as the story of the Planetarium in Yoshkar Ola: an under-funded public institution kept alive by an ageing group of enthusiasts as the country's leaders concentrated on enriching themselves.

Anna Yakovlevna, however, was energetic and enthusiastic. She had curly hair and soft, puffy cheeks and there was warmth in her eyes. She also talked nineteen to the dozen. Though in her seventies, she was still alert, eager, hungry for experience. The problem was that once again I had no idea who she was, or what she did. I had asked to talk to the theatre's director. It wasn't her. Not wanting to betray my ignorance, I launched into my pre-prepared spiel: 'I'd like to find out about Udmurt literature. Who are the great writers, the poets of your people?'

The lustre in Elena Pavlovna's eyes faded. 'I can't help you there,' she said. 'I'm not a specialist. You should talk to someone in the Philology department of the University. Or maybe the head of the Udmurt Writers' Union. I only know about the theatre. I'm the literary director here.'

'No, no, that's fine. Maybe you can tell me about the theatre.'

v

The Udmurt Theatre is less than a hundred years old. It was born in the 1920s, and before that there was nothing.

It had its origins in the Udmurt Club, a group of newly urbanized Udmurt proletarians keen on self-improvement. The members embraced socialism: it gave them opportunities they could never have dreamed of under the Tsar. Their ancestors had languished in poverty, slaves to tyranny, superstition and a primitive religion. Under the Bolsheviks, however, the Udmurt had the same cultural possibilities as Russians; the

286

members of the club were electrified by their sudden access to literature and art. They organized poetry readings and amateur theatrics. Anna Yakovlevna's father, Yakov Nikolaevich Perevoshikov, was a member, one of the first generation of Udmurt actors. 'He was a great Communist,' she said. 'He loved Lenin.'

The first professional troupe was formed in the 1930s, when some members of the club returned from the drama schools in St Petersburg and Moscow. With the aid of Udmurtia's Russian cultural commissar they set up a theatre, and the golden age began. Gavrilov, their greatest dramatist, was writing then and their great director, Kuzma Alexeeich Lozhkin, put on show after show of outstanding quality.

VI

By the 1950s, when the theatre's second generation of actors took to the stage, it already had a rich repertoire. Anna Yakovlevna told me of many plays: there were productions of *Buzh Multan*, *Shundi Mumi*, *Zibeg Zurka* and *Valo Op Kyasheta*. She translated the titles, but I chose not to write them down. I preferred them in Udmurt. They were better that way, inaccessible, retaining a sense of their otherness. One, however, I did put in my notebook. Its theme was the clash of the modern world with the old. *Chagir Sinyos* ('Blue Eyes') told the story of a socialist doctor coming to a village to perform an operation and his struggle to overcome the superstition and fear of the Udmurt peasants, who were frightened by his new methods.

There were also plays about the cruelty of the Tsar. Gavrilov wrote an acclaimed and much revived play about the Russian radical Korolenko, who successfully defended in court a group of Udmurt peasants accused of sacrificing

287

human victims to their pagan gods in the nineteenth century. This is a true story.* Korolenko had been exiled by the Tsar and had lived among the Udmurt. He knew they were kind and peace-loving people, and that the accusations of murder were Imperialist slander. From its inception the theatre produced plays by the great Russian dramatist Ostrovsky, and also Carlo Goldoni. Shakespeare, however, has never been translated into Udmurt, and thus has never been performed on the stage.

There was, however, a successful play about Lenin himself. The role of the Father of the Revolution was played by Vasili Yakovlevich Perevoshikov (1928–1986), the greatest actor in the history of the Udmurt theatre. He, coincidentally, was Anna Yakovlevna's brother.

VII

But they are all dead now, these great ones. As she told the story and showed me photos, old sepia pictures, curling at the edges, she kept repeating this phrase: 'But he has left this world'; 'She has left this world'; 'He also has left this world'. Everyone from the first generation had left this world. The same for the second. The only survivor was Anna Yakovlevna's sister-in-law, Nina Bakusheva, who is now retired. Anna Yakovlevna showed me some photographs of Bakusheva: 'Look at the transformations,' she said. 'They are amazing.'

And it was true, they were. Bakusheva was a peasant in one picture, a flapper in the next, a mourning wife in the next, a

---

* It took place on the territory of modern Tatarstan. Indeed, I mentioned it in on page 50. It took place in Elabuga, one of the cities I never visited. When I didn't go there, however, I didn't know that it was a group of Udmurt who had allegedly committed ritual murder. Not that it would have made any difference, of course. I still wouldn't have gone.

fairytale character in another . . . She seemed to flit from face to face, from identity to identity, with incredible ease, adopting and shedding roles like a snake does its skin. Suddenly, sitting there, I felt the power of the theatre, the magic of the actor, who shifts, slides from role to role, like a Corinthian, a chameleon. So much history! So much magic! Here in this dirty old building in this lost quarter of the earth . . . it was like a whole cosmos. Sitting there with Anna Yakovlevna I felt privileged and excited, like I had discovered a secret world of wonders. My doubts vanished. This was what I had come for, this, discovery, surely, was the point of all journeys. I felt honoured to have seen her brother, the first Udmurt Lenin . . . I was proud that I would carry his memory out there, into the world beyond, and keep it alive a little longer at least . . .

x

Afterwards I asked Anna Yakovlevna to take me backstage. I remembered how I had felt a sense of missed opportunity at the Youth Theatre in Kalmykia. There I had simply shaken hands and smiled coyly at the performers, too dumb and inexperienced to know what else to do. This time, I resolved, I was not going to fail. I was going to see what I had missed. I was going to connect.

I took pictures of wigs, rehearsal rooms, dressing rooms, costumes, actors and actresses. Many of the actors, however, were reluctant to be photographed. Even when Anna Yakovlevna asked them to 'do it for the people of Scotland' they scurried away, into rooms, down steps, avoiding my camera's eye.

One girl, however, was willing. Her name was Olga, and she knew exactly how she wanted to be pictured: sitting at her dressing table, looking into the mirror, applying lipstick. It was a classic pose – one I'd seen it before, in magazines, in

Olga Gavrilova, artiste of the Udmurt State Theatre

pop-music videos, though I couldn't remember which ones. I knew she'd rehearsed it many times.

Another woman allowed me to photograph her in national dress. She stared down at me, fierce and proud, against a backdrop of Lenin heads and theatrical posters. However, she shared her dressing room with another actress, who was openly hostile.

'This is all very pathetic for you, isn't it?'

'Excuse me?'

'You see our poverty, you see how little we have. You think it's pathetic, don't you? That's why you want to take pictures: to record our squalor.'

'No,' I said. 'It's not true.'

'You deny it, but I see it in your eyes. We are pathetic; this is pathetic. You are laughing at us.'

Perhaps I could have told her that I had lived in Russia for years, and that I was no longer shocked or titillated by poverty, that, on the contrary, it was very banal to me. However, I found that after listening to Anna Yakovlevna for three hours, my brain had seized up and I couldn't articulate a defence of myself. All I could do was say, *No*.

It wasn't true: I wasn't laughing at anybody. That wasn't why I was taking the pictures. I had never been backstage at a theatre before and I wanted a memento. My motive was simple and pure, naive even. But how could I explain myself? She wouldn't have believed me.

Anyway, what did it matter if one person chose to dislike me? Not at all. She was welcome to her hate.

29

Foreigners

There was a foreigner in the room next to mine. I think he was German, though I only ever heard him speak English. Every morning at 8 a.m. there was a knock at his door and he'd open it to two Russian guys, who walked with heavy footsteps and spoke in deep voices. One of them had no English at all and was silent, emitting only the occasional grunt. The other always said, 'Now you are coming with us. Let us have breakfast.'

I saw them only once, and very briefly, on my last night in the hotel. Two big Russian guys in suits marching at either side of a skinny, crewcut foreigner with specs, as if they were afraid he might break free. They were marching him to the lift. He looked like a child with his minders.

What was he doing? What were they after? No doubt he

was in town on business. Udmurtia has oil and guns and therefore carpet-bagging foreigners are interested in the place. Of all the places I went to for this book, the people of Izhevsk were most indifferent towards outsiders. We were not shocking or surprising at all.

But the question is: were his business ideas as good as mine? While I was rotting in my hotel room I had two stunners, which I list here to attract investors. The first was a simple idea good for a summer craze: cock hats. That's right – hats in the shape of a floppy cock. The second was for a channel called 'Tits'. Twenty-four hours of tits, soapy tit-kneading, small tits, big tits, etc. I reckon it could be a hit in hotel rooms.

30

Film 2004

Talking about business and getting rich, have you ever noticed how, though even good writers are often poor, shit film directors always have decent houses? Michael Winner, for example, lives in a mansion. That's why I continued to think up movie scenarios.

I had an idea for a movie in Izhevsk, too. In fact, I had two, but the second was definitely superior and we need not talk about the first. It was about the life of lesbians in Stalinist Russia. Unlike my other films, however, it was filled with sadness. I saw Izhevsk in the 1930s, deep in winter, a grim factory town, with the fumes of the factory drifting lazily over the frozen pond, over the few streets of brick apartments and the many wooden hovels. Against this backdrop, I wove a love story about the forbidden lesbian tryst between an actress, a singer at the Udmurt Theatre, and a Communist functionary. The actress would be soft and feminine; the functionary, of course, hard and masculine. They'd meet and then, for a few brief months, explore a kind of love that wasn't supposed to exist in a Communist utopia. There would be scenes of unbearable intimacy, tenderness and mutual self-discovery in the private world of the Communist's flat. Indeed the first half of the film would be a quiet evocation of the possibility of the private, the intimate, in an utterly politicized world.

The second half would be much darker, however. The actress is arrested and deported to Siberia, and then her lover too falls under suspicion. The Communist struggles to keep her position, but is also desperate to find out if her beloved is still alive. One day she's caught rifling through classified Party files and is brought up before Izhevsk's Chief Interrogator. She refuses to confess to anything. Indeed, she has nothing to confess: she's been a faithful servant of the Party all her life.

The Chief Interrogator is not concerned with trivialities such as guilt or innocence, however. He attaches a special helmet with rats in it to her head. Terrified, she agrees to sign a confession which pinpoints herself as a member of a plot to kill Stalin. She is sent to the terrible prisons of the Gulag.

But as she travels there in the crowded cattle wagon she realizes she is happy, almost. Crazy as it sounds, at last she feels free. She has nothing to lose. And she is anxious to see her beloved again, and prays to God that she is still alive.

On arriving in the Gulag she is reunited with the actress. But as her lover believes it was she who informed on her (she was arrested after a quarrel), there is no joy in their meeting. Quite the contrary. The film ends after the Communist's failed attempts at reconciliation. She commits suicide by stepping out of line while marching, inviting a shot. Her lover, shocked, runs out to help her, and is also shot. They fall together, united in death.

The music: very mournful.

Set design: bleak; sepia tones.

31

The Ministry

Andrei also set up an appointment for me at the Ministry of Foreign Relations. This was a big, modern building that was almost Western inside. It made a marked contrast to the sorry, dark Soviet hole Andrei himself worked in.

I got there just after the museum ethnographer had raped my brain, however, and I was tired. As usual, I didn't know who I had come to see and I no longer cared. I met the press officer. She asked me lots of questions about my journalistic status. I decided to experiment with frankness.

'Do you have accreditation?' she asked.

'No.'

'Who do you write for?'

'Nobody.'

'What about your book? Who is publishing it?'

'I don't have a publisher.'

'So who would you like to see?'

'I don't know.'

I did like the idea of penetrating a Russian government building and meeting a minister. It made me feel like a spy. Sitting there, however, with the press officer smiling at me in a faintly embarrassed way, I just knew I wasn't going to get far. I didn't feel up to it. I couldn't cook up an exciting alternative identity. In the end she found me a man with floppy hair called Andrei Baryshnikov. Mr Baryshnikov had a book in which was listed every single item the Udmurt Republic had exported in the year 2003. He read to me pages from the book. I found out, for example, that Udmurtia had sold seven thousand dollars' worth of lathe machines to the outside world in 2003. I also discovered that the republic had exported five cars to China, and one to Germany.

It was quite frightening actually to think that every car had been traced. That one car in Germany was particularly unpleasant. I realized that the world was full of ledgers tracing things, that men and women devoted the best years of their lives to tracing things. Was there, I wondered, a ledger tracing me? And had it followed me to this office in Izhevsk?

He started on about chemical plants and polyethylene and brought me some samples of plastics. While he was doing this my mind drifted. I started thinking about Zorro . . . and how cool it would be to be Zorro . . . leaping around in a black mask and cape thwarting evil-doers. The coolest thing, without question, would be slashing a 'Z' in their chests. Slash! Ha-ha! I am Zorro!

Baryshnikov looked at me. 'Any more questions?

'Er . . .' I said, 'why doesn't Izhevsk have a McDonald's?'

32

From *The Mig Mag Diaries,* or *How Mig Mag Fucked Me Up*

DAY 1: ROYALE CHEESEBURGER
OK. Tastes like meat. Way too many gherkins, however. Also, an excess of mayonnaise, a very Russian flaw. Fries ace – McCain oven chips, with plenty of salt. Apricot pie a disappointment. Crust very chewy.

DAY 2: ROYALE SUPREME
Not cheap – two dollars, that's a lot of money in Udmurtia. Shock: real tomatoes and cucumbers, in generous portions.

Reminiscent of short lived McFresh in McDonald's. Burger definitely tastes of meat. Two bags of fries this time – definitely superior to McDonald's. Nearby there were two kids playing, running around. That was nice. Their happy laughter made me love children.

DAY 3: DOUBLE ROYALE CHEESEBURGER
Problems setting in. All-burger diet taking its toll. Double Royale Cheeseburger: dry, bland patty. Two plasticky cheese thins. Limp lettuce leaf. Tomato sauce too sweet. Only onions acceptable.

Mig Mag, the burgers of my undoing

When I was a kid me and my dad used to have burger-eating competitions. We'd go to McD's, order a pile and see who could eat the most. Usually he won, but now and again I could get that last Big Mac down and claim the trophy. 'Climbing the cancer mountain,' he called it. They were our bonding sessions. That's what the Double Royale Cheeseburger was like – but without the filial love.

DAY 4: MAG CHICKEN.
Looked rubbish. Flat burger. Predicted it would be chewy and crispy. In actual fact, it was fairly inoffensive. Passed down throat with minimum resistance. Less fear of cancer. On the other hand, very insubstantial. After a day of not eating, only an invitation for my hunger to grow worse.

DAY 5: MAG FISH
To be honest, I almost backed away from the Mag Fish challenge. But I saw it through, Dad. Ate the fries first – no problems there. But the burger could not be postponed indefinitely. First bite: pleasant. More reconstituted than McDonald's fish burger and a little greasier. The grilled bun added some much needed flavour. One disappointment: I had now been served by Ksenia three days running. She showed no sign, however, of recognizing me. Ksenia, why do you ignore me thus? Your bright eyes, your perky little smile – for everyone but me. Speak to me, Ksenia . . . speak to me . . . just give me a sign . . .

33

The homeless collector

I

It was a miserable, damp day, and I can no longer remember where I was coming from or where I was going. But I do remember them, dancing in the underpass near the Central House of Metallurgists. I heard the music first – some cheerful Europop, synthesized and banal with lyrics about freeing your mind or somesuch crap, sung over a stomping techno beat. A homeless man and woman were performing a strange, slow-motion dance, as if underwater. Their faces were innocent, blissful even. The woman in the tape kiosk pumping out the music was smiling, bemused. Most passers-by reacted in the same way. Just after I passed them, however, a group of youths stopped and started to mock and guffaw. The alcoholics continued dancing for a minute, but then understood what was happening. The bliss left their faces, and they looked miserable, picked on, like children bullied at school.

'Piss off and leave us alone,' said the man. But the bullies kept laughing. As for me, I wished I could preserve the alcoholics in that moment of joy and forgetfulness for ever; but obviously I couldn't. I walked on.

II

I'd heard the Izhevsk church used to be a cinema, and that it had the same architect as the admiralty in St Petersburg. I went there, driven by a feeling that I'd been woefully neglectful of Russia's main religious confession in my travels, and that here, in Izhevsk, I ought at least to try to get to grips with it. I wandered around inside for a while. I knew there was a church the Christian Udmurt preferred. This wasn't it. Nor was it the one where the priest who was translating the Bible into Udmurt worked. I'd actually thought about tracking him down and talking to him, but it seemed an awfully *National Geographic*-type of thing to do, the kind of stuff I'd sworn off.

But I digress. Anyway, I was wandering around inside the church and it was pleasant, clean, filled with the devout lighting candles and kissing icons. But, equally, everything inside was new. The iconostasis was new, the icons were squeaky clean, the frescoes yet to be repainted. I sat down and tried to imagine watching a film there, with the screen in the place of the iconostasis. Of course, most of the films would have been Soviet, but the odd Western movie was shown in the Soviet Union from time to time. I know, for example, that in the 1980s Stanley Kubrick's *Spartacus* was popular. *Some Like It Hot* was also much loved by Soviet film fans. Had Marilyn Monroe jiggled her hips here, in the house of God? Had Tony Curtis and Jack Lemmon hammed it up in drag before audiences of factory-weary proletarians?

My reverie was broken by the sudden appearance of a bearded priest in black robes. He was a tall man with broad shoulders, thick arms and huge hairy hands emerging from the sleeves of his robes. A voice told me to follow him. I did. He was making straight towards a homeless guy who was bothering the old woman selling candles at the entrance of the church.

'Shit, arse, cunt-flap!' said the homeless.

'No, not you, out!' declared the priest. He seized him by the shoulder and marched him briskly out. The homeless put up no resistance.

I followed. Out on the Cathedral steps she turned to me (for suddenly I realized the homeless was a woman) and started jeering and cursing.

'Faggot! Arse-wipe! Ha-ha-ha!'

She was very young, perhaps still a teenager. She was thin and wasted-looking, and had black teeth and a pimply complexion. Probably a junkie.

'Fucker!' she said. 'Ha-ha!'

III

I do not think my third homeless was actually homeless, but he was certainly finding it difficult to get home. I passed him en route to the Udmurtia cinema, where I was rushing to catch a showing of the Yugoslavian film *Tragedy of a Telephone Operator*. I had seen it advertised on a small flyer peeling off a lamp-post. The details of the flyer were difficult to make out, but I thought I saw an image of a naked girl. That, and the fact that there was nothing else to do in Izhevsk on a Monday evening were enough to persuade me to go.

I found the drunk lying half on, half off the pavement, his legs projecting on to the road, his upper half spread over the pedestrian section. He was trying, every now and then, to get up, but in his advanced state of drunkenness was unable to. I spotted him from about twenty or thirty metres away, so as I approached I was able to watch him flip and flop around like a tired fish, long beached, approaching death. And as I approached I was also able to deliberate upon helping him. Would I? Or would I not? There were numerous reasons to help, not the least of which being that it was the kind, humane thing to do. On the other hand, I had helped drunks get up before and usually they cursed at me and then fell over again. I decided not to bother. Instead I walked on, and, after crossing the road, stopped to see if anyone else would. First a mother and her son passed him; they did nothing. Indeed, the mother told her son to stop staring and thus sent the man into the realm of the invisible.

Next came a young man who walked right on by.

Then came another young man, who spotted the flailing alkie, slowed down and even paused briefly, to stand over him. For a second I thought he might do it, he might help, but then – no – he walked on, too. Alas, there was a shortage of Good Samaritans in Izhevsk that day. I walked on to the cinema where, for 25p, I sat in a cold hall with a mob of adolescents watching a video recording of *Tragedy of a Telephone Operator*. It wasn't bad, and I was surprised by the amount of tits and arse in it: I thought Yugoslavia in the 1960s was a censorious country. Its bleak ending also took me a little by surprise. I did think the naked girl sitting stroking the black pussy purring in her lap was a bit much, however.

IV

My final homeless came to me as I walked to Mig Mag for my lunch on my last day in Izhevsk. He was middle-aged, wore a long overcoat and had slanted eyes and a long ginger beard. For the first time, I was able to identify someone definitively as Udmurt.*

'Brother,' he said, 'how about a few kopecks?'

I was about to ignore him, but suddenly I realized there was no reason to. I had money to spare, and he didn't. Even if he spent it on drink, what did it matter? It wasn't as if sobriety held out any glittering prizes for him. So I fished around in my pockets and pulled out ten roubles, and placed the note in his dirty, outstretched claw.

'Thanks, brother,' he said. 'Do you recognize me?'

'Sorry?' I said. I had understood, but the question was so strange, I had to have it repeated.

'You don't? You don't recognize me?'

'No, I don't. Who are you?' I asked.

'I was at the Cathedral yesterday. I saw you walking around. Do you remember?'

'No, I don't. I don't remember.'

'You don't. But I do. I saw you.'

And with that he burst out laughing. And it was a full laugh, a dry, hoarse crackle that erupted from inside of him. He was still laughing some time after I'd said goodbye and walked on.

I could hear him.

* See Udmurtspotting 1.

34

It was very good of Andrei to organize all these interviews for me and I was grateful to him. Certainly I hadn't reached the heart of the Udmurt nation, but then I never thought I would and nor did I want to. I wasn't sure if I'd found out much about the assimilated Udmurt either. But then I'd never known exactly what I was looking for there; it was more a pretext, an idea to give shape to my journey, another anti-quest like the hunt for Chess City or a sacred grove. Some people had revealed a few things to me: that's about the best you can ask for.

I wasn't worried. I knew that I was writing about Russia only on one level. In fact, I was and had always been writing a book about something else: the secret underground resistance of nonentities, about those who stand up and are not counted, those who ask but do not receive, those who knock but for whom the door will never open. The invisible dwellers in invisible cities. The ghosts haunting the ruins of collapsed empires, howling and moaning, with nobody to listen except other ghosts. From the list of Tatar geniuses to the desperate attempts of President Ilumzhinov to meet celebrities, from the Kalmyk Youth Theatre singing and dancing in the void to Alexei's twilight struggle for the greatness that had so long eluded him – the theme had always been there.

And I believed their lives and experiences reflected all our lives and experiences. Do not think you are any different, just because you live in the prosperous West. You, dear reader, are also one of these nonentities. So am I.

For example, I come from an old, tired town in a provincial corner of western Europe. Furthermore, I belong to a race that is becoming extinct: more Scots die each year than are born. I haven't said much about this because there's nothing to say. It is emptiness; it is nothingness. I grew up with a profound sense of absence, feeling life was elsewhere. Hence I can understand a people like the Kalmyks with great ease.

But all that is hardly the point. You may or may not be Scottish, but regardless of who you are you certainly don't matter very much. You might kid yourself you do, but you don't. The universe is huge and you are a speck of dust. Furthermore, soon you'll be dead. A few years after that you'll be forgotten and no one will know you ever were here. All your struggling, your striving, gone – *puff* – like a fart in a sock. Not that it's anything to get upset about. Personally, I think it's something of a relief.

However, it's better to forget and keep on acting as if you do matter. It makes it easier to get up and go to work in the morning. And I think that's the problem the denizens of these lost zones have, why their condition is more severe than ours. They don't see their lives reflected in the media, in stories, in the books they read or study. They don't have the illusion of connectedness to the hum, the throb, the buzz of the modern world, or a sense that their history is of any significance. They are merely footnotes to another, greater history, that of the Russian people. And so they know that nobody knows who they are. They are already forgotten, already not seen. And though that's bearable when you're dead, if you're still alive, it is extremely unpleasant.

We always hope our actions have meaning; that we matter. Each one of us stars in the movie of his own life. Alas, nobody's watching. The people of Tatarstan, Kalmykia, Mari El, Udmurtia feel this, in their atoms, every second of the day.

35

I was grateful to Andrei for another reason. I said earlier that

I had contacted the City Administration in the hope that he'd arrange a meeting with the President or Kalashnikov, or some other local big cheeses. He hadn't, and that was good, because it would have been pointless. While researching this book I read a few travel narratives to see what they were like. I won't mention any names but there was one, perhaps the best, and it was about the Soviet Union, its life and demise. I greatly enjoyed it – right up until the author started interviewing wise men. He dug up writers and film-makers – 'somebodies' – and asked them what they thought about the future of Russia. I was struck only by the staggering banality of their thoughts: 'I hope the future of the Ukraine is democratic', for example. Yeah, me too. You could have asked a guy in a pub the same questions and got the same level of analysis. The guys in the pub read the same newspapers after all. Not that this is a criticism of that one book *per se*. It's a criticism of all books. They all interview people with titles as if their opinions have added weight.

Fuck these wise men. I didn't need the local big shots. It was only vanity that made me want to meet them. Fortunately Andrei had ensured I had always remained safely underground in the realm of the unknown. He had rounded up a tour guide, a fully assimilated Udmurt ethnographer, the sister of the Udmurt Theatre's greatest actor and a man with a book listing everything the republic had exported the year before.

Andrei had kept me obscure, he had kept me lost. He had kept me pure. For that I thank him.

36

And yet he tempted me. I was sitting in his office towards the end of my stay in the city when a tiny blonde named Svetlana with huge blue eyes entered the room. She worked for

Udmurt State TV, which had its offices next to Andrei's. Andrei had told me the TV people wanted to meet me, though he hadn't said what about. I assumed I was going to get a tour of their facilities and maybe talk to one or two of the journalists.

'Hello,' said Svetlana, smiling. 'Sorry for the delay. Please wait a few minutes.'

'What do the TV people want from me?' I asked Andrei. He was sitting at his desk, in the dark, looking haunted and unhappy.

'Don't know,' he replied. 'They just said they wanted to meet you. You're a journalist, right? You ought to know what journalists do.'

'Er . . . yes. But I'm a print journalist.'

'Well, then. It'll be interesting for you to study another medium.'

'Probably,' I said. Though I had known him for a few days only I saw that rude sarcasm was a weapon Andrei employed frequently to prevent people from asking him questions. It had a challenging, defensive undertone as if to say: *Why are you asking me? Why don't you know the answer if you're so smart?*

At that moment, Sveta returned.

'Please come with me.'

I got up and followed her out.

37

As we stood in the lift Sveta tried a few words of English on me.

'How old are you?' she asked.

'Twenty-nine,' I replied. 'And you?'

'Eh?'

It appeared that she could ask questions in English, but

couldn't understand the replies.

'*Skolko tebye let*?' I asked.

'*Tridsat dva.*' Thirty-two. She looked a lot younger.

Sveta led me and my interpreter Feodor out of the building and towards a purple Russian car, inviting us to climb in the back with her. There were two guys already sitting in front. One of them, a Tatar, was the driver. He had hung some words in Arabic from his rear-view mirror. The other guy, Igor, was a Russian, and he was holding a huge camera in his arms.

I still didn't know what was going on, but as I was sitting there I began to suspect something strange: that it was not I who was about to interview them but rather they were about to interview me. I didn't say anything, however, as I was afraid of making a fool of myself.

The driver took us back to the central square and Sveta ordered everyone to pile out. I was standing in front of the hotel when Sveta produced a small radio mike.

'Please put this in your jacket pocket,' she said. 'We're going to film me asking you questions as we walk around the square.'

'OK,' I said.

I did as I was commanded. I wasn't prepared, and had never been interviewed before. I had no idea what they were going to ask me. But it was too late now. There was only one thing for it: to allow myself to be carried along, and trust that I wouldn't make an ass of myself.

Igor heaved the camera on to his shoulder. Sveta said, 'OK.' We began.

'So, Daniel . . .'

Immediately, however, Igor started gesticulating. He couldn't hear me or her. This was a problem. The media professionals huddled together for a confab.

Sveta took the radio mike from out of my jacket pocket. The battery was flat. 'You see the problems we have in Russia?' she said.

38

Fortunately Sveta had another mike, a long black cone which she held in her hand. This meant that we couldn't walk around the square as planned. We'd have to stand still in front of the hotel. We moved so that we'd have the opera house behind me. Then she began speaking.

'Today we're interviewing Daniel Kalder, a journalist from Scotland who is in Udmurtia to research a book he is writing.' Sveta turned to me. 'So Daniel, what is your book about?'

Ah, I thought. *This question is easy. I'll give her the same spiel I gave Andrei when I wrote asking for help.*

'Well,' I said. 'A few years ago I visited Tatarstan. And while I was there I realized that the image people had in my country of Russia as a Slavic country was all wrong. Of course, there is Asia, and people know that in Asia there are shamans, Buddhists, that sort of thing. But Tatarstan is in Europe. And suddenly I became aware that there were lots of different nationalities, cultures, ethnicities in the European part of Russia also, but nobody knew about them. I became fascinated by this and I decided that I'd write a book about them to reveal this fascinating world to a British readership.'

Sveta smiled, nodded. Yes, that was good, I could see that I had pleased her.

'I see. So you're writing about the *deep regions* of Russia. Good, good. So tell me, where have you been so far?'

'Well,' I said. 'I've been to Tatarstan, Kalmykia, and Mari El. You see, I wanted a mix of nationalities and religions. The Tatars are Turkic Muslims. The Kalmyks are Mongol

Buddhists. The Mari are Finno-Ugric pagans. It's very interesting. Udmurtia is my fourth republic.'

'And why did you choose Udmurtia?'

'Er . . . well . . .' Suddenly my mind dried up. I still didn't really know. Or at least I didn't feel comfortable explaining why. Why had I chosen Udmurtia? It had been so long I'd almost forgotten. Standing there with Sveta's mike up my nose I remembered staring at a map about four years beforehand and forming a desire to go there. I remembered reading that Izhevsk was crawling with serial killers and I had a vague desire to see what kind of city young Russians were dying in. The truth, however, was rather embarrassing. Nevertheless, I decided to produce it.

'I liked the name.'

'Excuse me?'

'I liked the name. It sounds very strange to my ears. *Ud-moor-tee-ya.*'

'And what does the name suggest in English?'

'Er . . .' I said. 'Er . . . absolutely nothing. That's why I liked it, it was that suggestion of nothingness. I wanted to see that nothing place.'

I had a feeling she'd be editing that out.

39

Sveta, however, was a professional. Dogged. She stuck to the programme. Ignoring the strangeness, shall we say, the almost tortured frivolousness of my reply, she chuntered on with her next cheery question.

'And what about Izhevsk? Do you like our city?'

'Yes . . .' I said. But actually I hated this question. You couldn't just say yes. You had to qualify it. I'd been asked it everywhere I'd gone, and the answer had always been yes, but not for the reaons people wanted to hear. 'Yes, I like it because it's grim and depressing. Because it reveals truths about the bleakness of human existence, about how lost and pitiful we all are.' No, I couldn't say that. So instead I said this:

'As the taxi took me to my hotel I saw the huge smoke-stacks rising above the city . . . I saw the smoke drifting lazily up towards the heavens. The factory struck me as being very beautiful. I like industrial cities, you see.'

Sveta was looking at me kind of sceptically, however, as if even that was too much. Suddenly I thought of the viewers. I didn't want them to think I was a pretentious arse-crack. I changed tack.

'Also, I saw lots of pretty girls and babies on the street yesterday. That was nice.'

That was better. Sveta liked that.

'And so, when you get back to Scotland and start writing . . . what will the first sentence of your book be?' she asked.

I was impressed by Sveta. She asked her questions with gusto and force, almost innocence, no matter how banal they were. I remembered my interview with Maxim where I had stared at him until he spoke. *So this is how you do it*, I thought.

'"It was my friend Joe who suggested going to Kazan, the capital of Tatarstan."'

That, of course, made no sense at all to her.

40

It was at this point that Sveta stopped beating about the bush and asked me to be wise.

'So, Daniel,' she said, 'you've travelled around Russia.'

'Yes,' I said.

'You've seen the way we live.'

'I have.'

'Well then: what advice do you have for the Russian people?'

'What?' I said, startled.

'You know, have you read Chernishevsky? Alexander Solzhenitsyn's *The Russian Question*?'

I nodded.

'It's the eternal question of Russia. What is to be done?'

It was a dangerous question. An insane question even. How could I presume to lecture a people on the country in which I was only a visitor? They lived there. For a brief second, tempted perhaps by vanity, I flirted with something glib and shitty, like 'Don't trust your leaders.' But then I heard myself speaking.

'I don't have any advice,' I said. 'I travel. I look. I record what I see. Then I describe it. I am not a preacher.'

Yes. I liked that. I had nothing to say. I knew nothing.

41

I wasn't trying to get out of a tricky question, by the way. I had no advice. My answer disappointed her, however. Undaunted, Sveta took another stab at getting profundity out of me.

'OK . . but, Daniel – you've travelled around Russia.'

'I have.'

'You've seen how we live.'

'Yes.'

'Then . . . why? Why is Russia like this? Why is it so back-ward? Why isn't it a normal European country?'

Sveta had surprised me again. This honest expression of self-loathing was something I had forgotten about. In the UK we don't like to air our despair openly. Especially in front of strangers. But Sveta had laid it on me. In all those cities I'd visited: Kazan, Elista, Mari El and now Izhevsk. Why? Why were they so . . . rubbish?

Again, I was conscious of the assembled people of Udmurtia watching me, waiting for my answer. Yes, I was a wise man. I was somebody. I was a foreign journalist. My opinions mattered. Bullshit.

Sveta had really set me up. I hesitated, but I didn't have time to think. I told the truth.

'You know, years ago, before the collapse of the Soviet Union there were schools of sovietologists in the universities of the West, and they spent their whole lives studying Russia and the Soviet Union. Their whole lives. And do you know: not one of those "experts" predicted the collapse of the Soviet Union. Not one. As for me, I've been in Russia for only seven years . . . what can I say? I think I am only beginning to understand your country.'

Yes, I thought. *That's nice. That'll flatter them.*

'Oh,' said Sveta.

And that was that: the interview was over. Afterwards Sveta and Igor the cameraman decided to get some shots of me looking writerly. I sat on a bench and chewed on my pen, while staring into the distance. 'Great!' said Igor. Then I had to look surprised, as if I had just had a great idea for my book. They also filmed me walking down a flight of steps, paying special attention to my shoes, which I had not polished.

42

I wasn't just being evasive, by the way. I had no comments to make on Russia and Her Destiny. I have no comments to make on Russia and Her Destiny. I have no comments to make on anything like that. My goal is simply to describe, to try and communicate a little of what I've seen, what I've felt. Sometimes I've said what I think, but generally I'd prefer to leave it up to you to draw your own conclusions about what it all amounts to. They probably won't be any less profound than mine would be.

When I think of all the newspaper columns I've read, all the discussion shows I've seen, with all those pontificating blowhards pronouncing judgements and analyses from their armchairs I feel only ire. These people lose nothing by their pontification, and they certainly can't be proven wrong. They produce nothing except wind, air, flapdoodle, hokum and blabber. Nay, when you listen to experts it's mostly vanity talking.

I'll say it again. Fuck wise men.

43

The next day I drifted through the streets in a strange paranoid state. I kept wondering if anyone had seen me on TV the night before. Consequently I stuck to back alleys where I spent my time making a list of shop names. There are no chains in Udmurtia, so each shop has a unique name.

I like drawing up lists, I find them easy to read and aesthetically pleasing. As soon as you draw up a list you imply a connection. But what is the connection? Sometimes it's clear, other times less so. Sometimes it's logical. Other times it's nonsense. I prefer nonsense.

The shop names, for some reason, struck me as significant. Some of them were named after women: 'Diana', 'Aigerim', etc. Others geographical objects such as 'Ural'. Still others incorporated foreign words, such as 'Déjà Vu'. I noticed, meanwhile, that there need be no connection between the name and what is sold inside.

Linza	optician
Art of Life	DVDs
Adam and Eve	furniture
Albina	furniture
Alaska	fur
Vivaldi	jewels
Spring	shoes
Harlequin	kids' stuff
Contour	photo
Megapolis	real estate

After a while I realized my list was going nowhere. Perhaps I was making it as a defence against what would definitely happen in the future. Perhaps not yet, but in a few years Russian and international chains would appear here. For example, since I had been to Kazan, an Ikea superstore had opened there. In fact, it was opening the weekend I was in Izhevsk. The days of Mig Mag were numbered. I didn't care much: the chains would probably bring better quality and better service to the people of Izhevsk. Their lives would improve. Yet nevertheless, I wanted to record for history, this trivial, insiginificant detail: that at one point all the shops had unique names. Someone thought them up. Someone worked there. Someone passed it every single day.

Nobody was staring at me and I was feeling more relaxed, so I began to walk in the open. As I did so I saw the towers of Izhmash and remembered my original thoughts about the city. That I'd find serial killers, people dying in the shadows of the smokestacks. It hadn't turned out that way. In fact, I'd found only one story about an Izhevsk serial killer and it was pretty dismal, revealing only the unimaginable extent of the idleness and incompetence of the Izhevsk police force:

When twenty-two-year-old Yuri Artomonov walked into the local police precinct in his Izhevsk neighbourhood last January with the intention of confessing, he expected to be greeted as a much-sought-after serial killer. After all, Artomonov had killed five people in a one-square-kilometre area with an axe over a two-year period and had, in addition, attempted and failed to kill four others with that very same axe before a combined total of thirteen witnesses, at least half of whom knew him by first and last name. (Artomonov's objective in each attack was the victim's VCR.) On confessing, however, Artomonov was surprised to learn that police weren't even on the trail of a serial axe-murderer. Izhevsk homicide detectives had simply chalked it up to 'coincidence' that so many elderly residents of the same neighbourhood had been decapitated for their VCRs in such a short period of time.

It was time for lunch. I wandered down to Mig Mag and ate something foul. It damaged me. On the way back to the hotel I passed two young guys. One of them leaned over and whispered to his friend, 'See that guy? He's a journalist from Scotland. He's writing a book about Russia.'

And that's how I became briefly famous in an obscure province of a crumbling empire. My travels were finished.

And so is this book.

Acknowledgements

Thanks to:
Joe Davies
Yoshi Iwamura
Jared Levy
Paul Richardson
Shamil Biktash
Dr. Alexander Salagaev
Stanislav Dzhavrunov
Natalia Anichkina
Maxim Sitnikov
Konstantin Sitnikov
Andrei Chulkin
Feodor Lapin
Ilya Morozov
Semyon Stankevich
Fabio Mazzarella
Alan Franks
Steve Tomlinson
Camilla Hornby at Curtis Brown
Lee Brackstone and all at Faber

Thanks also to:
Maxim Introductions (www.yoshkar-ola.com/e/) for permission to reprint material from their website.
The eXile newspaper (www.exile.ru) for permission to reprint material from their website.
David Sutton, editor of *Fortean Times* magazine, in which parts of Tatarstan chapter 18 originally appeared.
Andrei Fomin, sculptor of the Kalder Cosmonaut.

Extraordinary thanks to:
David Humphries
Nik White
Nancy Humphries

'The Holy Mountain' from *Strange Telescopes*, the forthcoming
(February 2008) book by Daniel Kalder

*In the early 1990s Sergei Torop, a traffic policeman living in
the industrial town of Minussinsk, Siberia received the revelation that he was the Christ. Taking the name Vissarion, he
moved several hundred kilometres from the city to the taiga
and mountains of southern Krasnoyarsk. From this base he
spent the next fifteen years developing a complex message of
apocalypse and salvation, blending together religion, science
and New Age environmentalism. Today four thousand of the
faithful live in villages surrounding the holy mountain where
Vissarion himself resides with his family and several hand-
picked assistants. At the mountain's peak is a shrine; each
Sunday the citizens of the village below trek up to the top to
worship their God and commune with Vissarion himself.
The following text is excerpted from an account of my journey to meet Vissarion in November 2005, and begins at the
top of the mountain, at the climax of the liturgical pilgrim-
age . . .*

There was a temple at the top of the mountain, erected on
a mystical stone that symbolized harmony between earth and
heaven. And yet that temple was surprisingly humble: made
of cedar, unpainted, following essentially the same design as
an orthodox chapel. Only the cross had been modified to fit
Vissarion's teachings, with the four points enclosed in a unifying circle. Sanya told me that this little shrine was only temporary, that it was but a model of the future *khram,* which
would be made of granite and would stand, tall and grand,
for centuries to come.

There was a set of bells under the dome, and beneath them,
five wooden angels, captured in flight. They represented the

317

five origins of universe: the Absolute Creator, the Material Spirit, the Heavenly Father, the Holy Spirit and . . . I forget the last one. I had tuned out again. Too many symbols, too much interpretation. Thinking about it now, the fifth one might have been Mother Earth. The Vissarionites were big on Mother Earth. As Sanya explained: 'The earth is the cradle of all mankind.' The symbols didn't end there, however. The stained glass incorporated little Yin-Yangs, and the angels themselves were circling a 'Star of Bethlehem', given 14 points because the saviour was born on the 14th of January. Inscribed on the side of the dome was the legend 'Glory to the Living God' and the date of construction, year 38 of the new era.

The priest took the cords of the bells in his white-gloved hands and pulled. The bells chimed, softly, tunefully, sending out invisible sonic pulses to the treetops and higher, to the clouds, and beyond, heaven itself. Everyone turned to face the temple. Some dropped to their knees in the snow, others remained on their feet. 'There are no strict rules here,' said Sanya. 'You may stand, or you may kneel. But most choose to kneel.'

The priest began intoning the next phase of the liturgy, facing away from the congregation, towards the star and the angels. Periodically he would break into song, and the followers around him would join in, swaying on their knees or standing firm, eyes closed or wide open, hands outstretched or by their sides, smiling blissfully or with faces set deep in concentration, each worshipper responding as his spirit prompted him.

Nobody took any notice of me. Nobody even saw me. Standing on the outskirts of the holy circle, I was invisible.

But then, why should they have seen me? God was love, and they were all acting out of love, love surrounded them absolutely – so there was nothing to fear. And yet I felt awkward standing there, as if I was violating something private. But nobody felt that violation except me.

I decided to put a little more distance between myself and the Vissarionites. I stepped backwards, towards the trees, close to the edge of the mountain. Below was a steep drop, thick with pines. And just over there, beyond that other mountain, was Mongolia.

Sanya followed, whispering more explanations in my ear. 'Before we built this temple, there was nothing here, except pine trees and a post marking the height of the mountain. We are now 965m above sea level, and 3km from our settlement, the City of the Shining Star.'

'Did you make this clearing yourself?'

'Yes,' he nodded. 'We cut the path up the mountain, felled the trees and erected the temple. Before that, there was no way to the top, except through thick *taiga*.'

The priest was praying now and an atmosphere of hushed reverence had descended. Sanya wasn't bothered, though. I kept waiting for him to be silent, to cross himself or bow, but he clearly had total freedom to ignore all the sacred rites we were witnessing, and attend to me instead. He explained more of the symbolism of the temple. 'There are four sides, representing what the Teacher tells us are the four main world religions – Christianity, Islam, Buddhism and Taoism. And then, if you look in the glass you will see the Yin and the Yang, which are a symbol of . . .'

'I know what they mean,' I said. Politeness didn't extend to listening to an explication of what is probably the most banal symbol in the history of human thought. But Sanya had already moved on, and was now explaining that everyone was welcome at the top of the mountain, that anyone, no matter what confession he professed, could pray according to his own rite in front of the temple. Hindus, Jehovah's Witnesses, Scientologists – they would all be received warmly. I considered asking about Satanists, but decided against it.

The Vissarionites were singing now. I listened in, to try to get a sense of the words: 'Holy Father, Your Warmth, Your spirit, Your breath . . .' Vissarion's god, it seemed, was an enormous hippy in the sky, raining down good vibes on his people. All around me were expressions of bliss, of tranced out ecstacy, of drugged joy. A lot of the women had that semi-glacial Hare Krishna smile, Antonina especially. Her eyes were turned upwards, and her hands were outstretched. She looked as though she was having an orgasm, but a supernatural one, where the ecstacy was caught, suspended, strung out in time. And at that moment the devil sidled up to me and whispered in my ear: *Look at her face, lost in rapture. She's being fucked by the Holy Mountain.*

And then I turned, and saw that in the midst of this joyous communion there was one who seemed excluded. Next to Antonina a middle-aged guy with a black beard was rocking back and forth, but not in ecstacy. He was looking around nervously. I knew he was some kind of engineer. He had approached me the day before about helping translate the instructions for a solar battery. I had looked at them, and, although they were in English, they were totally incomprehensible. Now I wondered what he was doing up here, with the truest of the true believers. He was totally out of sync with God's infinite grooviness.

'Father God,' sang the priest, 'Happiness and love are Your creation, and the light on Earth is Your creation, our Father, O Father God we sing to you.' And so it went on. There was no grandeur, no pain in these hymns. Nothing about the Potentate of the Rolling Spheres, nothing about our fear and trembling as we walk through the valley of the shadow of death. Just praise for the really nice big guy in the sky.

Then they started praying to Mother Earth. Adrian leaned forward, as if he were about to kiss the ground. That was too much for me. It was embarrassing. I had to get away. I wandered off, went behind the altar, turned my back on the ceremony. In the distance, beyond the dense *taiga* I could see the grey smear of Lake Tiburkul. It didn't look very inviting in November, but I knew that in the summer the Vissarionites went swimming there. And the fish, recognizing their inner harmony, would swim alongside them, for they knew that there was no need to fear these friends to all God's creatures, who do not eat the flesh of living things . . .

They sang one more song, thanking the Holy Father for his light and warmth, and then lapsed into silence. This was the *sliyaniye,* the confluence, merging, amalgamation with the Teacher. Eyes were closed, palms raised to the skies, and souls troubled and souls blissful alike were now reaching out to the shining, radiant warmth of the man who they all hoped was waiting for them on the lower stage of the mountain, the Son of God Himself: Vissarion.

The day before, in our private encounter, Vissarion had told me he was against meditation. But the *sliyaniye* . . . well, it looked a lot like meditation to me. I raised the point with Sanya.

'No: the *sliyaniye* is different. Meditation is about leaving life, whereas the Teacher stands for living life, the right way. He says that if you meditate, certainly you will feel the breath of the universe – but you shall not develop spiritually . . . Here, in the *sliyaniye,* our souls communicate with the Teacher Himself.'

Sanya continued, but his explanation was getting very involved, so I decided to leave it at that, where I just about understood him. The *sliyaniye* lasted a full minute, then the kneeling Vissarionites got up, shook the snow off their legs and boots and crossed and circled themselves. And then I thought of another question: in the Russian Orthodox Church there are strict rules about crossing yourself – both how many fingers you use, and which direction you cross in. Had Vissarion also laid down rules? Sanya laughed.

'You can do it any way: from right to left, left to right, up, down, whatever. We have no canon, no dogma. Our rituals are always evolving. Life is movement, life is change, life is growth.'

One guy was still deep, deep in the *sliyaniye*, his head thrown back, an ecstatic grin on his bearded face, his gloved hands resting on his knees. He was so happy, so blissful. God's light was flooding his soul.

'What about the cross?' I asked. 'What does it represent for you?'

'The cross is an ancient symbol,' said Sanya. 'It predates Christianity. Long before Jesus came it represented positive energy.'

'So what is it for followers of Vissarion? A symbol of Christ's death and resurrection or positive energy?'

'Er . . .'

'Christ or pre- Christ?'

'Ah . . .'

Sanya looked flummoxed. I decided to help him out. 'Or is it both?'

'Yes!' he said. 'Both, both.'

We started our descent, trailing behind the dwellers in the City of the Shining Star, who were making their way through the deep snow to the lower level, the place of communing with the Teacher. I was concentrating hard on staying upright, as the way was steep and treacherous. But it wasn't easy. Something in me was reacting with violence against what I'd seen. That guy kneeling in the snow with the idiotic grin on his face – what was wrong with him? And Antonina – how could she fall for this bullshit? And Adrian, an astrophysicist with two degrees, praying to Mother Earth, for fuck's sake . . .!

But I wasn't comfortable with this anger. Why couldn't I just be happy for them, or if not happy, at least accept that they had found a meaning to life that worked, that gave them direction, a path to transcendence? I wasn't sure, but I knew it had something to do with the absence of darkness. There was something wrong with the banishing of evil, of pain from their ritual. In the Judaeo-Christian tradition, God has a diabolical shadow, Satan. Paradise is mirrored by Hell. The heroes in the Bible are frequently flawed individuals who commit sins: adulterers, liars, killers. King David, beloved of God, arranged for Bathsheba's husband to die in battle so that he could nail the other man's wife. And then what about the innocent men, the good men, like Job? God actually granted Satan permission to torment him. There is plenty in the Bible that is obscure and terrifying, even to true believers. Pain, suffering, fear are central to the message of scripture. Christians drink the blood of Christ and eat his flesh in Holy Communion. But here . . . where was the blood? Where was the terror? What was going on?

'Sanya,' I said.

'Yes?'

'In the Old Testament it says 'Fear of the Lord is the beginning of all wisdom.'

'Yes?'

'What does Vissarion say about this?'

Sanya smiled. 'The Teacher says that only a fool or a child

323

would fear God.' He laughed. 'The Old Testament is talking about another God, God the Creator, not God the Father. Our God, his nature is pure love. What is there to fear?'

Of course: I'd forgotten Vissarion's great revelation, that there is not one God but two, and that it's the second one who loves us; the first doesn't give a fuck. And that was that: problem solved. No need to fear God, not the one that counts, at least. The wisdom of old eliminated with a snap of the fingers and a chuckle.

Sanya motioned to me to stop. Below us, the worshippers had reached the platform for meetings with the teacher and now another *sliyaniye* was taking place. Through the trees, I could see the assembled figures dropping to their knees. Total silence had descended. This could only mean one thing: Vissarion had come. The Messiah was present.

'We can't go any further,' said Sanya. 'Unbelievers are not permitted near this *sliyaniye*. And for the next nine minutes we must be silent, while the people commune with the Teacher.'

At last, I thought, *prohibition!* Finally I had been prevented from doing something. After so much tolerance, it came as a relief. This was more like it: religion that reserved privileges for the elect, for the true believers. A religion that excluded. None of this lovey-dovey, everyone- is-welcome crap. And so I stood there, in the snow, in the cold, shivering for nine minutes as down below, Antonina, Adrian, Alim and all the others closed their eyes and did what I could not: sent their souls reaching out towards the warm pulsating light of the Teacher.

There was no wind, there were no birds. I didn't have any new thoughts, I had no insights. I was aware of myself as a waiting organic thing only, and the longer this thing stood still, the more the cold infiltrated its outer garments.

Periodically I would shift my feet and crush some snow, or listen to my own intake of breath, or watch my breath drifting away in white clouds . . .

But then, just as the cold was beginning to kill the feeling in my toes, it was over. Through the trees I saw an arm drop, a head turn. The man at the foot of the slope waved us on, and Sanya and I began the descent to join the group.

The meeting with the Teacher was already in progress; the crowd of Vissarionites were standing or kneeling in the snow. And separated by thirty metres of untouched, sparkling white crystals, at the foot of a wall of solid rock, the Messiah, Vissarion himself, was sitting on a boulder. But he was not exposed to the elements: no, a cushion shielded his semi-divine rear from the boulder's roughness, and a red umbrella shut off the overcast sky. He looked regal in his long red robe, yes, although the woolly gloves and the tea-cosy on his head detracted slightly from the effect.

There was something startling about seeing him again, like this. At our meeting the day before he had been warm, witty. He had smiled. He was strange yes, but there, amid his paintings, with his wife at his side and the parrot squawking away, there had been something human about him. Something approachable. I don't know if I'd go so far as to say likeable, but . . .

Here, however, the whole situation was different. Vissarion was far away, sitting on what was effectively a throne, in what were effectively royal robes. He was a King, an absolute monarch of both the physical and spiritual realms, and it was forbidden to come close. I felt an urge to rush forward, to touch the hem of his garment, just to see what would happen.

My guess was that I'd be wrestled to the ground by the guys

standing under the pine trees, and given a good kicking. But I didn't do it, so we'll never know.

Sanya wanted me to go forward, to stand close to the Teacher, but I opted to stay at the back.

'Now the people have an opportunity to ask the Teacher for advice regarding situations and problems in their lives. But we must formulate our questions very precisely before asking, as if we are describing our symptoms to a doctor. For the wrong question will lead to the wrong answer. As the Teacher says – in learning how to ask the right question we learn how to live.'

'I see.'

'The people will pass the microphone among themselves and ask their questions. All the Teacher's replies are recorded and edited for inclusion in the Last Testament. That is why we must forbid you from recording what you hear today. There cannot be two versions of the Teacher's wisdom in existence. We must be very precise, and ensure that there is only one official Word of God. There must be no schisms, no debates, as there have been in other religions. There must only be clarity . . .'

As I was not permitted to record the meeting with the Teacher, the following account was put together 24 hours later in Abakan airport, over a cheap cup of coffee. The flight to Moscow had been grounded due to thick fog, so I had plenty of time to reconstruct the questions and answers in detail. In order to achieve the greatest accuracy, the questions were reconstructed with the aid of Semyon Stankevich, a native Russian speaker, who was present throughout the whole meeting with the Teacher. Though I could not capture the precise words, I have done my best to capture the essence of the petitioners' questions and Vissarion's replies.

I apologize to any members of the Church who may be reading this should they detect any inaccuracies.

As Vissarion answered the first question I realized that I had already forgotten the sound of his voice, that it had slipped away from me somehow. But now, here it was again, in my ears, and I was glad, because it was somehow central to his . . . *phenomenon*, to the experience of Vissarion. He spoke in soft, sing-song tones that mirrored the dreamy, other-worldly look in his eyes. There was something soothing about it, as if you were listening to a lullaby. Yet at the same time, there was also a weariness, as if being the Christ really was the great and heavy burden he said it was. But primarily it was soothing, hypnotic. So hypnotic, in fact, that I forgot to listen to what he was actually saying. All I heard were the whispered vowel sounds, the hushed, softened consonants . . .

But then Semyon, who had been hanging back all this time, stepped forward. 'Do you know what he's saying?'

'No.' I replied. 'I haven't been listening.'

'He's pretty angry.'

First Question: (*from a man kneeling in the front row*)
Teacher, can my wife leave the mountain so she can earn some money to pay for vital dental work? Her teeth are causing her a lot of pain.

Vissarion: In the past, many women have left the mountain to earn money. This causes problems for the husbands left behind, who have to keep house *and* work. But it's worse when men leave, while our town is still under construction. *That* amounts to criminal negligence.

Until now, I have given you a lot of freedom in letting you

327

come and go. You did not appreciate how free you have been. You abused it. But from now on I want to stop it. I am going to be much stricter. And when I am strict, you are not to ask why, only to accept it.

(*Questioner takes the microphone in hand again, leans forward slightly*)

Will the committee decide who can leave, or will it be you?

Vissarion: In the first days of our life on the mountain it was I who decided. Then I delegated to the committee. Now I shall be the one to decide again. In some cases, such as emergency dental work, I shall make exceptions. But too many people are leaving the town. This must stop.

Second Question: (*From a woman in the third row. Is it Antonina? It sounds like her. She's nervous and harried enough. But I'm not sure. The microphone distorts voices, makes them too loud, too abrasive.*)

Teacher, if someone tells me an offensive joke, should I tell them that they have offended me?

Vissarion: No. If you take offence at a joke, it's egoism. Confronting the joker will only create antagonism. You should look for the good in the joke.

(*The questioner is not satisfied. Her voice rises in pitch.*)

But Teacher, what if it's *really* dirty! I mean – (*Vissarion cuts her off.*)

Vissarion: Then you are to go away, and think carefully, and look for the good in the joke, even if it's difficult.

(*The questioner is really harassed now, keeps going.*)

But teacher, it was a really filthy joke!

Vissarion replies, at length, but basically says: We must be careful what we joke about. But you are not to confront the joker.

328

Third Question: (*A woman at the end of the second row, with blonde hair, takes the microphone.*)

Teacher, my four-year old son asked if he could play with my breasts. I let him, for about 15 minutes. Then he asked if he could play with them for another 20 minutes. Should I let him?

Vissarion enquires: How old is the boy?

Four.

Vissarion: Let him play. There's a difference between four and thirty-four, after all. (*He laughs, and the assembled community laugh also at the Teacher's joke.*)

Fourth Question: (*A man, middle aged takes the microphone. I can't see him.*)

Teacher, if I ask my hostess for extra helpings at dinner, but she says no, won't you explode? And then I say, in that case, stand back – will I get the food?

(*This is a reference to a popular Russian TV ad in which a little girl gulps down buckets of tasty fruit juice. A boy walks up to her and asks: won't you explode? The little girl replies: in that case, stand back*)

Vissarion: Yes.

Fifth Question: (*From the bearded man who looked so out of place at the sliyaniye on top of the mountain, the one who was not in sync, whose eyes were not closed, who was not swaying back and forth in cosmic harmony, but rocking nervously in agitation.*)

Teacher, Lyuba (*Vissarion's wife*) came to the meeting in town last night and said that you said it is now OK to use (*names certain brand of washing powder*).

Vissarion: I never said that. It is not OK to use (*certain brand of washing powder*). You are lying to me.

(*The questioner shrinks back, nodding vigorously, as if the more eagerly he receives his chastizement, the faster it will end. The curious thing is the lack of a change in Vissarion's tone. When he is mellow he sounds hypnotic, when angered he sounds hypnotic. A non-Russian speaker would have no idea that this follower had just received a dressing down . . .*)

Sixth Question: (*A woman, adding fuel to the fire . . .*)

Teacher, is it permitted to use cleaning products that contain chlorine?

Vissarion: Yes.

But I seem to recall that in 1995 or 1996 you said it wasn't.

Vissarion, now slightly roused from his hypnotic torpor: I did not say that. Categorically, I state that I never said that. You may use products with chlorine, but you should always study the chemical constituents of the powder, and be mindful that whatever you pour out you will eventually drink again.

Seventh Question: (*From a woman, not far from the one who had asked the breast question earlier*)

Teacher, my fouteen-year-old daughter is dating a twenty-seven-year-old man. They say they love each other and are ready to be married. They are becoming more intimate. They have already kissed with tongues. Is this acceptable?

Vissarion: No it is not. This is not good. She's too young to make these decisions. They may meet, and talk, but they must not touch or kiss. How old is this man?

Twenty-seven.

Vissarion: Then he should be spanked in public. (*The crowd laughs.*)

Eighth Question: (*From a man in the middle of the kneeling audience*)

Teacher, if I eat only once a day, will this act of self-denial help me to forget the taste of something I used to enjoy in my old life, but am no longer permitted to eat by our community's rules?

Vissarion: You eat only once a day?

Yes, but I eat a lot.

Vissarion: Won't you explode? (*Audience laughs*) No, this is not right. You shouldn't try to forget the taste of something you once liked. It was a positive experience and it's imprinted on your soul, so be grateful for it. Also, unless there's something wrong with you and you have to force yourself to eat and once a day is the most you can manage, then you shouldn't live like this. You should eat more often. It's bad for your health otherwise.

Ninth Question: (*A woman, kneeling right in front of me*)

Teacher, if I let my neighbour keep her horses and goats in my barn, and then when she takes them out again, there's shit on the ground from her animals, can I use it to fertilise my field? Or should I give the shit to her? Is it my shit or is it her shit? Can I use the shit?

Vissarion: Use it.

And then it was over. The meeting had lasted about an hour, but now Vissarion was blessing his children, he was rising from the boulder, and walking away, waving, towards the pines, where some men were waiting for him. They let him reach them, he moved in front, and then they followed the Teacher into the trees. And just like that, the whole procession vanished. The Teacher was gone.

The kneeling Vissarionites got to their feet, brushed the snow off their clothes, and started the descent back towards the settlement. Some were talking, chatting about Vissarion's answers, while others were silent, perhaps pondering the day's wisdom, or perhaps thinking about what they were going to eat. I didn't know what to think; I needed time to reflect on all this. The thing was, most of the questions were banal, and most of Vissarion's answers were banal. I would have said the same things, had it been me sitting on the rock.

Except, now that I come to think of it, for the one about the four-year-old groping his mother's titties: that was dodgy.

But that wasn't the problem, that wasn't what was nagging at me. It was this: if the questions and answers were so banal, then why did they need to be asked at all?

But then the guy with the beard, who had been out of sync on the mountain-top, and who had subsequently been slapped down over his question regarding which brand of washing powder to use, came up to me.

'Did you read those instructions about the solar panel?
'Yes I did.'
'Did you manage to translate them?'

The truth was, I hadn't tried all that hard. First, I studied poetry and novels at university, so technical (i.e. practical and useful) texts are pretty much impossible for me to understand. But second, and more importantly, as there was no reliable source of electricity on the mountain the lights in my hut had been switched off at 8 o'clock, and it was impossible to read the manual by moonlight.

'I tried,' I said, 'But I didn't get them all done. They were difficult.'

'Yes, he said, nodding. 'They're tricky. Damned tricky . . .'

But I couldn't discuss the problem any longer. Vadim was waiting for me on the lower stage of the mountain. It was time to take tea with the writer of Vissarion's gospel.